The Gospel According to Matthew

VOLUME III

The Gospel
According to Matthew

VOLUME III
(Chapters 11–15)

by

Oliver B. Greene

The Gospel Hour, Inc., Oliver B. Greene, Director
Box 2024, Greenville, South Carolina 29602

First printing, July 1972—25,000 copies
Second printing, November 1973—15,000 copies
Third printing, June 1975—15,000 copies

$6.00

Foreword

Continuing our verse-by-verse commentary on *The Gospel According to Matthew,* we now present Volume III, covering chapters 11 through 15. In chapter 11, we see the clouds of rejection and hatred beginning to gather around Israel's promised Messiah. Some of His miracles are recorded in chapter 12, but it is concerned chiefly with various exhortations as He continues His teaching ministry. This teaching continues through chapter 13, which presents the seven great mysteries of the Kingdom of Heaven in parable form. In chapter 14 are recorded the imprisonment and death of John the Baptist, the forerunner of our Lord. Also included in that chapter are two of the Lord's greatest miracles—the feeding of the five thousand and His walking on the stormy waters of Galilee. Chapter 15 records a very severe rebuke of the scribes and Pharisees by Jesus, after which He continues on His public ministry, performing various miracles. In these five chapters we are reminded again what a mighty, compassionate, all-sufficient Saviour we serve.

Because of the length already attained in this study, we deemed it wise to close this volume at this point, taking up with chapter 16 in the next volume. It is our sincere prayer that through the truths presented here hearts will be challenged, strengthened, and blessed.

—The Author

Contents

Chapter XI

1. And it came to pass, when Jesus had made an end of commanding his twelve disciples, he departed thence to teach and to preach in their cities.

2. Now when John had heard in the prison the works of Christ, he sent two of his disciples,

3. And said unto him, Art thou he that should come, or do we look for another?

4. Jesus answered and said unto them, Go and shew John again those things which ye do hear and see:

5. The blind receive their sight, and the lame walk, the lepers are cleansed, and the deaf hear, the dead are raised up, and the poor have the gospel preached to them.

6. And blessed is he, whosoever shall not be offended in me.

7. And as they departed, Jesus began to say unto the multitudes concerning John, What went ye out into the wilderness to see? A reed shaken with the wind?

8. But what went ye out for to see? A man clothed in soft raiment? behold, they that wear soft clothing are in kings' houses.

9. But what went ye out for to see? A prophet? yea, I say unto you, and more than a prophet.

10. For this is he, of whom it is written, Behold, I send my messenger before thy face, which shall prepare thy way before thee.

1

11. Verily I say unto you, Among them that are born of women there hath not risen a greater than John the Baptist: notwithstanding he that is least in the kingdom of heaven is greater than he.

12. And from the days of John the Baptist until now the kingdom of heaven suffereth violence, and the violent take it by force.

13. For all the prophets and the law prophesied until John.

14. And if ye will receive it, this is Elias, which was for to come.

15. He that hath ears to hear, let him hear.

16. But whereunto shall I liken this generation? It is like unto children sitting in the markets, and calling unto their fellows,

17. And saying, We have piped unto you, and ye have not danced; we have mourned unto you, and ye have not lamented.

18. For John came neither eating nor drinking, and they say, He hath a devil.

19. The Son of man came eating and drinking, and they say, Behold a man gluttonous, and a winebibber, a friend of publicans and sinners. But wisdom is justified of her children.

20. Then began he to upbraid the cities wherein most of his mighty works were done, because they repented not:

21. Woe unto thee, Chorazin! woe unto thee, Bethsaida! for if the mighty works, which were done in you, had been done in Tyre and Sidon, they would have repented long ago in sackcloth and ashes.

22. But I say unto you, It shall be more tolerable for Tyre and Sidon at the day of judgment, than for you.

23. And thou, Capernaum, which art exalted unto heaven, shalt be brought down to hell: for if the mighty works, which have been done in thee, had been done

in Sodom, it would have remained until this day.

24. But I say unto you, That it shall be more tolerable for the land of Sodom in the day of judgment, than for thee.

25. At that time Jesus answered and said, I thank thee, O Father, Lord of heaven and earth, because thou hast hid these things from the wise and prudent, and hast revealed them unto babes.

26. Even so, Father: for so it seemed good in thy sight.

27. All things are delivered unto me of my Father: and no man knoweth the Son, but the Father; neither knoweth any man the Father, save the Son, and he to whomsoever the Son will reveal him.

28. Come unto me, all ye that labour and are heavy laden, and I will give you rest.

29. Take my yoke upon you, and learn of me; for I am meek and lowly in heart: and ye shall find rest unto your souls.

30. For my yoke is easy, and my burden is light.

Jesus Turns His Face Toward the Cross

In chapter 11, we see clearly the clouds of rejection and hatred gathering around Israel's promised Messiah. Indeed He had come unto His own and they "received Him not" (John 1:11). The Jews had looked for a King who would bring deliverance to the nation of Israel, and this Man was as a "root out of dry ground." In their hearts they thought surely He could not be their Messiah. He had "no form nor comeliness," and there was "no beauty" such as they desired in their King; therefore they despised Him and rejected Him.

3

They had been looking for a majestic, powerful ruler, but this One was "a Man of sorrows, and acquainted with grief." Israel, His own people according to the flesh, "hid (their) faces from Him."

The Lamb of God was definitely on His way to Calvary. He came into the world "not to be ministered unto, but to minister, and to give His life a ransom for many" (Matt. 20:28). He came as the sin offering for His people; therefore He must die "without the camp" (Heb. 13:11-13). He would bear their griefs and carry their sorrows even though they hated Him and said all manner of evil against Him. They thought He was an impostor, they thought He was suffering for His own sins; but Jesus was the sinless One, "holy, harmless, undefiled, separate from sinners" (Heb. 7:26). Upon enduring "such contradiction of sinners against Himself" (Heb. 12:3), He was fulfilling every jot and every tittle of the law. He was indeed being wounded for *their* transgressions and bruised for *their* iniquities, because *in Him* there *was* no iniquity. The chastisement of their peace was laid upon Jesus, and with His stripes they were healed. The whole nation, with the exception of a very small remnant, had sadly gone astray— they had turned everyone to their own way. The Father had sent His Son, the Lamb of God, into the world; and even though He was the Son of God, He was "smitten of God," and the Lord "laid on Him the iniquity of us all"—not only the

4

Jew but the Gentile as well. (Please study Isaiah chapter 53 carefully.)

Someone may ask if the Jews were not justified in looking for a great and glorious King to deliver them from their enemies. Had not Jehovah spoken to the prophets that the coming One would sit exalted on the throne of David and rule over the nations of the earth? Was it not written in the Old Testament Scriptures that God would raise unto David "a righteous Branch" and that a King should reign and prosper and execute justice and judgment right here upon this earth? Was it not prophesied that in the days of this glorious King, Judah would be saved and Israel would dwell safely? (Jer. 23:5, 6). Was it not prophesied over and over again in connection with the coming of the King that the nation of Israel should be gathered unto their land and there dwell forever, delivered from the rule of the heathen? (Zech. chapter 14; Deut. 30:1-6; Isa. chapters 11 and 12; Ezekiel chapters 36 and 37).

Yes, the prophets did foretell that Jehovah would send a glorious King; God promised all this and much more. But what the Jews failed to see was that the Scriptures which prophesied of the glorious Kingdom also declared that the Messiah would be a vicarious sufferer, that He would bear the sins of His people. The Psalmist clearly prophesied that the Messiah would be crucified, as did the Prophet Zechariah. Daniel declared that He would

5

be "cut off"—not for Himself, but for others. (Please study Isaiah 53, Psalm 22, Zechariah 12:10 and 13:6, and Daniel 9:26.)

It was perfectly in order for the Jews to believe in the coming of a Messiah who would be glorious and powerful, who would reign over the whole earth; but they were fools, according to Jesus, not to believe *all* that the prophets had said concerning the Promised One: "Then He said unto them, *O fools, and slow of heart to believe all that the prophets have spoken: ought not Christ to have suffered these things, and to enter into His glory?* And beginning at Moses and all the prophets, He expounded unto them in all the Scriptures the things concerning Himself" (Luke 24:25-27).

I wonder what the risen Lord is saying today as He sits at the right hand of God the Father and looks down upon this earth. He witnesses in the pulpits around the world men who are preaching that God has finished with Israel and that the promises made to Abraham have been given to the Church. I am persuaded to believe that He is saying again, *"O FOOLS, and slow of heart to believe ALL THAT THE PROPHETS HAVE SPOKEN."* God is now visiting the Gentiles and calling out a people for His name—the New Testament Church, of which Jesus is the head and the foundation. When the Church is complete, He will return and will build again the tabernacle of David, "that the residue of men might seek after the Lord": "After this I will return, and will build again the tabernacle of David, which is fallen down; and I will build again the ruins thereof, and I will set it up: that the residue of men might seek after the Lord, and all the Gentiles, upon whom my name is called, saith the Lord, who doeth all these things" (Acts 15: 16, 17). God will keep *every promise* He has made to Abraham and to his children. (Read Romans chapter 11.)

Here in chapter 11 of Matthew's Gospel (and in chapter 12) the rejection of Jesus by the nation Israel is clearly manifested. This immediately follows the instruction and sending forth of the twelve apostles by the Lord, which we studied in chapter 10.

Verse 1: *"And it came to pass, when Jesus had made an end of commanding His twelve disciples, He departed thence to teach and to preach in their cities."*

When Jesus had finished His instructions to the twelve disciples, He departed and began *"to teach and to preach in their cities."* The Lord Jesus is always intimately associated with His ministers and servants in their work. We may not see Him, but He is always with us—yea, in the Person of the Holy Spirit, He abides within us and helps us in our labors for Him. When Jesus was bodily present with the disciples upon the

7

earth, He traveled in their cities preaching and teaching. He is not present today in bodily form, but nevertheless He is always with His servants in this day and hour. We have the promise, *"I will never leave thee, nor forsake thee."* Therefore "we may boldly say, The Lord is my helper, and I will not fear what man shall do unto me" (Heb. 13:5, 6).

John the Baptist Sends Disciples to Question Jesus

Having given a general account of the Lord's journeys about Galilee with important examples of His teaching and miracles, and having added an account of His instructing and sending out the twelve apostles, Matthew now advances to other topics. The first is the remarkable message in question form from John the Baptist, and the Lord's answer (chapter 11:2-30).

Verses 2 and 3: *"Now when John had heard in the prison the works of Christ, he sent two of his disciples, and said unto Him, Art thou He that should come, or do we look for another?"*

Herod had arrested John the Baptist and thrown him in prison because John had declared that it was not lawful for Herod to have his brother's wife. We have the record in Matthew 14:3, 4. Although John was in prison he was allowed some intercourse with his followers. In Luke 7:18, we learn that the disciples of John brought to him messages concerning the works and miracles of Jesus. We see in our present verse that *when he "heard in the prison the works of Christ, he sent two of his disciples"* to Jesus with a question.

The disciples asked, *"Art thou He that should come?"* — or, "the coming (One)." *"Thou"* is expressed in the original at the head of the sentence, so as to be strongly emphatic; and this corresponds to the emphatic position in the Greek of *"another"* in the last part of the question. The statement, "the coming One," had become a very familiar designation of the Messiah. We find this designation in Matthew 3:11, 21:9, 23:39; John 6:14, 11:27; and Hebrews 10:37. No doubt the phrase was derived from Psalm 118:26: "Blessed be *He that cometh* in the name of the Lord: we have blessed you out of the house of the Lord." Jesus was the coming One and there was no other.

The question continued, *". . . or do we look for another?"* *"We"* speaks of those who had longed for the coming of their Messiah—not just John and the disciples, but all who had lived with the Messianic hope.

It is not known why John sent these disciples to Jesus to ask the question they did. Personally, I believe it was to satisfy his *disciples* that Jesus was the Messiah. I do not believe that John the Baptist ever doubted that Jesus was the Promised One. It *could* be that his faith had been shaken,

9

but I do not believe that the faith of John the Baptist ever wavered. I believe he knew that Jesus was the Messiah, the Son of God, because he clearly announced Him as such and he gave the reason why he was so sure of it. We have the record in John 1:15-37:

"John bare witness of Him, and cried, saying, This was He of whom I spake, He that cometh after me is preferred before me: for He was before me. And of His fulness have all we received, and grace for grace. For the law was given by Moses, but grace and truth came by Jesus Christ. No man hath seen God at any time; the only begotten Son, which is in the bosom of the Father, He hath declared Him.

"And this is the record of John, when the Jews sent priests and Levites from Jerusalem to ask him, Who art thou? And he confessed, and denied not; but confessed, I am not the Christ. And they asked him, What then? Art thou Elias? And he saith, I am not. Art thou that prophet? And he answered, No. Then said they unto him, Who art thou? that we may give an answer to them that sent us. What sayest thou of thyself? He said, I am the voice of one crying in the wilderness, Make straight the way of the Lord, as said the prophet Esaias.

"And they which were sent were of the Pharisees. And they asked him, and said unto him, Why baptizest thou then, if thou be not that Christ, nor Elias, neither that prophet? John answered them, saying, I baptize with water: but there standeth One among you, whom ye know not; He it is, who coming after me is preferred before me, whose shoe's latchet I am not worthy to unloose.

"These things were done in Bethabara beyond Jordan, where John was baptizing. The next day John seeth Jesus coming unto him, and saith, *BEHOLD THE LAMB OF GOD, which taketh away the sin of the world.* This is He of whom I said, After me cometh a Man which is preferred before me: for He was before me. And I knew Him not: but that He should be made manifest to Israel, therefore am I come baptizing with water.

"And John bare record, saying, I saw the Spirit descending from heaven like a dove, and it abode upon Him. And I knew Him not: but He that sent me to baptize with water, the same said unto me, UPON WHOM THOU SHALT SEE THE SPIRIT DESCENDING, AND REMAINING ON HIM, THE SAME IS HE WHICH BAPTIZETH WITH THE HOLY GHOST. AND I SAW, AND BARE RECORD THAT THIS IS THE SON OF GOD.

"Again the next day after John stood, and two of his disciples; *and looking upon Jesus as He walked, he saith, BEHOLD THE LAMB OF GOD!* And the two disciples heard him speak, and they followed Jesus."

With this clear testimony of John the Baptist

concerning Jesus and who He was, I cannot believe that he ever doubted that Jesus was the Son of God. We must remember that John was a special servant of Almighty God. God gave him to Elisabeth and Zacharias, and he was filled with the Holy Spirit before birth. (Read Luke 1:5-15.) He was to announce the coming of the Messiah; and when his ministry was finished, God permitted him to be put in prison (and later to be put to death). God did get glory—and will still get glory —out of that which happened to the forerunner of Jesus. Christ had this to say about John: "I say unto you, *Among those that are born of women THERE IS NOT A GREATER PROPHET THAN JOHN THE BAPTIST . . ."* (Luke 7:28).

There are great Bible teachers who believe that John sent the two disciples to ask this question (here in Matthew 11:3) to satisfy his own heart. But I cannot believe that the devil was successful in causing John to doubt for one moment that he had announced the true Messiah. I will admit, however, that the devil is a powerful being, and I will admit that we dare not trust our own strength. The Apostle Paul warned: "Wherefore let him that thinketh he standeth take heed lest he fall" (I Cor. 10:12). If it were possible, the devil would deceive the very elect of God (Matt. 24:24), but I am thankful that it is not possible for him to do so.

John the Baptist was called and anointed by God to announce the coming of the Messiah as "the Lamb of God"—which meant suffering, humiliation, and death. John had also been sent by God to proclaim Jesus as Judge and King: "Whose fan is in His hand, and He will throughly purge His floor, and gather His wheat into the garner; but He will burn up the chaff with unquenchable fire" (Matt. 3:12). What did all of this mean? John knew what a lamb suffered as a type under the law, and he knew that Jesus had come as "the Lamb of God" to take away "the sin of the world" (John 1:29). John knew that all of the Old Testament offerings were shadows of that which was to come, and Jesus had come to make good God's promises to take away not only the sin of Israel but of the whole world. That Jesus was the Coming One, the Messiah, the Son of God, John never doubted.

In John 3:22-36 we have recorded the last testimony of John the Baptist concerning Jesus, the Messiah whom he announced:

"After these things came Jesus and His disciples into the land of Judaea; and there He tarried with them, and baptized. And John also was baptizing in Aenon near to Salim, because there was much water there: and they came, and were baptized. For John was not yet cast into prison. Then there arose a question between some of John's disciples and the Jews about purifying. And they came unto John, and said unto him, Rabbi, He that was with thee beyond Jordan, to whom thou barest witness, behold, the same baptizeth, and all men come to Him.

"John answered and said, A man can receive nothing, except it be given him from heaven. Ye yourselves bear me witness, that I said, I am not the Christ, but that I am sent before Him. He that hath the bride is the bridegroom: but the friend of the bridegroom, which standeth and heareth him, rejoiceth greatly because of the bridegroom's voice: this my joy therefore is fulfilled. *He must increase, but I must decrease.*

"He that cometh from above is above all: he that is of the earth is earthly, and speaketh of the earth: He that cometh from heaven is above all. And what He hath seen and heard, that He testifieth; and no man receiveth His testimony. He that hath received His testimony hath set to his seal that God is true. For He whom God hath sent speaketh the words of God: for God giveth not the Spirit by measure unto Him. The Father loveth the Son, and hath given all things into His hand. He that believeth on the Son hath everlasting life: and he that believeth not the Son shall not see life; but the wrath of God abideth on him."

According to this passage of Scripture, John's disciples were envious because Jesus was having what seemed to them greater success than their leader; so John set them straight immediately and reminded them exactly what he had said concerning

Christ. John the Baptist was instructed by God that the One on whom the Holy Spirit descended and remained, was the Messiah. Jesus did not receive the Spirit "by measure"; the Spirit came upon Him in the form of a dove and remained upon Him. John the Baptist knew who Jesus was, and I believe that he lived and died with perfect assurance in his heart that he had announced the true Messiah.

Verse 4: *"Jesus answered and said unto them, Go and shew John again those things which ye do hear and see."*

Notice that Jesus did not tell John's disciples He was the Messiah, the Promised One, and they need not look for another. Instead He said, *"Go and shew John again THOSE THINGS WHICH YE DO HEAR AND SEE."* Luke tells us, "And in that same hour He cured many of their infirmities and plagues, and of evil spirits; and unto many that were blind He gave sight" (Luke 7:21). Therefore, Jesus performed many miracles while these two messengers from John the Baptist looked and listened.

Verse 5: *"The blind receive their sight, and the lame walk, the lepers are cleansed, and the deaf hear, the dead are raised up, and the poor have the Gospel preached to them."*

Blind men's eyes were opened, lame men began

15

to walk, lepers were cleansed, the deaf could hear, the dead were raised, and the poor had the Gospel message of glorious free salvation delivered unto them. Jesus was doing all that the promised Messiah was supposed to do when He came. There is no excuse for any who were there that day to have doubted that they were in the presence of the true Messiah whom God had promised in the Old Testament Scriptures.

The Prophet Isaiah, speaking of Jesus, declared: "The Spirit of the Lord God is upon me; because the Lord hath anointed me to *preach good tidings unto the meek;* He hath sent me to *bind up the brokenhearted, to proclaim liberty to the captives, and the opening of the prison to them that are bound;* to proclaim the acceptable year of the Lord, and the day of vengeance of our God; to comfort all that mourn" (Isa. 61:1, 2). In Isaiah 61:3-11, we have the prophecy concerning the Kingdom, when peace will reign and the earth will be filled with the knowledge of the Lord as the waters now cover the sea. But the Kingdom peace and blessing will come only after the day of vengeance. (Please study Isaiah 61:3 through 65:25.)

Note Luke's account of the return of Jesus to Galilee and His visit to the synagogue there:

"And Jesus returned in the power of the Spirit into Galilee: and there went out a fame of Him through all the region round about. And He taught in their synagogues, being glorified of all.

And He came to Nazareth, where He had been brought up: and, as His custom was, He went into the synagogue on the sabbath day, and stood up for to read.

"And there was delivered unto Him the book of the prophet Esaias. And when He had opened the book, He found the place where it was written, *The Spirit of the Lord is upon me, because He hath anointed me to preach the Gospel to the poor; He hath sent me to heal the brokenhearted, to preach deliverance to the captives, and recovering of sight to the blind, to set at liberty them that are bruised, to preach the acceptable year of the Lord.*

"And He closed the book, and He gave it again to the minister, and sat down. And the eyes of all them that were in the synagogue were fastened on Him. And He began to say unto them, *This day is this Scripture fulfilled in your ears.* And all bare Him witness, and wondered at the gracious words which proceeded out of His mouth. And they said, Is not this Joseph's son? And He said unto them, Ye will surely say unto me this proverb, Physician, heal thyself: whatsoever we have heard done in Capernaum, do also here in thy country. And He said, Verily I say unto you, No prophet is accepted in His own country" (Luke 4:14-24).

It is interesting to notice that when Jesus read this Old Testament Scripture (Isaiah 61:1, 2), He read down to the comma in verse 2 and stopped.

He did not read "and the day of vengeance of our God . . ." because this points to the "time of Jacob's trouble," or the Great Tribulation period. Jesus read the Scriptures concerning His *first* coming—that is, when He came to "give His life a ransom for many" (Matt. 20:28). He opened the Day of Grace and proclaimed "the acceptable year" of Jehovah. But in His first coming He did not fulfill the day of vengeance and wrath. That will take place when Jesus comes the *second* time: "And to you who are troubled rest with us, when *the Lord Jesus shall be revealed from heaven with His mighty angels, in flaming fire taking vengeance on them that know not God, and that obey not the Gospel of our Lord Jesus Christ: who shall be punished with everlasting destruction from the presence of the Lord, and from the glory of His power; when He shall come to be glorified in His saints,* and to be admired in all them that believe (because our testimony among you was believed) in that day" (II Thess. 1:7-10).

Jesus was doing exactly what Isaiah prophesied seven centuries before His birth. The Spirit of God was upon Him—the Holy Spirit descended at His baptism and remained upon Him. He was anointed, He was preaching good tidings to the meek, He was binding up brokenhearted men and women. He was setting at liberty many who were bound with demons and diseases, He was opening the prison for many who were in the chains of sin and ungodliness, and certainly He was proclaiming the acceptable year of the Lord.

Anyone who knew anything at all about the Old Testament Scriptures had no excuse for missing the identification of the Lord Jesus Christ. Someone has said that He had so many "labels" on Him it is mysterious that anyone could have missed His identity. He did everything that the Old Testament prophets said He would do up to the time when He will come as King of kings and Lord of lords, when He will judge in righteousness. He did not come the first time to sit on the throne; He came the first time to be nailed to a cross. The brazen serpent lifted up by Moses in the wilderness, the rock that was smitten, and all of the offerings and types in the Old Testament economy pointed to the coming of the spotless Lamb of God who would shed His blood for the remission of sins. Jesus fulfilled all of this, and it was as clear as could be—yet the Jews missed their Messiah.

John the Beloved speaks of the miracles of Jesus, the mighty works that He performed, and the wonderful words of life that He uttered in this way:

"And many other signs truly did Jesus in the presence of His disciples, which are not written in this book: but these are written, that ye might believe that Jesus is the Christ, the Son of God; and that believing ye might have life through His name.... *AND THERE ARE ALSO MANY OTHER*

THINGS WHICH JESUS DID, the which, if they should be written every one, I suppose that EVEN THE WORLD ITSELF COULD NOT CONTAIN THE BOOKS THAT SHOULD BE WRITTEN. AMEN" (John 20:30, 31; 21:25).

I have been asked if I believe the statement in John 21:25 is to be taken literally. *Yes,* I believe exactly what is recorded in this last verse of the Gospel of John. I believe that if every word Jesus said and all that He did had been put in books, *the world could not contain the books that would be written!* We have recorded in the four Gospels some of His miracles and His mighty works—*but not all of them.* How many blind men were healed, how many lepers were cleansed, how many lame were made to walk, how many deaf were made to hear, how many dumb were given their speech, how many dead were raised, we do not know. The record tells us that He did heal all kinds of diseases, He raised the dead, and He performed every miracle that the Messiah was supposed to perform. He did that which no other prophet had ever done. The prophets performed miracles by the power of God—but *Jesus* performed miracles *by His own power and in His own name.*

We find in the fourteenth chapter of John's Gospel that the disciples were troubled because Jesus had just revealed to them that He would be betrayed into the hands of His enemies and that He was going away. He told them, "Let not your heart be troubled." Then Thomas asked Him where He was going and how they could know how to come where He would be. Jesus answered, "I am the Way, the Truth, and the Life: no man cometh unto the Father, but by me. If ye had known me, ye should have known my Father also: and from henceforth ye know Him, and have seen Him.

"Philip saith unto Him, Lord, shew us the Father, and it sufficeth us. Jesus saith unto him, Have I been so long time with you, and yet hast thou not known me, Philip? he that hath seen me hath seen the Father; and how sayest thou then, Shew us the Father? Believest thou not that I am in the Father, and the Father in me? The words that I speak unto you I speak not of myself: but the Father that dwelleth in me, He doeth the works. *Believe me that I am in the Father, and the Father in me: or else BELIEVE ME FOR THE VERY WORKS' SAKE"* (John 14:6-11).

"THE POOR have the Gospel preached to them." This meant much more to the men of that day than it does to us. The Messiah would bring good tidings to the lowly; that is, the poor. The word translated *"poor"* or "lowly" in the Hebrew language signifies those who are oppressed, afflicted, and of humble circumstances. For this great mass of people, the Messiah would bring good tidings. The masses of mankind in that day were poor and ignorant and were neglected by the

21

philosophers and teachers, even by the Jewish rabbis. The rabbis often spoke of the masses of ignorant and poor people with the greatest contempt. They said, "But this people (rabble) who knoweth not the law are *cursed*" (John 7:49). The rabbis and religious leaders delighted to stigmatize the masses of the poor as "country folks," since ancient culture was almost entirely confined to the cities. It was quite different in the days of our Lord than in this day. Therefore, it was remarkable that Jesus pointed out clearly that He had come to bring good tidings to the poor, to the suffering, to the despised, to those who were looked upon as the scum of the earth.

The Scripture in John chapter 7 referred to above is most interesting. After Jesus spoke of the prophecy concerning the coming of the Holy Spirit (John 7:37-39), many people said, "This is the Prophet." Others said, "This is the Christ," and still others asked, "Shall Christ come out of Galilee?" Then they pointed out that the Scriptures declared that Christ would be of the seed of David and would come out of the town of Bethlehem. The people were divided among themselves, and some would have taken Him and thrown Him in prison, but they were afraid to lay their hands on Him. Some officers of the chief priests had been sent to take Him but returned without Him. When asked why they had not brought Jesus, they answered, *"Never man spake like this Man."* Then the Pharisees

said, "Are ye also deceived? Have any of the
rulers or of the Pharisees believed on Him? *But
this people who knoweth not the law are cursed"*
(John 7:46-49). "This people" speaks of the masses
who were attending the meetings of Jesus and were
being healed, blessed, and delivered from demons
and evil spirits—"the *common* people" who "heard
Him gladly" (Mark 12:37).

Verse 6:   *"And blessed is he, whosoever shall
not be offended in me."*

The miracles that Jesus was performing and the
good tidings He was bringing to the meek and
lowly proved beyond any shadow of doubt that
He was the prophesied Messiah.   He declared,
*"Blessed (or happy) is he, whosoever shall not be
offended (or find occasion of stumbling) in me."*
Isaiah speaks of the same thing in his prophecy:
"And He shall be for a sanctuary; but for *a stone
of stumbling and for a rock of offence* to both the
houses of Israel, for a gin and for a snare to the
inhabitants of Jerusalem" (Isa. 8:14).

The statement by Jesus here in Matthew means,
"Whosoever does not find in me anything that will
keep him from believing that I am the Messiah and
thus reject me as Saviour, will be blessed."   Jesus
was doing and saying that which had been prophesied concerning Him, but the Jews stumbled
because in their eyes He failed to do various other
things they expected the Messiah to do.

John 5:30-47 records these words of Christ: "I can of mine own self do nothing: as I hear, I judge: and my judgment is just; because I seek not mine own will, but the will of the Father which hath sent me. If I bear witness of myself, my witness is not true. There is another that beareth witness of me; and I know that the witness which He witnesseth of me is true. Ye sent unto John, and he bare witness unto the truth. But I receive not testimony from man: but these things I say, that ye might be saved. He was a burning and a shining light: and ye were willing for a season to rejoice in his light. But I have greater witness than that of John: for the works which the Father hath given me to finish, *the same works that I do, bear witness of me, that the Father hath sent me.* And the Father Himself, which hath sent me, hath borne witness of me. Ye have neither heard His voice at any time, nor seen His shape. And ye have not His Word abiding in you: for whom He hath sent, Him ye believe not.

"Search the Scriptures; for in them ye think ye have eternal life: and they are they which testify of me. And ye will not come to me, that ye might have life. I receive not honour from men. But I know you, that ye have not the love of God in you. I am come in my Father's name, and ye receive me not: if another shall come in his own name, him ye will receive. How can ye believe, which receive honour one of another, and seek not the honour that cometh from God only? Do not think that I will accuse you to the Father: there is one that accuseth you, even Moses, in whom ye trust. For had ye believed Moses, ye would have believed me: for he wrote of me. But if ye believe not his writings, how shall ye believe my words?"

Notice in verse 36 of John chapter 5, Jesus declared to the religious leaders of His day that He had a greater witness than that of John—*the works,* or the *miracles,* that He did. He told them to search the Old Testament Scriptures—for in these Scriptures "ye think ye have eternal life: and they are they which testify of me. And ye will not come to me, that ye might have life." They *did* search the Scriptures, and they did refuse to come to Jesus that they might live. He reminded them that if they had believed Moses, they would have believed *Him*, because Moses wrote about Him. They were willingly ignorant, blinded by the god of this age—the devil.

The two disciples who came to Jesus asking if He was the promised Messiah were instructed to return and tell John what they heard and saw. But they were not to stop there. They were to bear the message to John, "Happy is he to whom I shall not prove a stumbling block. Happy is he who shall not take offence at what I am doing or because of my poverty and my lowliness. There is no reason for anyone to reject me, because I am

doing exactly what your prophets said the coming
Messiah would do." To the very men whom John
sent, and to other disciples of John, Jesus had
proven to be a stumbling block, because they were
jealous. Jesus was recruiting more followers than
John, and they were envious. He was a stumbling
block—they could not believe that He was the
Messiah.

Verse 7: *"And as they departed, Jesus began
to say unto the multitudes concerning John, What
went ye out into the wilderness to see? A reed
shaken with the wind?"*

John had borne testimony to Jesus, and now
Jesus uses this opportunity to bear testimony to
John the Baptist. Great crowds had gone out to
hear John when he preached in the desert (Matt.
3:1-6). It is probable that many had been attracted
to his desert meetings by the novelty of his dress
and also by the unusual doctrine he declared of
the coming King. It is true that some of the Jews
were looking for their King, but not all the people
by any means. And there is no doubt that many
who followed John the Baptist had now begun to
follow Jesus. Therefore, Jesus took this occasion
to ask some unique and striking questions concerning John the Baptist in order to examine the mo-
tives which prompted their attraction to the ministry of John.

"What went ye out into the wilderness to see?

A reed shaken with the wind?" The area where John the Baptist had preached was overflowed each spring by the flood waters of the Jordan River. Great quantities of reeds or canes of a very fragile nature grew there, and these reeds were easily shaken by the wind. They were a picture of a flippant, light, inconsistent man—that is, one who is constantly changing. The fact that John the Baptist in prison had sent messengers to Jesus asking if He was Christ might lead some to think that *John* was an inconsistent man like a reed. John had preached fervently, "Make straight the path, the King is coming"—and now he sends messengers to ask if the One he had announced as King was really the One they were looking for. But by asking the question here in verse 7, Jesus declared that John the Baptist was *not* a man of wavering character.

Verse 8: *"But what went ye out for to see? A man clothed in soft raiment? behold, they that wear soft clothing are in kings' houses."*

Jesus continues the questions by asking the people if they had gone out to see *"a man clothed in soft raiment."* Soft raiment would be light, thin, and worn by an effeminate person—not a ruddy, stalwart man like John the Baptist. The soft raiment to which Jesus referred was made primarily of very fine linen. John wore a very rough garment that was just the opposite—leather

27

instead of linen, camel's hair instead of lace. Jesus points out that where they went to hear John was not a place to find soft raiment; such clothing is found *"in kings' houses."* This kind of garment denoted riches, splendor, and lack of character. Jesus was telling these people that John was a *different* man, a singular man—coarse in his exterior, but firm, solid, in his character and virtue. He was a man equipped to endure trials and tribulations and thus qualified to be the forerunner of the suffering Messiah who was to come according to their prophets.

Verse 9: *"But what went ye out for to see? A prophet? Yea, I say unto you, and more than a prophet."*

Jesus continues His questions to the multitude by asking, *"What went ye out for to see? A prophet?"* The masses regarded John as a prophet, and the fact that there had been no prophet for so many centuries made them even more interested in his words. The fact that he was regarded as a prophet is borne out in Matthew 21:23-27:

"And when He (Jesus) was come into the temple, the chief priests and the elders of the people came unto Him as He was teaching, and said, By what authority doest thou these things? and who gave thee this authority? And Jesus answered and said unto them, I also will ask you one thing, which if ye tell me, I in like wise will tell you by what authority I do these things. The baptism of John, whence was it? from heaven, or of men? And they reasoned with themselves, saying, If we shall say, From heaven; He will say unto us, Why did ye not then believe him? But if we shall say, Of men; we fear the people; *for all hold John as a prophet.* And they answered Jesus, and said, We cannot tell. And He said unto them, Neither tell I you by what authority I do these things."

"Yea, I say unto you, and more than a prophet." Jesus tells the multitude that indeed John *was* a prophet—but he was exceedingly more than just an ordinary prophet. He was an inspired man who had come to announce the coming King, the Messiah. He was the fulfillment of prophecy uttered by their prophets in the days of their fathers. John held a unique and singular position that no other man had ever known—he was the forerunner of the Messiah. John the Baptist not only announced the coming of the King—he *baptized* the King. John not only said, "He will come," but he had the glorious opportunity of announcing, "He *has* come, and *there He is! Behold the Lamb of God!"*

The Lord Jesus was exalting His own mission by exalting the mission of John the Baptist. John had clearly announced to the multitudes that he must decrease and Christ must increase. John made it clear that he was not "that Prophet," but he was just a *voice* announcing the coming of that Prophet. Therefore, Jesus is saying, in effect,

"You should listen to me and to my words because I am the One of whom John spoke. If you believe that John was a prophet, then you should obey the One John announced as the Messiah."

It is most interesting to study the messages delivered by Jesus from the very outset of His ministry. Notice here how He uses introductory questions to lead up to the one great question. He uses illustrations of things that the people were accustomed to and knew about—a shaking reed and a man clothed with fine, soft raiment. These people knew what Jesus meant when He spoke of these things. Then He asked them the great question: "Did you really go out to see a reed or a man dressed in soft raiment in the wilderness, or did you go out to see a prophet?" Those who knew anything at all about the Old Testament Scriptures knew that the Messiah was coming and they knew that it was prophesied that Elijah would precede the Messiah; therefore, they went out to see a prophet.

All through His ministry, Jesus used illustrations understood by the people. He talked about the sower, the seed, the lilies of the field, the sparrows, and the mother hen protecting her chickens. Jesus preached messages that were down to earth, that anyone could understand. We need in the pulpits today words easily understood.

The Apostle Paul was also such a minister. He said, "So likewise ye, except ye utter by the tongue *words easy to be understood,* how shall it be known what is spoken? for ye shall speak into the air" (I Cor. 14:9). Paul gave this admonition to the Corinthians, of whom it was said, "Every one of you has a tongue, a song, a message," and then Paul rebuked them for the confusion in the church and declared that they needed to speak words easily understood. If the minister or the speaker did not use words that could be understood, then he was simply speaking "into the air." (Read I Corinthians 14:9-26.)

Verse 10: *"For this is he, of whom it is written, Behold, I send my messenger before thy face, which shall prepare thy way before thee."*

"This is he, of whom it is written . . . ." It is interesting to notice how many times Jesus quotes from the Old Testament in His messages to the people. The passage of Scripture quoted here is found in the prophecies of Isaiah and Malachi. In Isaiah 40:3 we read, "The voice of him that crieth in the wilderness, Prepare ye the way of the Lord, make straight in the desert a highway for our God." Malachi 3:1 states: "Behold, *I will send MY MESSENGER, and he shall prepare the way before me:* and the Lord, whom ye seek, shall suddenly come to His temple, even the messenger of the covenant, whom ye delight in: behold, He shall come, saith the Lord of hosts."

In this prophecy Jehovah speaks as if He Himself

31

is coming as the Messiah—which is true, because Jesus was God in flesh: "In the beginning was the Word, and the Word was with God, and *the Word was God.... And the Word was made flesh, and dwelt among us,* (and we beheld His glory, the glory as of the only begotten of the Father,) full of grace and truth" (John 1:1, 14). The Apostle Paul brings out the same truth in II Corinthians 5:19: "To wit, that *God was in Christ,* reconciling the world unto Himself, not imputing their trespasses unto them; and hath committed unto us the word of reconciliation."

Verse 11: *"Verily I say unto you, Among them that are born of women there hath not risen a greater than John the Baptist: notwithstanding he that is least in the Kingdom of Heaven is greater than he."*

"Among them that are born of women there hath not risen a greater than John the Baptist." Luke says, "a greater *prophet"* (Luke 7:28). We know that *Jesus* was born of a woman—the Virgin Mary—and we know that *He* was greater than John. However, the fact that Matthew leaves off the word "prophet" does not damage or contradict the Scripture. Jesus had just asked if the people had gone out to see a reed, one from a king's court, or *a prophet,* and it is understood that Jesus is declaring here that *no greater prophet* than John the Baptist had ever been born of women.

The testimony given by the Lord Jesus here concerning John the Baptist is unequaled; there is nothing else like it in all the Word of God or recorded in secular history. It is a glowing testimony. John was not a reed shaken with the wind. He was not a prophet in the ordinary sense of the word; he was an extraordinary prophet. He was the greatest of the prophets and the greatest of men up until that hour. To him God gave the exalted privilege of announcing the coming of the King and then proclaiming that the King was already present. No other man had ever had such a wonderful ministry up until that hour.

I think it will be well worth our time to read the account of the birth of John the Baptist as given in Luke 1:57-80:

"Now Elisabeth's full time came that she should be delivered; and she brought forth a son. And her neighbours and her cousins heard how the Lord had shewed great mercy upon her; and they rejoiced with her.

"And it came to pass, that on the eighth day they came to circumcise the child; and they called him Zacharias, after the name of his father. And his mother answered and said, Not so; but he shall be called John. And they said unto her, There is none of thy kindred that is called by this name. And they made signs to his father, how he would have him called. And he asked for a writing table, and wrote, saying, His name is John. And they

33

marvelled all. And his mouth was opened immediately, and his tongue loosed, and he spake, and praised God.

"And fear came on all that dwelt round about them: and all these sayings were noised abroad throughout all the hill country of Judaea. And all they that heard them laid them up in their hearts, saying, *What manner of child shall this be!* AND THE HAND OF THE LORD WAS WITH HIM.

"And his father Zacharias was filled with the Holy Ghost, and prophesied, saying, Blessed be the Lord God of Israel; for He hath visited and redeemed His people, and hath raised up an horn of salvation for us in the house of His servant David; as He spake by the mouth of His holy prophets, which have been since the world began: that we should be saved from our enemies, and from the hand of all that hate us; to perform the mercy promised to our fathers, and to remember His holy covenant; the oath which He sware to our father Abraham, that He would grant unto us, that we being delivered out of the hand of our enemies might serve Him without fear, in holiness and righteousness before Him, all the days of our life. *And thou, child, shalt be called the prophet of the Highest: for thou shalt go before the face of the Lord to prepare His ways;* to give knowledge of salvation unto His people by the remission of their sins, through the tender mercy of our God;

whereby the dayspring from on high hath visited us, to give light to them that sit in darkness and in the shadow of death, to guide our feet into the way of peace.

"And the child grew, and waxed strong in spirit, and was in the deserts till the day of his shewing unto Israel."

"Notwithstanding he that is least in the Kingdom of Heaven is greater than he." The last part of verse 11 is very confusing to some believers, but it need not be if we study and rightly divide the Word. I believe this Scripture has a twofold meaning. Primarily Jesus is speaking of the *position* of John the Baptist; i. e., not greater morally, but greater *positionally.* John the Baptist was the forerunner of the King and he announced that the Kingdom was at hand. However, the Jews *rejected* the King—and instead of crowning Him with a crown and placing Him on the throne of David, they crowned Him with thorns and nailed Him to a cross. So the Kingdom was not set up at that time but will be in the future. And the least in the Kingdom of Heaven will have a greater position than John the Baptist had in announcing the coming of the King. Jesus is not saying here that the least in *heaven* is greater than John, but He is talking about the *Kingdom of Heaven* which will be set up right here upon this earth.

But it is also true that the *new dispensation* brought in by the sacrifice of the Lord Jesus was on a higher plane than the dispensation of the law. The least in this glorious new dispensation is on higher ground than the greatest under the law. We are kings and priests unto God; we are sons of God by birth, heirs of God and joint-heirs with Christ. The most privileged person ever to live is one who by virtue of the shed blood is permitted to enter into the Kingdom of God by faith and to become a son of God through the miracle of the new birth. Such a person possesses divine nature and therefore can see and understand things which even the greatest of prophets, John the Baptist, did not fully understand.

Peter exclaims, "BLESSED BE THE GOD AND FATHER OF OUR LORD JESUS CHRIST, which according to His abundant mercy hath begotten us again unto a lively hope by the resurrection of Jesus Christ from the dead, to an inheritance incorruptible, and undefiled, and that fadeth not away, reserved in heaven for you, who are kept by the power of God through faith unto salvation ready to be revealed in the last time. Wherein ye greatly rejoice, though now for a season, if need be, ye are in heaviness through manifold temptations: that the trial of your faith, being much more precious than of gold that perisheth, though it be tried with fire, might be found unto praise and honour and glory at the appearing of Jesus Christ: whom having not seen, ye love; in whom, though now ye see Him not, yet believing, ye rejoice with joy unspeakable and full of glory: receiving the end of your faith, even the salvation of your souls.

"OF WHICH SALVATION THE PROPHETS HAVE INQUIRED AND SEARCHED DILIGENTLY, who prophesied of the grace that should come unto you: searching what, or what manner of time the Spirit of Christ which was in them did signify, when it testified beforehand THE SUFFERINGS OF CHRIST, AND THE GLORY THAT SHOULD FOLLOW. Unto whom it was revealed, that not unto themselves, but unto us they did minister the things, which are now reported unto you by them that have preached the Gospel unto you with the Holy Ghost sent down from heaven; *WHICH THINGS THE ANGELS DESIRE TO LOOK INTO"* (I Peter 1:3-12).

According to Peter, the men who prophesied in the Old Testament searched in an attempt to understand what was meant by words they themselves penned down concerning the sufferings and then the glory of Christ. *Angels* desired to look into these things but, of course, they were not allowed.

In I Peter 2:9, 10, it is declared that believers are a highly privileged people: "But *ye are a chosen generation, a royal priesthood, an holy nation, a peculiar people;* that ye should shew forth the praises of Him who hath called you out of darkness into His marvellous light: which in time

37

past were not a people, but are now the people of God: which had not obtained mercy, but now have obtained mercy."

Verse 12: *"And from the days of John the Baptist until now the Kingdom of Heaven suffereth violence, and the violent take it by force."*

The words of Jesus recorded in verses 12 through 15 have caused commentators much anxiety and have greatly troubled outstanding Bible teachers. They do not agree whether the *"violence"* mentioned here is external—that is, violence against John the Baptist and Jesus—or whether it points to the extreme opposition of the religious leaders of that day, so that only the violently resolute would dare press into the Kingdom. That is, only those who were daring, determined, and bold would dare follow Jesus and declare faithful allegiance to Him. Personally, I believe both positions are correct. John the Baptist, the forerunner of the King, and Jesus, the King, did suffer violence; and, no doubt, this is the primary meaning of the words here. However, we also know that when the going became difficult and rough, only those who were determined and resolute in their hearts continued to follow the Lord. We know that many suffered in prison and many were martyred because of their faithfulness to Christ.

Luke gives us this light on the passage: "The law and the prophets were until John: since that time the Kingdom of God is preached, and every man *presseth into it*" (Luke 16:16). The meaning here is that John preached the Gospel of the Kingdom with such power that some forgot the sacrifice they would be called upon to make to become a part of the Kingdom. In spite of the persecution, in spite of every obstacle, in spite of all opposition, they pressed, or *entered violently,* into the Kingdom. In other words, they had striven to enter in "at the strait gate." These had been so determined in their heart, so eager and so much in earnest about the Kingdom that nothing could keep them from becoming disciples of John the Baptist and later of the Lord Jesus Christ. These men had become in their deep, determined, intense desire, men of violence, and had taken the Kingdom *"by force."*

Verse 13: *"For all the prophets and the law prophesied until John."*

"The law" points to the five books of Moses, the first five books in our Bible. *"All the prophets"* indicates the rest of the books of the Old Testament. So we see that God had not left Himself without a witness here upon the earth throughout the silent years between Malachi and Matthew. The prophets had spoken, and the law was present. John the Baptist ended the chain of prophets, and our Lord draws a line by saying, *"UNTIL JOHN."*

Now the Lord Jesus Himself was present—and

His presence was truly the presence of God among men. Paul reveals the message to us in these words:

"God, who at sundry times and in divers manners spake in time past unto the fathers by the prophets, *hath in these last days SPOKEN UNTO US BY HIS SON, WHOM HE HATH APPOINTED HEIR OF ALL THINGS, BY WHOM ALSO HE MADE THE WORLDS; who being THE BRIGHT-NESS OF HIS GLORY, and THE EXPRESS IM-AGE OF HIS PERSON, and upholding all things by the word of His power, when He had by Him-self purged our sins, sat down on the right hand of the Majesty on high;* being made so much better than the angels, as He hath by inheritance ob-tained a more excellent name than they" (Heb. 1:1-4).

Verse 14: *"And if ye will receive it, this is Elias, which was for to come."*

"If ye will receive it." The message of God is the channel of salvation, edification, joy, assurance, peace; that is, *if* the message is received by faith. If the message is rejected, then it will stand to condemn the one who heard but refused to receive. John the Beloved makes this crystal clear in these words:

"But though He had done so many miracles before them, yet they believed not on Him: that the saying of Esaias the prophet might be fulfilled, which he spake, Lord, who hath believed our report? and to whom hath the arm of the Lord been revealed? Therefore they could not believe, because that Esaias said again, He hath blinded their eyes, and hardened their heart; that they should not see with their eyes, nor understand with their heart, and be converted, and I should heal them. These things said Esaias, when he saw His glory, and spake of Him" (John 12:37-41).

"This is Elias . . . ." Elias is the Greek for the Hebrew name, *Elijah.* We find the life and ministry of the great prophet, Elijah, recorded in the books of I and II Kings.

". . . which was for to come." Among the last words in Old Testament Scripture we read: "Behold, *I will send you Elijah the prophet before the coming of the great and dreadful day of the Lord:* and he shall turn the heart of the fathers to the children, and the heart of the children to their fathers, lest I come and smite the earth with a curse" (Mal. 4:5, 6). The Jews were not looking for one to come in the *spirit* of Elijah (see Luke 1:17). They looked for Elijah *literally,* expecting him to appear *in person* before the coming of the Lord.

We know there are two comings of the Lord Jesus Christ. When He came the first time, He offered Himself to Israel as their Messiah, their King; but He was rejected. As a result He was crucified, and the Kingdom was postponed until

41

His *second* coming, at the end of the Tribulation period. Of course, the Lord knew all of this from eternity, even though He came and offered Himself and the Kingdom to Israel.

The Scriptures clearly declare that the King is to be heralded by a forerunner; and from the passage in Malachi chapter 4, we know that forerunner will be *Elijah* when Jesus comes as King of kings and Lord of lords.

If you will notice, the word *"it"* in this verse in our Bible is in *italics,* indicating that this word is not in the original text but was supplied by the translators in order to make better sense. All such italicized words should be carefully watched, however, for sometimes they *confuse* the sense rather than clarifying it. This is true here, for I think Jesus is really saying, "If you will receive *Him* (meaning Jesus Himself), this *would have been* Elijah, which was for to come." In other words, if the nation Israel had accepted Christ at His first coming, then Elijah would indeed have come in person to announce the coming of the Lord. However, since God knew that they would not receive His Son, He sent John the Baptist instead, who was the "Elijah" of the first coming. According to Luke 1:17, John came *"in the spirit and power of Elias (Elijah)."* When Jesus comes to set up His Kingdom, Elijah himself will come, as we read in Malachi 4:5, 6. (In this connection read Revelation 11:3-12.)

42

Verse 15: *"He that hath ears to hear, let him hear."*

Jesus used this expression often. It implies that the highest and most undisturbed attention should be given to what was being spoken. Jesus regarded the doctrine about John the Baptist of the greatest importance. Those who were willing to listen attentively and allow the words spoken to enter their ears, their minds, and down into their hearts, would believe and clearly understand. What a solemn declaration— *"He that hath ears to hear, let him hear."*

John the Baptist and Jesus Rejected

As we look at verses 16 through 19, we will see that John the Baptist and Jesus the Messiah were both rejected by Israel. John was unsurpassed in the dignity of his calling, position, and ministry. The greatness of his work could never be estimated in words; but He whom John heralded was *even greater.* John declared that he was not even worthy to untie the shoes of the One whom he announced —but both were rejected by the nation Israel. John and Jesus had different—even opposite—peculiarities and modes of life; but the stubborn, willful, unreasonable generation to whom they appeared rejected both. The attitude and the spirit displayed by the people showed a determined opposition to the heavenly wisdom which John the Baptist and Jesus sought to make known to the nation Israel concerning the promised Messiah. The people had no excuse for rejecting John and Jesus, because what these two did and what they said had undeniable effects on the lives of all who received the message.

Verses 16 and 17: *"But whereunto shall I liken this generation? It is like unto children sitting in the markets, and calling unto their fellows, and saying, We have piped unto you, and ye have not danced; we have mourned unto you, and ye have not lamented."*

"Whereunto shall I liken this generation?" Earlier we pointed out that Jesus used unique and extraordinary illustrations; however, the conduct of these people was so strange and inconsistent that even Jesus seemed at a loss to find anything to which He could liken the people. (We find similar words in Mark 4:30: "And He said, *Whereunto shall we liken* the Kingdom of God? or *with what comparison shall we compare it?"* And in Luke 13:18-20 we read: "Then said He, Unto what is the Kingdom of God like? and *whereunto shall I resemble it?* It is like a grain of mustard seed, which a man took, and cast into his garden; and it grew, and waxed a great tree; and the fowls of the air lodged in the branches of it. And again He said, *Whereunto shall I liken* the Kingdom of God?")

When Jesus said, *"this generation,"* He did not

mean every individual without exception. He was
speaking in general of the masses and especially
the leaders, the scribes and the Pharisees. Luke
informs us that of the persons present on that
particular occasion, the common people and the
publicans justified God, having received John's
baptism: "And all the people that heard Him,
and the publicans, justified God, being baptized
with the baptism of John" (Luke 7:29). However,
the Pharisees and the lawyers declared void the
message given by Jesus, proclaiming themselves
the custodians of the counsels of Almighty God.
They refused the baptism of John.

(The Lord Jesus was not at that moment ready
to openly denounce the scribes and Pharisees,
calling them by name; but a little later He did so.
You will not find words anywhere in the Bible
with such scorching power as the words uttered
by the tender Lamb of God against these religious
leaders and recorded in Matthew 23.)

*"It is like unto children sitting in the markets,
and calling unto their fellows."* The markets
spoken of here were open places primarily. They
were not enclosed and did not have roofs. Pro-
visions of all kinds were bought and sold there.
It was at these market places the children gathered
to play. They came with their parents, some
probably from quite a distance; and some of them
did not see other children often except at the
market places.

This question and answer by Jesus reproves the religious leaders concerning the inconsistency and fickleness of their standards, both in religion and life in general. He said that they were acting like children—nothing pleased them. Children can be dancing and laughing one moment, sullen and dissatisfied the next. They can play in perfect harmony in a group one moment, and the next moment one may drop out and refuse to play at all. A group of children can be gathered in perfect harmony, laughing, talking, filled with joy—and in five minutes have a big fight, grumbling and accusing one another of being responsible for the discord. Also, children are imitators. Many times little girls dress in their mother's garments and act like grown-up ladies; and, of course, boys like to imitate their fathers. Children act out in play what they see in the home and in the life of their parents or other adults.

"We have piped unto you, and ye have not danced; we have mourned unto you, and ye have not lamented." Instrumental music and dancing were used in marriages, festivals, and many kinds of joyous community gatherings. (Please study Judges 11:34; II Samuel 6:14, 15; Job 21:11, 12; and Luke 15:25.) We also notice in Matthew 9:23 that music was used at *funerals,* as were mourning, lamentations, and howling. Men were paid to mourn and scream at a funeral. It is possible that these children in the streets and market places

imitated the funeral procession. One group is represented as being sullen, pouting, discontent, and dissatisfied. These would not enter into play with the other children; they could not be pleased, nothing suited them. The other group complained about it. They said, "We have piped to you, we have played music for you, we have engaged in several sports—but you have refused to join us. You have refused to play our games, to join in our singing and in our music. You have not lamented when we played funeral, but have refused to join in with us." In like manner, Jesus said, the generation of men present at that time were acting like these children.

Verses 18 and 19: *"For John came neither eating nor drinking, and they say, He hath a devil. The Son of man came eating and drinking, and they say, Behold a man gluttonous, and a wine-bibber, a friend of publicans and sinners. But wisdom is justified of her children."*

John came as a Nazarite, *"neither eating nor drinking,"* abstaining from food and drink in which other men indulged. His diet was locusts and wild honey (Matt. 3:4). But John did not please the Jews. They were dissatisfied with him and accused him of having a demon. By this they meant that he had a bad spirit. He was unusual—and he could not be a good man because he was so different!

47

Then Jesus said, "I, the Son of man, have come in a manner that is totally different from John. I have come *eating and drinking* and trying to live as you live, but you are just as unhappy and dissatisfied with me as you are with John. You slander him for not eating and drinking, and you abuse me for doing the very thing that you slander him for *not* doing. You cannot be pleased; you are fickle, inconsistent, abusive, changeable, stubborn, and hardhearted."

Had these religious leaders known their Scriptures they would have recognized that the peculiarities of both John the Baptist and Jesus the Messiah were appropriate and effective, producing works the truly wise would recognize. John's mode of life was suitable to his ministry and message. He came out of the wilderness clothed in camel's hair and a leather girdle, eating locusts and wild honey. He was the rugged forerunner, thundering out the warning to prepare the way for the coming King. Then *Jesus* came, moved in and out among the people, and lived with them. He visited in their homes, sat at their tables, and ate their food. He conformed to their way of life—but He did not partake of their sins.

John's way of life as the forerunner of Jesus was very unusual—and when *Jesus* came, the scribes and religious leaders thought it strange and unusual that He would sit with publicans and talk to harlots, being *"a friend of publicans and sinners."* The methods of both John and Jesus were condemned by the people, but both were of God. God sent John, and God sent Jesus. The peculiarities of their modes of life and their methods of working were strictly ordained of God.

"The Son of man came eating and drinking." Lest someone misunderstand, let me assure you that Jesus did not drink the kind of wine which is sold today in the liquor store or the supermarket. The Son of man came "eating and drinking"—but He did not drink fermented wine that would make one drunk. It is a known fact that in the days of our Lord, people had *new* wine and *old* wine. (Some authorities tell us that even the grapes still on the vine were referred to as wine.) Jesus said that men do not put *new wine* in old skins. If grape juice is placed in a stiff skin and left to the natural atmosphere, it will ferment and burst the skin. New wine is pure grape juice— and grape juice is good for anyone.

The Jews declared that Jesus was gluttonous and a winebibber. A winebibber is one who drinks much wine, and we know that Jesus did not indulge in drinking grape juice to excess or eating to excess. He was certainly temperate in all things. These people were inconsistent beyond words. John did not eat the natural food that they did in that day. He did not drink their wine or their grape juice, and they said he had a devil. Jesus ate with them and drank their new wine, and they said He was a drunkard and a winebibber, a friend of publicans and sinners.

"But wisdom is justified of her children." Thanks be unto God, there was a little remnant of true believers. Wisdom had a few children, and by them wisdom was justified. In Proverbs chapter 8, wisdom is a figure of the Lord Jesus Christ. This truth is also declared in Paul's letter to the Corinthian believers:

"Base things of the world, and things which are despised, hath God chosen, yea, and things which are not, to bring to nought things that are: that no flesh should glory in His presence. But of Him are ye in *Christ Jesus, who of God is MADE UNTO US WISDOM, and righteousness, and sanctification, and redemption:* that, according as it is written, He that glorieth, let him glory in the Lord" (I Cor. 1:28-31).

When God imputes wisdom into one's heart, that individual possesses the "power of judging rightly and following the soundest course of action" (Webster). Children of God are "children of wisdom" because they possess Christ (Col. 1:27).

"The fear of the Lord is the beginning of knowledge: *but FOOLS DESPISE WISDOM and instruction"* (Prov. 1:7). In Luke's Gospel we read that as Jesus gave testimony to John the Baptist, "All the people that heard Him, and the publicans, justified God, being baptized with the baptism of John. *But the Pharisees and lawyers rejected* the

counsel of God against themselves, being not baptized of him" (Luke 7:29, 30). The ministry of
John the Baptist was not a failure but a great and
glorious success. All who received his message
and were baptized of him also received the message
of Jesus and justified God. All those who failed
to receive the message of John the Baptist also
rejected the message of the Lord Jesus and, therefore, were lost eternally.

It is true that it was just a very small remnant
that showed any love for the message delivered by
John or Jesus. The masses have always rejected
the Word of God. They "heap to themselves
teachers, having itching ears" (II Tim. 4:3). They
cry to the prophets to speak smooth things—good
words. The great crowds rejected John and Jesus,
but thanks be unto God for the few that received
the message and the Messiah.

I am so glad the Lord Jesus was *"A FRIEND
OF PUBLICANS AND SINNERS"*—and I am glad
that Jesus is *still* the friend of sinners and it is
His desire to save all who will come to God by
Him. If you have not received His Word, I beg
you to "receive with meekness the engrafted Word,
which is able to save your souls" (James 1:21). It
is with the Word of truth that we are begotten of
God (James 1:18). Jesus declared to Nicodemus
that "except a man be born again, he cannot see
the Kingdom of God" (John 3:1-7). And Peter tells
us that we are "not redeemed with corruptible

things, as silver and gold," but we are redeemed "with the precious blood of Christ . . . being *born again,* not of corruptible seed, but of incorruptible, *by the Word of God,* which liveth and abideth for ever" (I Pet. 1:18-23).

Jesus said, "Verily, verily, I say unto you, He that heareth *my Word,* and believeth on Him that sent me, hath everlasting life, and shall not come into condemnation; but is passed from death unto life" (John 5:24). One must *hear the Word, believe the Word,* and *receive the Word* to be born again. The Word is the power of God unto salvation (Rom. 1:16). The Word is life (John 6:63). When we receive the Word of God, the Word brings faith (Rom. 10:17). Faith brings grace (Eph. 2:8), and grace brings salvation (Tit. 2:11).

Can you remember an experience when you received the Word of God by faith and invited Jesus to come into your heart? If you cannot remember such a time, let me urge you to have such an experience this moment. Just bow your head, close your eyes, and talk to Jesus as you would talk to your doctor about your physical needs or to your lawyer about your legal needs. Jesus is willing, anxious, and ready to tell the Father that you have heard the Word, received the Word, believed the Word, and that you do this moment trust Him as your Saviour. If you will tell Jesus that you want Him to forgive your sins and save you and take up His abode in your heart, He will.

Jesus Rejected; Judgment Is Sure

Verse 20: *"Then began He to upbraid the cities wherein most of His mighty works were done, because they repented not."*

"Then" (or immediately) Jesus *"began . . . to upbraid the cities . . . ."* That is, He began to reprove, to rebuke, to denounce their sin and their rejection of Him, and to make it clear that judgment was sure to follow. John the Baptist had announced that the Kingdom of Heaven was at hand. The Lord Jesus Himself and His twelve disciples had made the same announcement. The fact that the Kingdom was at hand was proven by many miracles and *"mighty works,"* but the message went unheeded. The announced Kingdom having been rejected, there was nothing left for Jesus to preach but judgment. When one man, a family, or a nation rejects the Gospel, *judgment is inevitable.*

Verse 21: *"Woe unto thee, Chorazin! woe unto thee, Bethsaida! for if the mighty works, which were done in you, had been done in Tyre and Sidon, they would have repented long ago in sackcloth and ashes."*

Chorazin and Bethsaida were towns not too far from Capernaum. We know the general locality according to historians, but we cannot pinpoint their exact location. The name *"Chorazin"* appears only in the woe pronounced upon it by our Lord. *"Bethsaida"* means literally "a house of hunting, or of game." This city was probably located on the banks of the Sea of Galilee, and the people earned their livelihood by fishing and hunting. We are told in John 1:44 that Philip, Andrew, and Peter lived there: "Now Philip was of Bethsaida, the city of Andrew and Peter." These two cities and Capernaum (v. 23) are named as the principal scene of Jesus' miracles. Matthew calls them "the cities wherein *most of His mighty works* were done" (v. 20).

Jesus said that if those "mighty works . . . *had been done in Tyre and Sidon, they would have repented . . . ." Tyre* and *Sidon* were cities of trade and were distinguished for their merchandise. These cities were situated on the shore of the Mediterranean Sea in the western part of Judaea and were well known to the Jews. The city of Tyre is mentioned often in the Old Testament as the place where Solomon purchased many of the materials for building the temple. (Please study II Chronicles 2:11-16.) Tyre was also a place against which outstanding and clear prophecies of judgment were directed. (Please study Isaiah 23 and Ezekiel 26.)

Located about twenty miles south of Sidon, Tyre was luxurious and extremely wicked. It was beseiged on many occasions by enemies and finally taken by Nebuchadnezzar after thirteen years of bloody war. Afterwards it was rebuilt, but later it was conquered again by Alexander the Great in a battle lasting five months. Tyre never regained its former glory, and for centuries it has been a "bare rock" where fishermen "spread their nets." This is an amazing fulfillment of the prophecy found in Ezekiel chapters 26 through 28.

Sidon was also a very famous city. Its inhabitants were the first remarkable merchants in the world. They were very able and wealthy merchants, known throughout the world for their luxury. When Jesus tabernacled among men here upon this earth, Sidon was probably a city of splendor and expansive trade. The name of the city now is Saida. It is not as large today as it was in the days of Jesus, and certainly not as luxurious. The city was first conquered by Babylon, later by Egypt, and then by the Romans, who completely took away their freedom.

"Sackcloth and ashes." Sackcloth was a very coarse cloth similar to canvas. The poor used it for their garments, and it was also used for domestic coverings. Sackcloth was worn as a sign of grief and mourning when someone died, and the Jews also frequently threw *ashes* on their heads to express their grief at a time of mourning. In this regard, please study the following passages in the Old Testament: II Samuel 13:19; Esther 4:3; Job 2:12; Jeremiah 6:26; Lamentations 2:10; Jonah 3:6; Micah 1:10. Job said, "I abhor myself, and repent *in dust and ashes*" (Job 42:6). Daniel

prayed "with fasting, and *sackcloth, and ashes*"
(Dan. 9:3). This and other various modes of mani-
festing sorrow and extreme grief among the Israelites were natural. In some eastern nations, people
still express their grief in this manner.

*"They would have repented long ago in sack-
cloth and ashes."* By this statement Jesus meant
that if Tyre and Sidon had been as privileged as
were Chorazin and Bethsaida—if they had seen
His miracles, His "mighty works"—they would
have repented with deep sorrow and anguish over
their sins. Like Nineveh, they would have seen
the coming judgment and would have turned from
their sin and cried out to God for forgiveness.
Jesus is saying that heathen cities would have received Him better than the religious cities of the
Jews, even His own native land.

The wicked city of Nineveh actually repented
in sackcloth and ashes as the result of the preaching of Jonah, the prophet:

"So the people of Nineveh believed God, and
proclaimed a fast, and *put on sackcloth,* from the
greatest of them even to the least of them. For
word came unto the king of Nineveh, and he arose
from his throne, *and he laid his robe from him,
and covered him with sackcloth, and sat in ashes.*
And he caused it to be proclaimed and published
through Nineveh by the decree of the king and his
nobles, saying, Let neither man nor beast, herd
nor flock, taste any thing: let them not feed, nor

drink water: but *let man and beast be covered
with sackcloth,* and cry mightily unto God: yea,
let them turn every one from his evil way, and
from the violence that is in their hands. Who can
tell if God will turn and repent, and turn away
from His fierce anger, that we perish not?

"And God saw their works, that they turned
from their evil way; and God repented of the evil,
that He had said that He would do unto them;
and He did it not" (Jonah 3:5-10).

Verse 22: *"But I say unto you, It shall be more
tolerable for Tyre and Sidon at the day of judgment, than for you."*

Jesus clearly teaches here that men will be
judged according to the opportunities they have.
The heathen are lost, for no man can enter heaven
except he receive Jesus. To enter heaven one must
be born again. For one to be born again, he must
hear the Gospel; therefore, the heathen who have
never heard the Gospel cannot be born again. They
are lost and they will not enter heaven. But they
will not suffer the intense suffering that people
from America will suffer—people who have had
opportunity after opportunity to be saved but have
rejected the message.

Tyre and Sidon are not *excused* because they
did not have the opportunity of witnessing the
mighty miracles of the Lord Jesus Christ, but it
shall be *"more tolerable"* for them *"at the day of*

judgment" than for the people of Chorazin and Bethsaida. The same is true today. If you are not saved, every opportunity that you turn down to receive Jesus will make your suffering more intense in hell. Men will be judged according to the opportunities and the light rejected. Those who live in darkness and have never had the opportunity to walk in the light will be judged and will be lost, but they will not suffer the intense suffering of those who had the light of the Gospel but refused to walk in that light.

The term *"day of judgment"* is found in Matthew 10:15; 11:22, 24; 12:36; II Peter 2:9; 3:7; and I John 4:17. Please compare these Scriptures with the following words: *"He hath appointed a day, in the which He will judge the world in righteousness* by that Man whom He hath ordained; whereof He hath given assurance unto all men, in that He hath raised Him from the dead"* (Acts 17:31). In Jude 6 we read: "And the angels which kept not their first estate, but left their own habitation, He hath reserved in everlasting chains under darkness unto *the judgment of the great day."*

"The day of judgment" is also referred to in the Word of God as "the day of God," "the day of the Lord," "the day of Christ," "the last day," "the day of wrath," "that day." Please study Matthew 7:22, I Thessalonians 5:4, and Hebrews 10:25.

Jesus will be the righteous Judge in that day.

He said, "Many will say *TO ME in that day*, Lord, Lord, have we not prophesied in thy name? and in thy name have cast out devils? and in thy name done many wonderful works?" (Matt. 7:22). (He is also seen as the Judge in Matthew 25:34 at the judgment of the nations: "Then shall the King say unto them on His right hand, Come, ye blessed of my Father, inherit the Kingdom prepared for you from the foundation of the world.") Let me assure you that you will be judged righteously. All you deserve will be given to you; and if you are lost eternally, there will be nothing put upon you that you do not deserve. Jesus will judge in righteousness and His judgment will be fair. In I Corinthians 4:5 we are instructed to *"judge nothing before the time,* until *the Lord* come, who both will bring to light the hidden things of darkness, and will make manifest the counsels of the hearts: and then shall every man have praise of God."

The statement made by Jesus concerning the judgment of these cities no doubt startled the Jews. They thought themselves safe from judgment because they were descendants of Abraham. They looked with contempt upon all Gentiles, and because *they* were *the elect* they thought nothing could happen to them.

Verse 23: *"And thou, Capernaum, which art exalted unto heaven, shalt be brought down to hell: for if the mighty works, which have been done in thee, had been done in Sodom, it would have remained until this day."*

Jesus makes a stronger statement concerning Capernaum than He made concerning the other cities. Capernaum was more prosperous than Chorazin and Bethsaida and more favored with the Saviour's presence, miracles, and teachings. Jesus visited the city of Capernaum many, many times. According to Matthew 4:13, Jesus dwelt in Capernaum at least for a time and traveled out of that city, using it as His headquarters. In Matthew 9:1 it is called "His own city." Therefore, He declares judgment upon the city with even stronger terms than He had on the previous cities.

Some of Jesus' most outstanding miracles were performed at Capernaum. In John 4:46-54, we have the account of the healing of the nobleman's son. In Mark 1:23-28 is recorded the healing of the demoniac in the synagogue. In Matthew 8 we find the healing of the centurion's servant and the healing of Peter's wife's mother. Matthew 9 records the healing of the paralytic who was carried on a cot to Jesus, the raising from the dead of the daughter of Jairus, the healing of the woman with the issue of blood, and the healing of the two blind men and the dumb demoniac. Jesus did these and many other mighty works in the city of Capernaum.

"Which art exalted unto heaven" denotes great privileges. Capernaum had been favored in an

unusual way by the presence of Jesus and in many other ways. It was a very prosperous and wealthy city. Some authorities think these words may well refer to the excessive pride of the inhabitants in their city.

"*. . . shalt be brought down to hell.*" This prosperous, wealthy city which was "exalted unto heaven" would be debased. Jesus was not speaking of every person in the city of Capernaum dropping into hell. The city which had flourished and was so wealthy would lose its prosperity; it would be completely demoted, occupying the lowest place among the cities of that day. Jesus uses the word "hell" here in contrast to heaven. Heaven is the most glorious of places and hell is the lowest. Hell is a place of desolation and destruction—and desolation and destruction would come upon Capernaum because of their pride and their sin. Their great privileges on earth and their prosperity would be taken away, and they would go as far down as they had ascended up. This was literally fulfilled, and the very site of this once great city is a matter of dispute today.

"*If the mighty works, which have been done in thee, had been done in Sodom, it would have remained until this day.*" If the mighty works that were done in Capernaum had been done in Sodom, Jesus declared that the city would not have been burned but would have remained until that day. Sodom was the most wicked city of its day, no doubt. The sin of *sodomy* is referred to with shame and humiliation. Sodom was destroyed completely because of its great wickedness (Gen. 19); however, if Sodom had had the opportunities that Capernaum had, they would have repented and the city would have been spared. Therefore, it would be easier for Sodom in the day of judgment than for Capernaum. The inhabitants of Sodom did not have the opportunities that the inhabitants of Capernaum had; therefore, they did not abuse the privileges that the people of the flourishing city of Capernaum abused. Sodom was never visited by the Lord Jesus Christ; Capernaum was.

What Jesus said about Capernaum can be said about an individual. A person who has been favored in a very singular way will be punished accordingly if that person refuses to use the opportunities and the privileges afforded him. If an individual is exposed to light in the spiritual sense and refuses to walk in that light, then he will be judged accordingly. If a sinner is given many gracious and glorious opportunities to become a Christian but refuses to receive the Lord Jesus and be saved, then he will be judged and punished in like manner.

Verse 24: *"But I say unto you, That it shall be more tolerable for the land of Sodom in the day of judgment, than for thee."*

"I say unto you . . . ." Here, as on many occasions and recorded in many other places, Jesus speaks from His own full divine authority. Jesus spoke truth because *He was (and IS) Truth.* He was the Word incarnate, and He will Himself be the righteous Judge.

"It shall be more tolerable for the land of Sodom in the day of judgment." We need not speculate concerning what the Sodomites will go through in judgment, but we know that it will be less than the penalty inflicted upon those who have sinned against light such as Capernaum enjoyed in the presence of the Lord Jesus Christ Himself. He was there in the city but they refused to see the light; therefore, they will be judged for rejecting the light that they could have known and could have seen if they would only have listened to His words. To reject the message of the glorious Gospel of the grace of God is to bring severe and added judgment upon oneself throughout eternity.

Verse 25: *"At that time Jesus answered and said, I thank thee, O Father, Lord of heaven and earth, because thou hast hid these things from the wise and prudent, and hast revealed them unto babes."*

The last six verses of chapter 11 contain the final remarks of Jesus occasioned by the message from John the Baptist. These last six verses are in two divisions—verses 25 through 27 and verses

28 through 30. The message recorded in verses 25 through 27 is also found in Luke 10:21-24; however, the message found in the final three verses is recorded by Matthew only.

"At that time" means "on that occasion." At that time Jesus ceased speaking concerning the scribes and Pharisees and the nations that had rejected Him. Now He turns to the Father and gives thanks because the Father has *"hid these things"* from the men who profess to be *"wise and prudent"*—that is, these religious leaders who announced themselves the custodians of the law and the prophets. They professed to be wise, but they were fools; they professed to be the men to whom God had given the light, and yet they rejected the light. Jesus thanks the Father that those who are humble as little children receive the message while those who profess to be wise and prudent reject the message.

In the words spoken by the Lord Jesus at this time, He tells of the unreasonable and determined rejection by the religious leaders, both of John the Baptist and Himself (verses 16 through 19). He speaks of the impenitence of even the cities where He performed many mighty miracles (verses 20 through 24). Yet these Jews—especially the teachers, the scribes, the chief priests, and other leading men—were intelligent. They were well acquainted with the words of the prophets and the Psalms. They knew much about the coming Messiah, and yet they failed to comprehend and appreciate the words and miracles of Jesus. However, those who were humble, lowly, and comparatively ignorant received His words. We see an example of this in Luke's account of the healing of the palsied man whose friends brought him to Jesus:

"And it came to pass on a certain day, as He was teaching, that *there were Pharisees and doctors of the law sitting by,* which were come out of every town of Galilee, and Judaea, and Jerusalem: and the power of the Lord was present to heal them. And, behold, men brought in a bed a man which was taken with a palsy: and they sought means to bring him in, and to lay him before Him. And when they could not find by what way they might bring him in because of the multitude, they went upon the housetop, and let him down through the tiling with his couch into the midst before Jesus. And when He saw their faith, He said unto him, Man, thy sins are forgiven thee. And *the scribes and the Pharisees began to reason, saying, Who is this which speaketh blasphemies?* Who can forgive sins, but God alone?

"But when Jesus perceived their thoughts, He answering said unto them, What reason ye in your hearts? Whether is easier, to say, Thy sins be forgiven thee; or to say, Rise up and walk? But that ye may know that the Son of man hath power upon earth to forgive sins, (He said unto the sick of the palsy,) I say unto thee, Arise, and take up thy couch, and go into thine house. And immediately he rose up before them, and took up that whereon he lay, and departed to his own house, glorifying God. *And they were all amazed, and they glorified God,* and were filled with fear, saying, We have seen strange things to day" (Luke 5:17-26).

In this account we learn that there were Pharisees and doctors of the law out of every town of Galilee and Judaea, and from Jerusalem there. Jesus openly declared that He had the power to forgive sins, yet they missed the truth of His statement. Why did these men—even though they witnessed that day a tremendous display of the power of God—not recognize their Messiah, that Prophet of whom their prophets spoke? But many people did recognize Him and went away glorifying God. These glorious truths were hidden from the doctors of the law, but God *"revealed them unto babes."*

Jesus is not speaking (here in Matthew 11:25) of little babies a few days old, but babes in wisdom, wealth, and social standing. And it is interesting to notice here that Jesus thanks the Father both for hiding these things from one class and for revealing them to another class. Jesus preached to all—the rich, the poor, the wise, the unwise, the bond, the free. The majority of the persons who received Jesus were poor, obscure, ignorant, simple, humble—and, therefore, teachable. The wise, the rich, the prudent, and the social crowd refused to hear His message. The proud, haughty Pharisees in Capernaum and throughout the land rejected His simple Gospel message. But it was the pleasure of Almighty God to reveal this wonderful good news to the poor, the humble, the obscure. Some ask, "Why? Why did God hide these things from the doctors of the law and reveal them unto the ignorant?" The only answer that anyone can give is recorded in the next verse:

Verse 26: *"Even so, Father: for so it seemed good in thy sight."*

Such is the will of Almighty God; and on many occasions the only explanation that can be offered is that it is God's will. Our understanding is often confounded, and we are frequently unsuccessful in all of our efforts at explanation. Our philosophy fails—and all that we can say is what Jesus said: *"Even so, Father: for so it seemed good in thy sight."* This enough; we need not say more.

When God does anything, the best answer that man can give for that which God does is that God has a right to do it. God cannot do wrong. God is righteous, God is holy, God is pure, and it is impossible for God to sin or do wrong. Therefore, whatsoever God doeth, it is for man's good and for God's glory. We need not through the wisdom of man attempt to reason out many of the things God does and allows. How comforting and assuring it is to know that our God cannot make a mistake. Jesus said to His disciples, "Have faith in God" (Mark 11:22). When you and I have faith in God, we will never question what He does, what He says, or what He commands us to do.

Verse 27: *"All things are delivered unto me of my Father: and no man knoweth the Son, but the Father; neither knoweth any man the Father, save the Son, and he to whomsoever the Son will reveal Him."*

"All things are delivered unto me of my Father." The doctrinal thought here is clearly taught often in the New Testament. (Please study John 3:35; 5:22; 13:3; I Corinthians 15:27, 28; Ephesians 1:22, 23.) At some time in the eternity behind us, all things were committed unto God's Son—in particular, all things pertaining to man in the truth of redemption, things pertaining to the Church. In Paul's letter to the Colossians, we read that "by Him were all things created, that are in heaven, and that are in earth, visible and invisible, whether they be thrones, or dominions, or principalities, or powers: all things were created by Him, and for Him: and He is before all things, and *by Him all things consist. And He is the head of the body, the Church:* who is the beginning, the first-born from the dead; *that in all things He might have the preeminence"* (Col. 1:16-18).

Christ has control over all things for the good of the Church—that is, the true Church made up

of all born-again believers. He is the head and
the foundation of the Church. We are bone of His
bone and flesh of His flesh, as revealed in Paul's
letter to the Ephesians: "For the husband is the
head of the wife, even as *Christ is the head of the
Church: and He is the Saviour of the body. . . .*
Husbands, love your wives, even as Christ also
loved the Church, and gave Himself for it; that
He might sanctify and cleanse it with the washing
of water by the Word, that He might present it
to Himself a glorious Church, not having spot, or
wrinkle, or any such thing; but that it should be
holy and without blemish. . . . *For we are members
of His body, of His flesh, and of His bones. . . .*
This is a great mystery: but I speak concerning
Christ and the Church" (Eph. 5:23-32).

It is another and distinct fact that the government of the universe is committed to Him (Eph.
1:20-22). We know that not all rulers are God-
fearing men; but God is Ruler over all, and in the
end all things will redound to the glory of God.
We know that many things are carried on by human governments that are not in accord with God's
righteousness and holiness. God *allows* this, but
it is not according to His *will.* However, it cannot
be denied that "the most High ruleth in the kingdom of men, and giveth it to whomsoever He will"
(Dan. 4:25).

All things in this universe will eventually glorify
God, and the Church will display His glory in the

Pearly White City throughout the ages of ages. Paul clearly indicates this in the following Scriptures:

Ephesians 1:15-23: "Wherefore I also, after I heard of your faith in the Lord Jesus, and love unto all the saints, cease not to give thanks for you, making mention of you in my prayers; that the God of our Lord Jesus Christ, the Father of glory, may give unto you the spirit of wisdom and revelation in the knowledge of Him: the eyes of your understanding being enlightened; that ye may know what is the hope of His calling, and what the riches of the glory of His inheritance in the saints, and what is the exceeding greatness of His power to us-ward who believe, according to the working of His mighty power, which He wrought in Christ, when He raised Him from the dead, and set Him at His own right hand in the heavenly places, far above all principality, and power, and might, and dominion, and every name that is named, not only in this world, but also in that which is to come: *and hath put all things under His feet, and gave Him to be the head over all things to the Church, which is His body, the fulness of Him that filleth all in all.*"

Ephesians 2:4-7: "God, who is rich in mercy, for His great love wherewith He loved us, . . . *hath raised us up together, and made us sit together in heavenly places in Christ Jesus: that in the ages to come He might shew the exceeding riches*

*of His grace in His kindness toward us through
Christ Jesus."*

"No man knoweth the Son, but the Father."
That is, none but God *fully* knows Him. The
finite mind of man cannot comprehend fully the
nature of the Son of God or the mystery of the
union between the human and the divine. God
is infinite and omniscient, man is finite and limited; therefore, no mortal man can fully comprehend God's Son. We accept Him by faith and
believe that He is Christ, the Son of God, the
Lamb without spot or blemish. We believe that
He was conceived of the Holy Ghost and born of
the Virgin Mary. The finite mind cannot understand these things, but we accept them *by faith.*
He was man—but He was *more* than man. Liberals and modernists refuse to accept the virgin
birth, the deity of Christ, or the Incarnation, because they cannot *explain* these things. But the
finite mind of man *cannot explain* our God and
cannot know His ways, except as it pleases God
to reveal His ways to us.

No one will ever accept Jesus as Saviour apart
from the enlightening power of the Word of God
and the drawing power of the Holy Spirit. The
Word of God brings light, the Spirit convicts and
draws; therefore, man can be saved only by God's
grace through faith. Faith that brings saving grace
comes only by hearing the Word. (Please study
Ephesians 2:8, 9 and Romans 10:17.)

"... *neither knoweth any man the Father, save the Son, and he to whomsoever the Son will reveal Him.*" Just as man cannot know *Christ* fully, the same is true concerning God the Father. No one knows the Father except the Son. Jesus said, "As the Father knoweth me, even so know I the Father . . ." (John 10:15). *No man,* regardless of how wise he may be, can clearly and fully understand God. Only the Son understands and knows the Father, and only through Jesus can any man know God. In John 1:1 we read, "In the beginning was the Word, and the Word was with God, and the Word was God." Later in that chapter we read, "And the Word was made flesh, and dwelt among us, (and we beheld His glory, the glory as of the only begotten of the Father,) full of grace and truth" (John 1:14). Then in verse 18 of that chapter we read, "*No man hath seen God at any time; the only begotten Son, which is in the bosom of the Father, He hath declared Him.*"

Christ was in the beginning with the Father. The Triune God has been from everlasting and will be to everlasting. Approximately two thousand years ago Jesus took a body of flesh and came into this world to declare God's love, God's grace, and God's mercy. Therefore, no man can come to God except through Jesus Christ (John 14:6). No man will ever accept God as the Father of our Saviour, Jesus Christ, unless He allows Jesus to reveal to him the truth of the Father.

The Apostle Paul tells us that "the natural man receiveth not the things of the Spirit of God: for they are foolishness unto him: neither can he know them, because they are spiritually discerned" (I Cor. 2:14). The Spirit of God makes known to the sincere soul the truth about spiritual things. No man can know God the Father or God the Son except as they are revealed to the individual through the Word as the Spirit enlightens the mind that has been blinded by the god of this age:

"If our Gospel be hid, it is hid to *them that are lost: in whom the god of this world hath blinded the minds of them which believe not*, lest the light of the glorious Gospel of Christ, who is the image of God, should shine unto them. For we preach not ourselves, but Christ Jesus the Lord; and ourselves your servants for Jesus' sake. For God, who commanded the light to shine out of darkness, hath shined in our hearts, *to give the light of the knowledge of the glory of God* in the face of Jesus Christ" (II Cor. 4:3-6).

The natural man is dead in trespasses and sins (Eph. 2:1). The natural man is blinded by the god of this world (II Cor. 4:4). The natural man cannot receive the things of God, for they are spiritual and he is carnal (I Cor. 2:14; Rom. 8:7, 8). Therefore, the natural man is hopeless, helpless, and hell-bound, apart from God.

The plan of salvation is clearly laid down in Romans 10:9-17: "That if thou shalt *confess with thy mouth* the Lord Jesus, and shalt *believe in thine heart* that God hath raised Him from the dead, *thou shalt be saved.* For with the heart man believeth unto righteousness; and with the mouth confession is made unto salvation. . . . For *whosoever shall call upon the name of the Lord shall be saved.* How then shall they call on Him in whom they have not believed? and how shall they believe in Him of whom they have not heard? and how shall they hear without a preacher? and how shall they preach, except they be sent? as it is written, How beautiful are the feet of them that preach the Gospel of peace, and bring glad tidings of good things! But they have not all obeyed the Gospel. For Esaias saith, Lord, who hath believed our report? *So then faith cometh by hearing, and hearing by the Word of God.*"

The lost, dead, blinded, helpless sinner must first hear the Word and believe the Word; then the light of the glorious Gospel breaks into the darkened and blinded mind. The Spirit, using the light of the Word, opens the darkened heart; and the individual seeking salvation is saved by hearing, believing, receiving, and confessing. Hearing the Word precedes all else. No one can be transformed from a sinner to a child of God apart from hearing the Word of God. Jesus came to declare God (John 1:18); and in declaring God, He declared the *love* of God and the *grace* of God (I John 4:8; Heb. 2:9).

The New Message of Jesus:
Not the Kingdom, but Personal Discipleship

Verse 28: *"Come unto me, all ye that labour and are heavy laden, and I will give you rest."*

There is no doubt in my mind that Jesus is referring primarily here to the Jewish system. The Jews groaned under the heavy weight of their ceremonies, laws, traditions, dogmas, and holy days. Peter asked the Church leaders in Jerusalem, "Now therefore why tempt ye God, to put *a yoke upon the neck of the disciples, WHICH NEITHER OUR FATHERS NOR WE WERE ABLE TO BEAR?"* (Acts 15:10). Jesus tells the Jews here in verse 28 of Matthew 11 that if they will come to Him and receive His message, they will be set free from these burdensome rites, ceremonies, feasts, and offerings.

There can be no doubt, however, that He also meant these words for the unsaved person. The poor sinner is weighed down, burdened down, with transgressions and sins. The sinner who sees his condition will tremble before God as he sees the heavy burden resting upon him. Jesus invites all— those who are burdened down with religion, ceremonies, laws, traditions; and those who are just poor, lost sinners who profess no religion but know they are burdened down with sin. He invites *all* to come to Him. He says, *"Come unto me, all ye that labour and are heavy laden, and I will give*

75

you rest." There is a beautiful picture of salvation here.

Christ's Gracious Invitation

When we step out at night and look up into the sky, it seems to be studded with gems—some sparkling a little brighter than others. We call them stars. The Bible is filled with spiritual gems —diamonds and rubies. To me *this* is one of the diamonds of the Bible—these words of Jesus: *"Come unto me, all ye that labour and are heavy laden, and I will give you rest."* In these words we have stated the entire purpose of the coming of the Lord Jesus Christ into this world. We have here the answer for every heartache, every need, and every want. *Any* and *all* who will come to Jesus will find rest.

Christ's invitation is SIMPLE:—

Many times ministers use much time preparing a sermon, attempting to prepare it homiletically so as to make a deep impression on educated people as well as the uneducated. But we have many of the sermons of Jesus recorded in the Gospels, and all of them were very simple. Here He said, *"Come unto me."* The religion of the Jews was a religion that demanded feast days, holy days, ceremonies, and offerings. (The same is true in modern religions and sects.) How refreshing it must have been to the poor and the heavy laden when Jesus said simply, *"Come."*

Has it ever dawned upon you that this is one of the first words in man's vocabulary? When the baby is born and the mother reaches into the bassinet to pick up the infant, she says, "Come to Mother." When the baby begins to sit in the playpen and the mother puts forth her arms to pick it up, she says, "Come." The first step the baby takes, the mother puts out her arms and says, "Come."

Jesus said, *"Come."* This word can be understood when other words are confusing and irritating. Religions declare that man must *quit, abstain, do, go, give,* and *be.* Religions demand that eternal life and rest depend upon what you *do* and what you do *not* do. But Jesus said, "Come. Simply come to me, and I will *give . . . ."*

His invitation was simple and understandable. Jesus said to Peter and Andrew, *"Come* ye after me, and I will make you to become fishers of men" (Mark 1:17). When the disciples were tired and weary, Jesus said, *"Come* ye . . . apart . . . , and rest a while" (Mark 6:31). When two of John's disciples asked Jesus, "Where do you live?" He said, *"Come* and see" (John 1:38-40). After the disciples had toiled all night and had not caught one fish, Jesus had breakfast prepared on the sands of the seashore of Galilee and He said, *"Come* and dine" (John 21:1-12).

Regardless of how wicked and ungodly the sinner may be, our Lord's invitation is "Come to

77

me." There is no one else to whom the sinner
can go. There is no other way, no other door, no
other name. He is the Way, the Truth, and the
Life, and no man can come to the Father but
by Jesus (John 14:6).

Christ's invitation is TO ALL:—

The Lord Jesus invited *all: "Come unto me,
ALL YE that labour and are heavy laden."* The
salvation that Jesus brought down to man is for
all—no one is excluded. This is revealed beauti-
fully in John 3:16: "For God so loved *the world,*
that He gave His only begotten Son, that *whosoever* believeth in Him should not perish, but
have everlasting life." And we see in John 6:37
that no one has ever been turned away: "All that
the Father giveth me shall come to me; and *him
that COMETH to me I will IN NO WISE cast
out."*

II Peter 3:9 reveals to us the longsuffering of
God: "The Lord is not slack concerning His promise, as some men count slackness; but is longsuffering to us-ward, *not willing that ANY should
perish, but that ALL should come to repentance."*
And the Bible closes with another invitation: "And
the Spirit and the bride say, *Come.* And let him
that heareth say, *Come.* And let him that is athirst
come. And *whosoever will,* let him take the water
of life freely" (Rev. 22:17).

There is not a club, an organization, or a man-made religion on earth to which all men could belong. All clubs, religions, and organizations instituted by man have requirements and stipulations that *some* persons cannot meet for various and sundry reasons. *But SALVATION is for ALL.* All anyone need do to become a child of God is to come to Jesus and receive Him by faith. He is God's love-gift to this world, and all who will receive Jesus *can be* and *will be* saved. No one is excluded. It is not God's will that any perish, but that all men repent. God has no pleasure in the death of the wicked (Ezek. 33:11)—but He rejoices in the salvation of the sinner.

Christ's invitation is SURE: —

All can *rely* on the invitation Jesus gives here: *"Come unto me, all ye that labour and are heavy laden, and I WILL GIVE YOU REST."* Jesus will give rest to all who come to Him. He cannot lie, He cannot break His Word, He cannot break His promise. (Let me point out that God reserved the sole right for *His Son* to give rest to all who will receive Jesus. This rest cannot be purchased or attained through human merit; it comes only by receiving Jesus.) This life is filled with disappointments, heartaches, and tears. Even the most reliable of people can fail, but *JESUS cannot fail!* One of the most heartbreaking things on this earth is for one to place confidence in the promises of an individual or an organization, only to discover at the most crucial moment that one's trust has been misplaced. This is sickening to the heart of any man.

Jesus said, *"COME UNTO ME . . . I WILL GIVE YOU REST."* That promise made by Jesus almost two thousand years ago has been put to the test by many and found to be true! No man or woman has ever come to Jesus in sincerity to find Him turn them away. No man or woman has ever put trust in the words of Jesus and found them disappointing. Jesus is God—and *it is "impossible for God to lie"* (Heb. 6:18). This is revealed to us again in Titus 1:2: "In hope of eternal life, which *God, that cannot lie,* promised before the world began." You can rest assured that the promises of God recorded in His Word are always true, trustworthy, and reliable.

Christ's invitation is SUBLIME:—

Jesus said, "Come to me, and I will give you rest"—a rare jewel in our Bible. It reveals to us that we can have *free,* simply by receiving, that which multi-billionaires cannot buy. Rest cannot be purchased with earth's money. It is freely *given* to those who come to Jesus.

Rest is not advice freely given by a friend; rest is not sympathy sincerely expressed by a loved one; rest is not financial assistance offered by a friend in time of need. Rest is healing for a broken heart, comfort for a troubled mind, fellowship for a lonely spirit. Rest is unspeakable relief for a soul that is haunted by sin and unbelief. Rest is the dawn after the stormy midnight, the calm after the billows have folded and lain down. Rest is laughter after bitter tears, glad reunion after a long heartbreaking separation. To sum it all up, rest is the gift of God to a weary, sin-sick, heart-broken, tear-stained, blood-drenched world.

No king on earth can supply his subjects with rest. No dictator or president can give rest to his people. No engineer can manufacture rest. It belongs exclusively to Christ, and He alone can give it to others. He said, *"Come unto me—and I will give you rest."* It does not matter how deep in sin one may be, how far into the darkness one may have gone, how wretched one's soul and spirit may be—if that dear one will come to Jesus, *he will receive rest.* He will receive rest for his soul *now*, and a glorious *future rest* promised to the children of God: *"There remaineth therefore A REST to the people of God"* (Heb. 4:9).

Verse 29: *"Take my yoke upon you, and learn of me; for I am meek and lowly in heart: and ye shall find rest unto your souls."*

"Take my yoke upon you." This is a figure taken from the yoke used with oxen, and therefore signifies labor or service. If you have ever seen a yoke on oxen, you know it is a beam that fits across the necks of the animals and binds them

together as they plow or pull the ox cart. In the Bible the yoke is used as an emblem of bondage, affliction, punishment, etc. Let me give you a brief outline of the use of the yoke in the Bible:

1. The yoke is used as an emblem of bondage or slavery: "I am the Lord your God, which brought you forth out of the land of Egypt, that ye should not be their bondmen; and *I have broken the bands of your yoke,* and made you go upright" (Lev. 26:13). Also, in Deuteronomy 28:48 we read, "Therefore shalt thou serve thine enemies which the Lord shall send against thee, in hunger, and in thirst, and in nakedness, and in want of all things: and He shall put *a yoke of iron* upon thy neck, until He have destroyed thee."

2. The yoke is spoken of in connection with the punishment of sin: "The yoke of my transgressions is bound by His hand: they are wreathed, and come up upon my neck: He hath made my strength to fall, the Lord hath delivered me into their hands, from whom I am not able to rise up" (Lam. 1:14).

3. The yoke is referred to concerning afflictions or crosses: "It is good for a man that he bear *the yoke* in his youth" (Lam. 3:27).

4. The yoke is used in connection with the commandments of God or of legal ceremonies: "Now therefore why tempt ye God, to put *a yoke* upon the neck of the disciples, which neither our fathers nor we were able to bear?" (Acts 15:10). And in Galatians 5:1 we read, "Stand fast therefore in the liberty wherewith Christ hath made us free, and be not entangled again with *the yoke of bondage."*

When Jesus said, *"Take my yoke upon you, and learn of me,"* He was speaking of the salvation that He had brought down to men. For one to take His yoke signifies obedience or uniting with Him. A yoke of oxen are fastened together and they walk side by side. Jesus is saying, "If you will embrace my doctrine, my Word, and the message that I bring, then you will find rest instead of burdens, crosses, afflictions, and bondage." That does not mean that all will be a flowery bed of ease, but it means rest and peace in the heart. When we are in the yoke with Jesus, He gives perfect peace even though we may be under heavy burdens.

". . . for I am meek and lowly in heart: and ye shall find rest unto your souls." It is true that Jesus was meek and lowly in personality or character—but this is not the full meaning here. Jesus is giving to the Jews the reason why they should receive Him and follow Him. His *doctrine* was not harsh, overbearing, and oppressive like that of the Pharisees, but meek, mild, and gentle. As compared to the Jewish system, His laws were very light, reasonable, and tender. It would be far easier for them to follow His rules of living than the yoke of bondage under which they lived as they followed the religion of the Pharisees.

We must remember that the system which the

Pharisees had set up in the days when our Lord appeared upon this earth was not true to the Law of Moses. They had changed it—added to it and taken from it—and were following dogmas, doctrines, and the traditions of men. However, even the law in its purest form was a yoke of bondage because the people were constantly called upon to bring sacrifices and observe days, feasts, and ceremonies. These things could never take away sin; they were simply shadows until the Lamb appeared. Jesus was the Lamb—and here He was inviting them to get in the yoke with Him.

Verse 30: *"For my yoke is easy, and my burden is light."*

The Jews were very definitely under the yoke or the bondage of the law. They were weary and burdened down with feasts, offerings, holy days, and rituals of their religion. Jesus is saying to the Jews that the laws of *His* religion, Christianity, are mild and gentle compared to the burden they were attempting to carry. They never did fulfill the law—*no* man ever did, except Jesus.

Christ said, "Think not that I am come to destroy the law, or the prophets: I am not come to destroy, but *to fulfil*" (Matt. 5:17). In Romans 3:20 we read, "Therefore *by the deeds of the law there shall no flesh be justified in His sight:* for by the law is the knowledge of sin." Compare Christianity with the ceremonies of the Jews, the

religious rites of the heathen, or with the requirements of man-made religion, and you will see how
true it is that the yoke of Jesus is *easy* and His
"burden is light" in comparison.

Let me point out here that the sinner is carrying
a very heavy yoke. Compare the laws that are
observed by sinners and the penalties for breaking
those laws, to Christianity and the rules of Christ,
and you will see that His yoke is indeed easy. If
the Son of God sets you free, you are *free indeed*
(John 8:36). The Christian life is much easier and
much less complicated than the life of a sinner.
If you do not believe this, go to the penitentiary
or the jail and talk to those behind the bars. You
will agree that it is much more expensive and
burdensome to serve sin than to serve God and
get in the yoke with Jesus. Of all the yokes im-
posed on men, the yoke of Jesus is by far the
lightest.

The Christian way is the best way, the *easiest*
way, simply because Christ lives in the heart of
the believer. The believer is led by the Spirit—
and He leads us in paths of righteousness for the
name's sake of Jesus and for the glory of God.
The Christian is the possessor of divine nature
(II Pet. 1:4).

Jesus said, "Come unto me, and I will give you
rest." When we come to Him, He does give us
rest—and *peace,* which passeth all understanding.
Note the words of Christ in John 14:27: *"Peace*

I leave with you, *my peace* I give unto you: not as the world giveth, give I unto you. Let not your heart be troubled, neither let it be afraid." Another great promise of peace is found in Philippians 4:7: "And *the peace of God, which passeth all understanding, shall keep your hearts and minds through Christ Jesus.*" And to believe on Jesus is to know *joy* that words cannot explain: "Whom having not seen, ye love; in whom, though now ye see Him not, yet believing, *ye rejoice with JOY UNSPEAKABLE and full of glory*" (I Pet. 1:8).

All who follow Jesus in true faith through good and evil find comfort, assurance, and stability which the world cannot give, neither can the world take away. If we suffer with Him, we will reign with Him. If we endure persecution, we will share His glory. In keeping His Word there is great reward; and if all we have to give is a cup of cold water, if we give it in the name of Jesus to the glory of God, we will not lose our reward.

Chapter XII

1. At that time Jesus went on the sabbath day through the corn; and his disciples were an hungred, and began to pluck the ears of corn, and to eat.

2. But when the Pharisees saw it, they said unto him, Behold, thy disciples do that which is not lawful to do upon the sabbath day.

3. But he said unto them, Have ye not read what David did, when he was an hungred, and they that were with him;

4. How he entered into the house of God, and did eat the shewbread, which was not lawful for him to eat, neither for them which were with him, but only for the priests?

5. Or have ye not read in the law, how that on the sabbath days the priests in the temple profane the sabbath, and are blameless?

6. But I say unto you, That in this place is one greater than the temple.

7. But if ye had known what this meaneth, I will have mercy, and not sacrifice, ye would not have condemned the guiltless.

8. For the Son of man is Lord even of the sabbath day.

9. And when he was departed thence, he went into their synagogue:

10. And, behold, there was a man which had his hand

withered. And they asked him, saying, Is it lawful to heal on the sabbath days? that they might accuse him.

11. And he said unto them, What man shall there be among you, that shall have one sheep, and if it fall into a pit on the sabbath day, will he not lay hold on it, and lift it out?

12. How much then is a man better than a sheep? Wherefore it is lawful to do well on the sabbath days.

13. Then saith he to the man, Stretch forth thine hand. And he stretched it forth; and it was restored whole, like as the other.

14. Then the Pharisees went out, and held a council against him, how they might destroy him.

15. But when Jesus knew it, he withdrew himself from thence: and great multitudes followed him, and he healed them all;

16. And charged them that they should not make him known:

17. That it might be fulfilled which was spoken by Esaias the prophet, saying,

18. Behold my servant, whom I have chosen; my beloved, in whom my soul is well pleased: I will put my spirit upon him, and he shall shew judgment to the Gentiles.

19. He shall not strive, nor cry; neither shall any man hear his voice in the streets.

20. A bruised reed shall he not break, and smoking flax shall he not quench, till he send forth judgment unto victory.

21. And in his name shall the Gentiles trust.

22. Then was brought unto him one possessed with a devil, blind, and dumb: and he healed him, insomuch that the blind and dumb both spake and saw.

23. And all the people were amazed, and said, Is not this the son of David?

Chapter 12

24. But when the Pharisees heard it, they said, This fellow doth not cast out devils, but by Beelzebub the prince of the devils.

25. And Jesus knew their thoughts, and said unto them, Every kingdom divided against itself is brought to desolation; and every city or house divided against itself shall not stand:

26. And if Satan cast out Satan, he is divided against himself; how shall then his kingdom stand?

27. And if I by Beelzebub cast out devils, by whom do your children cast them out? therefore they shall be your judges.

28. But if I cast out devils by the Spirit of God, then the kingdom of God is come unto you.

29. Or else how can one enter into a strong man's house, and spoil his goods, except he first bind the strong man? and then he will spoil his house.

30. He that is not with me is against me; and he that gathereth not with me scattereth abroad.

31. Wherefore I say unto you, All manner of sin and blasphemy shall be forgiven unto men: but the blasphemy against the Holy Ghost shall not be forgiven unto men.

32. And whosoever speaketh a word against the Son of man, it shall be forgiven him: but whosoever speaketh against the Holy Ghost, it shall not be forgiven him, neither in this world, neither in the world to come.

33. Either make the tree good, and his fruit good; or else make the tree corrupt, and his fruit corrupt: for the tree is known by his fruit.

34. O generation of vipers, how can ye, being evil, speak good things? for out of the abundance of the heart the mouth speaketh.

35. A good man out of the good treasure of the heart bringeth forth good things: and an evil man out of the evil treasure bringeth forth evil things.

36. But I say unto you, That every idle word that men shall speak, they shall give account thereof in the day of judgment.

37. For by thy words thou shalt be justified, and by thy words thou shalt be condemned.

38. Then certain of the scribes and of the Pharisees answered, saying, Master, we would see a sign from thee.

39. But he answered and said unto them, An evil and adulterous generation seeketh after a sign; and there shall no sign be given to it, but the sign of the prophet Jonas:

40. For as Jonas was three days and three nights in the whale's belly; so shall the Son of man be three days and three nights in the heart of the earth.

41. The men of Nineveh shall rise in judgment with this generation, and shall condemn it: because they repented at the preaching of Jonas; and, behold, a greater than Jonas is here.

42. The queen of the south shall rise up in the judgment with this generation, and shall condemn it: for she came from the uttermost parts of the earth to hear the wisdom of Solomon; and, behold, a greater than Solomon is here.

43. When the unclean spirit is gone out of a man, he walketh through dry places, seeking rest, and findeth none.

44. Then he saith, I will return into my house from whence I came out; and when he is come, he findeth it empty, swept, and garnished.

45. Then goeth he, and taketh with himself seven other spirits more wicked than himself, and they enter in and dwell there: and the last state of that man is worse than the first. Even so shall it be also unto this wicked generation.

46. While he yet talked to the people, behold, his mother and his brethren stood without, desiring to speak with him.

47. Then one said unto him, Behold, thy mother and

thy brethren stand without, desiring to speak with thee.

48. But he answered and said unto him that told him, Who is my mother? and who are my brethren?

49. And he stretched forth his hand toward his disciples, and said, Behold my mother and my brethren!

50. For whosoever shall do the will of my Father which is in heaven, the same is my brother, and sister, and mother.

Jesus Declares He Is Lord of the Sabbath

Verse 1: *"At that time Jesus went on the sabbath day through the corn; and His disciples were an hungred, and began to pluck the ears of corn, and to eat."*

The account given here in this passage is also found in Mark 2:23-28 and Luke 6:1-5.

"At that time . . . ." In Luke 6:1, we have a more definite statement concerning the exact time. Luke tells us that it was "on the second sabbath after the first." To understand the statement given by Luke, it is necessary to remember that the Passover was observed during the month of Abib (or Nisan), which was the latter part of March and the very first of April. The feast of the Passover began on the fourteenth day of the month and lasted seven days. (Please study Exodus 12:1-28 and 23:15.) The law stated that a sheaf (we would call this a *bundle* of barley) should be offered up as the firstfruits of the harvest. We find the account of this in Leviticus 23:10, 11. From the day that the sheaf of barley was offered, the Israelites

counted seven weeks to the feast of Pentecost (Lev. 23:15, 16). (The feast of Pentecost is called "the feast of weeks" in Deuteronomy 16:10 and "the feast of the harvest" in Exodus 23:16.) This second day in the feast of the Passover (or "the feast of unleavened bread") marked the beginning from which they reckoned toward the feast of Pentecost.

The Sabbath in the week following would be the second Sabbath after this first one, in the counting of time. This was doubtless the time mentioned when Jesus and His disciples *"went on the sabbath day through the corn"*—or through the grain fields. *"Corn"* here is not maize, or Indian corn, as we in America have confined it to mean, but the little grains of wheat and barley at the top of the stalk. The word "corn" in various European languages is applied to breadstuffs in general, especially to that most used in that particular nation—whether wheat, barley, rye, or oats. You remember that Jesus, speaking of a grain of wheat, said, "Except a *corn of wheat* fall into the ground and die . . ." (John 12:24).

Jesus and His disciples walked through the barley and the wheatfield—*"and His disciples were an hungred."* The heads of wheat and barley were fully grown and ready for harvesting; therefore, they plucked them, "and did eat, rubbing them in their hands" (Luke 6:1). That this was *grain* and not our Indian corn explains why they rubbed it in their hands—i. e., to separate the grains from the chaff. We should mention also that in Judaea the barley is ready for harvest about the first of May. Both the barley and the wheat harvests are over by the twentieth of the month of May. The grains of barley are fully developed in the ear by the first of April. Therefore, it is not unreasonable to take the account here literally—that the disciples did walk through a field of barley and wheat and pluck the heads and eat the grains.

The Sabbath

It is most interesting to note that the Sabbath is not mentioned in the Gospel of Matthew until our present verse. The complete rejection of Jesus as Messiah by the nation Israel is marked in this chapter by His break with them concerning the Sabbath day. This was the final thing remaining of their violated covenant with Almighty God. God made a covenant with Israel, and they had broken all of its rules. The Sabbath was given to Israel as a sign of the covenant, and now they had completely deserted the covenant. Therefore, Jesus was about to set aside the sign—that is, the Jewish Sabbath.

The reason God gave the Sabbath to the nation Israel is clearly stated in the Old Testament Scriptures:

"And the Lord spake unto Moses, saying, Speak thou also unto the children of Israel, saying, *Verily*

*MY SABBATHS ye shall keep: for it is A SIGN
BETWEEN ME AND YOU throughout your generations; that ye may know that I am the Lord
that doth sanctify you.* Ye shall keep the sabbath
therefore; for it is holy unto you: every one that
defileth it shall surely be put to death: for whosoever doeth any work therein, that soul shall be
cut off from among his people. Six days may work
be done; but in the seventh is the sabbath of rest,
holy to the Lord: whosoever doeth any work in
the sabbath day, he shall surely be put to death.
*Wherefore the children of Israel shall keep the
SABBATH, to observe the SABBATH throughout
their generations, for a PERPETUAL COVENANT.
IT IS A SIGN BETWEEN ME AND THE CHIL-
DREN OF ISRAEL FOR EVER:* for in six days
the Lord made heaven and earth, and on the
seventh day He rested, and was refreshed'' (Ex.
31:12-17).

The nation Israel had violated all the terms of
the covenant and had sinned constantly and grievously in the sight of God. In Ezekiel 20:12-26, God
states the case against the nation Israel in detail:

"Moreover also *I GAVE THEM MY SABBATHS,
TO BE A SIGN BETWEEN ME AND THEM,
that they might know that I am the Lord that
sanctify them.* But the house of Israel rebelled
against me in the wilderness: they walked not in
my statutes, and they despised my judgments,
which if a man do, he shall even live in them;

and *my sabbaths they greatly polluted:* then I said, I would pour out my fury upon them in the wilderness, to consume them. But I wrought for my name's sake, that it should not be polluted before the heathen, in whose sight I brought them out. Yet also I lifted up my hand unto them in the wilderness, that I would not bring them into the land which I had given them, flowing with milk and honey, which is the glory of all lands; because they despised my judgments, and walked not in my statutes, but *polluted my sabbaths:* for their heart went after their idols.

"Nevertheless mine eye spared them from destroying them, neither did I make an end of them in the wilderness. But I said unto their children in the wilderness, Walk ye not in the statutes of your fathers, neither observe their judgments, nor defile yourselves with their idols: I am the Lord your God; walk in my statutes, and keep my judgments, and do them; and *hallow MY SABBATHS; and they shall be A SIGN BETWEEN ME AND YOU, that ye may know that I am the Lord your God.*

"Notwithstanding the children rebelled against me: they walked not in my statutes, neither kept my judgments to do them, which if a man do, he shall even live in them; *they polluted my sabbaths:* then I said, I would pour out my fury upon them, to accomplish my anger against them in the wilderness. Nevertheless I withdrew mine hand, and

wrought for my name's sake, that it should not
be polluted in the sight of the heathen, in whose
sight I brought them forth. I lifted up mine hand
unto them also in the wilderness, that I would
scatter them among the heathen, and disperse them
through the countries; because they had not exe-
cuted my judgments, but had despised my statutes,
and had polluted my sabbaths, and their eyes were
after their fathers' idols. Wherefore I gave them
also statutes that were not good, and judgments
whereby they should not live; and I polluted them
in their own gifts, in that they caused to pass
through the fire all that openeth the womb, that
I might make them desolate, to the end that they
might know that I am the Lord.''

The Word of God clearly points out to anyone
who desires to know the truth that the Sabbath is
purely *a Jewish institution.* The law given to
Moses by Almighty God was given to Israel specifically and directly—never to the Gentiles nor
to the Church of God. The *Sabbath* is Jewish;
it is not for the Gentiles or for the Church. When
anyone speaks of the Lord's day as the Christian
Sabbath, that person is "pouring new wine into
old wineskins." He is doing what Jesus referred
to when He said a man will not sew new cloth
in old garments (Matt. 9:16). There is no such
thing as the Christian Sabbath. In this dispensation, the believer worships on *the Lord's day,* and
this is *immensely higher* than the Jewish Sabbath

ever was. The Lord's day is not a day of law but a day of grace.

Verse 2: *"But when the Pharisees saw it, they said unto Him, Behold, thy disciples do that which is not lawful to do upon the sabbath day."*

The Pharisees were always looking for something with which they could accuse the Lord and find fault with Him. They said that in plucking the grains from the stalk on the Sabbath day, His disciples had violated the commandment given to them concerning keeping the Sabbath. Moses had commanded the Jews to abstain from all labor of any nature on the Sabbath day—such as gathering food or working in the fields: "But the seventh day is the sabbath of the Lord thy God: *in it thou shalt not do any work,* thou, nor thy son, nor thy daughter, thy manservant, nor thy maidservant, nor thy cattle, nor thy stranger that is within thy gates" (Ex. 20:10). The command is repeated in Exodus 35:2, 3: *"Six days shall work be done, but on the seventh day there shall be to you an holy day, a sabbath of rest to the Lord: whosoever doeth work therein shall be put to death.* Ye shall kindle no fire throughout your habitations upon the sabbath day."

In Numbers 15:32-36 we have the record of the man who gathered sticks on the Sabbath:

"And while the children of Israel were in the wilderness, they found a man that gathered sticks upon the sabbath day. And they that found him gathering sticks brought him unto Moses and Aaron, and unto all the congregation. And they put him in ward, because it was not declared what should be done to him. And the Lord said unto Moses, The man shall be surely put to death: all the congregation shall stone him with stones without the camp. And all the congregation brought him without the camp, and stoned him with stones, and he died; as the Lord commanded Moses.''

Jesus and His disciples were probably on their way to the synagogue. On any other day of the week it would have been perfectly lawful for them to gather food from the field, for they were allowed by the law to take the heads of wheat for food as they passed along: "When thou comest into the standing corn of thy neighbour, then thou mayest pluck the ears with thine hand; but thou shalt not move a sickle unto thy neighbour's standing corn'' (Deut. 23:25). But the objection the Pharisees made was that they were doing this *on the Sabbath*. To the Pharisees, plucking the heads of wheat and barley was *reaping*, and rubbing the grains in their hands to remove the husks was *threshing*. The hypocritical minds of the Pharisees looked upon this as labor on the Sabbath, which was strictly forbidden.

These critics came directly to Jesus with their complaints. For once, at least, they had courage enough to deal with the leader instead of asking

His followers why they plucked the wheat and barley. These Pharisees, who were fanatics concerning the law, felt very strongly on the question of the Sabbath. They thought that they had found legitimate fault with Jesus; therefore they approached Him and asked why He permitted His followers to break the Law of Moses.

(It is interesting to me to learn from this account that Jesus did not perform a miracle to feed His disciples. These men who had left all and had followed Him were without food and were hungry. Jesus had the power and could have fed them in a miraculous way, but He did not. He did perform miracles to feed the multitudes [Matt. 14:15-21; 15:32-38], but neither here nor elsewhere in the New Testament did Christ work miracles to provide food for Himself or His disciples. I wonder how many of us would serve the Lord if it demanded hunger and many times we did not have food.)

There is something here that is most interesting when we carefully read this passage: Why did the Pharisees condemn the disciples for plucking the grains of wheat and barley and rubbing them in their hands on the Sabbath, when they themselves were breaking the Sabbath by making a journey? If they witnessed what the disciples did, then they of necessity traveled. Why did these religionists accuse men of breaking the law when they themselves were breaking the law? And if they were so pious, why did they not give these men bread?

If we see a neighbor hungry, we are supposed to feed him. If the Pharisees had given the disciples bread, they would not have found it necessary to pluck the wheat and the barley.

It is very easy to condemn others for doing things that we do not do ourselves. But when we examine ourselves carefully, we may be doing something just as wrong as the thing for which we condemn a brother—perhaps worse! It is much easier to see the faults of others than it is to see our own. God forgive us and help us not to judge others but to wait until that day when the righteous Judge will appear (I Cor. 4:1-5).

The meaning of the word *"sabbath"* is "cessation"—meaning, of course, complete rest or ceasing from all activity and labor. We have given the account in the Old Testament where a man was found gathering sticks on the Sabbath, and he was stoned. The Sabbath first appears in the Word of God as the day of God's rest in the finished work of Creation (Gen. 2:2, 3). For twenty-five hundred years of human history, there is no mention whatsoever of the Sabbath. Then the Sabbath was revealed. (Please study Exodus 16:23 and Nehemiah 9:13, 14.) The Sabbath was made part of the law (Ex. 20:8-11): God thundered out, "Remember the sabbath day, to keep it holy."

As I pointed out earlier in this discussion, the Sabbath was given to Israel as a sign between God and the nation Israel (Ex. 31:13-17). It was

100

given as a perpetual reminder to the nation of Israel of their separation unto God. They were not to mix and mingle with other nations, to inter-marry or to participate in their activities. During the Dispensation of Law, the Sabbath was ob-served by complete rest (Ex. 35:2, 3). As already mentioned, God clearly ordered a man put to death for gathering sticks on the Sabbath day (Num. 15:32-36).

Let me point out a Bible fact that most Chris-tians have not considered: Apart from continuing the burnt-offering (Num. 28:9, 10) and the connection with other animal feasts (Ex. 12:16; Lev. 23:3-8; Num. 28:25), the Jewish Sabbath was *not* a day of sacrifice, worship, or any manner of religious serv-ice such as we practice today in our local churches. The Sabbath was a day of complete rest for both man and beast. God created man, and "He know-eth our frame; He remembereth that we are dust" (Psalm 103:14). God knew that man must rest; so the Sabbath was a humane provision made by God for man's needs. In the words of Jesus, *"The sab-bath was made for man,* and not man for the sabbath" (Mark 2:27).

When Jesus appeared, the religious rulers and leaders of the day had added their dogmas and traditions to the pure Sabbath God gave to Moses in the Ten Commandments. They had added certain restrictions that were not included when Jehovah gave the law to Moses; therefore Jesus was declared to be a Sabbath breaker by the chief priests, the scribes, and the elders.

The Sabbath will be observed again during the Millennium, the time when Jesus will sit on the throne of David here on this earth and reign for one thousand years (Isa. 66:23)—but in this Dispensation of Grace we observe the *first* day of the week—Sunday. (Saturday is still the *Sabbath*, of course, according to Jewish law.) The believer remembers the first day as the day when we acknowledge that at least one-seventh of our time belongs to the Lord. In all other respects, the first day of the week is *in contrast* with the seventh day; that is, Sunday is in contrast with Saturday in the spiritual realm:

The Sabbath (the seventh day) commemorates God's rest after Creation; the Lord's day (the first day of the week) points to the resurrection of Jesus, because it was on that day that He came out of the grave. On the seventh day God rested; on the first day of the week Jesus was very active. He certainly did not *rest,* according to the account of His activities on the first day He was out of the tomb.

God's Sabbath commemorates the completion of Creation; Sunday, the first day of the week, points to the empty tomb and *finished redemption.* (The death, burial, and resurrection of Jesus according to the Scriptures was a divine necessity, that redemption might be ours.)

The Jewish Sabbath was a day of legal obligation, and if the people desecrated the Sabbath, they were put to death. The first day of the week is a day when we *voluntarily* worship the Lord Jesus in church services and in our homes. We worship Him by attending church, studying His Word, listening to the minister deliver the message from the Bible, and in many other ways. This would have been strictly forbidden on the Jewish Sabbath day.

In the book of Acts the Sabbath is mentioned only in connection with the Jews. As we study the rest of the books of the New Testament we find the Sabbath referred to only two times—in Colossians 2:16, 17, where Paul says it is a *type* "of things to come"; and in Hebrews 4:4-11, where it is a type of the present rest into which the Christian enters when he ceases from his own works and puts faith and trust in the Lord Jesus Christ.

Let me repeat: The Sabbath was never given to the Church, and the Church is not commanded to keep the Sabbath day. It is upon *the first day of the week* that we "lay by in store" as God has prospered us (I Cor. 16:2). On the first day of the week we go to the house of God to worship (Acts 20:7). We are not under law—we are living in the marvelous Day of Grace!

In the passages we have given it is clear to see that the Sabbath was a *sign* between God and *the nation Israel*—that the nation might know that He was their God and they were His elect nation. But the Jews did not know God's Son, and when He came, they refused to receive Him. He stood in their midst, He held out His hand, He desired to heal their backslidings—but they would have no part of Him. And when Jesus in their eyes broke their Sabbath, they cried out against Him.

Human nature does not change. It is now as it was then. Man has always been religious, but the natural man is at enmity toward God (Rom. 8:5-8). The flesh cannot please God—and yet the flesh longs for and seeks after *religion*. The masses have no desire to know the holy and righteous God. They have no desire to experience the power of godliness and righteousness in their lives, but they cannot get along without some form of religion. Almost all men are religious and belong to some religious organization. They ease their conscience by participating in some form of religious activity or giving to some religious cause.

The Messiah of Israel, the promised One, "that Prophet" of whom their prophets spoke, the very Son of God, stood in their midst—but the nation Israel did not seek their Messiah. Israel put the Sabbath of the Lord in the place of the Lord of the Sabbath. They defended the Sabbath of the Lord; they condemned the Lord of the Sabbath. They were blind and sat in darkness, but they refused to allow Jesus to open their blinded eyes.

104

Verses 3 and 4: *"But He said unto them, Have ye not read what David did, when he was an hungred, and they that were with him; how he entered into the house of God, and did eat the shewbread, which was not lawful for him to eat, neither for them which were with him, but only for the priests?"*

Our Lord's reply to this censure of the disciples and Himself contains, as here reported, four distinct arguments—verses 3 and 4; verses 5 and 6; verse 7; and verse 8. This first argument is an appeal to *history*—that is, to the conduct of David (I Sam. 21:1-6), which these Pharisees would admit to have been justifiable.

The law commanded that twelve loaves of bread (called *shewbread*) be placed on the table in the holy place in the tabernacle. The twelve loaves were to remain there for one week and then were to be eaten *by the priests only.* The loaves were then replaced with fresh bread. The instructions concerning this bread are given in Leviticus 24:5-9:

"And thou shalt take fine flour, and bake twelve cakes thereof: two tenth deals shall be in one cake. And thou shalt set them in two rows, six on a row, upon the pure table before the Lord. And thou shalt put pure frankincense upon each row, that it may be on the bread for a memorial, even an offering made by fire unto the Lord. *EVERY SABBATH he shall set it in order before the Lord continually,* being taken from the children of

Israel by an everlasting covenant. And it shall be Aaron's and his sons'; and they shall eat it in the holy place: for it is most holy unto him of the offerings of the Lord made by fire by a perpetual statute."

The incident referred to by Jesus occurred when David was fleeing from King Saul. He was tired, weary, and hungry, and he came to Ahimelech, the priest, in *"the house of God"* (the tabernacle). David asked for bread—*"and did eat the shew-bread,"* contrary to the letter of the Mosaic law:

"Then came David to Nob to Ahimelech the priest: and Ahimelech was afraid at the meeting of David, and said unto him, Why art thou alone, and no man with thee?   And David said unto Ahimelech the priest, The king hath commanded me a business, and hath said unto me, Let no man know any thing of the business whereabout I send thee, and what I have commanded thee: and I have appointed my servants to such and such a place.   Now therefore what is under thine hand? *Give me five loaves of bread in mine hand, or what there is present.*

"And the priest answered David, and said, There is no *common bread* under mine hand, but there is *hallowed bread;* if the young men have kept themselves at least from women. And David answered the priest, and said unto him, Of a truth women have been kept from us about these three days, since I came out, and the vessels of the young men are holy, and the bread is in a manner common, yea, though it were sanctified this day in the vessel. *So the priest gave him hallowed bread: for there was no bread there but the shew-bread, that was taken from before the Lord, to put hot bread in the day when it was taken away"* (I Sam. 21:1-6).

To the Jews David was a man of high authority for whom they had great respect. Therefore he was not condemned for what he did. This proved that *in cases of dire necessity* the law did not bind a man. This is a principle which all laws recognize. So the *necessity* of the disciples on this occasion justified them in doing on the Sabbath day what would otherwise have been unlawful. In their case, as in the case of David, it was a dire necessity.

"Have ye not read . . . ?" Jesus asked these men who were supposed to be authorities on the Old Testament Scriptures if they had not read about David eating the shewbread. He said to them, "Since you know so much about the Scriptures, it seems that you would remember how David entered into the tabernacle and ate shewbread, which was for the priests only. It seems that you would know that David did that which was not lawful for him to do, yet he was not condemned. Why do you condemn my disciples for doing what David did? You honor him very highly, so why do you denounce my disciples?"

Verse 5: *"Or have ye not read in the law, how that on the sabbath days the priests in the temple profane the sabbath, and are blameless?"*

The second ground of justification for the disciples was not drawn from sacred history, but from *the law.* Here, as in Matthew 5:17, Jesus shows that He is not violating the law, for He justifies Himself and His disciples out of the law itself. He reminds the Pharisees of the conduct of *"the priests in the temple"* on the Sabbath days. They were engaged in killing beasts for sacrifice on the Sabbath as on other days: "And on the sabbath day two lambs of the first year without spot, and two tenth deals of flour for a meat-offering, mingled with oil, and the drink-offering thereof: *this is the burnt-offering of every sabbath,* beside the continual burnt-offering, and his drink-offering" (Num. 28: 9, 10).

Two lambs were killed on the Sabbath day, in addition to the daily sacrifices that were offered. The priests, therefore, had to be engaged in slaying the lambs and making fires to burn the sacrifices, although God had commanded, "Ye shall kindle no fire throughout your habitations upon the sabbath day" (Ex. 35:3). The temple was the place of holiness where the law should have been most strictly observed. The priests did that which, if done by other persons, would have been *profaning the Sabbath day.* Yet the priests were *"blameless"* — they did what was commanded of them.

108

Verse 6:   *"But I say unto you, That in this place is One greater than the temple."*

Jesus here refers to Himself and is speaking of His own power, His deity, and His mission on the earth. He was the fulfillment of all that the temple typified. The temple was superior to the Sabbath, and *Jesus was "greater than the temple."* Much more, then, might the usual law of the Sabbath be set aside without blame, when it became necessary, for His disciples in His service.

Everything about the law—every sacrifice, feast, holy day, ceremony; the tabernacle, the temple, the ark of the covenant—*everything* pointed to Jesus. In the Sermon on the Mount He said, "Think not that I am come to destroy the law, or the prophets: *I am not come to destroy, but to FULFIL"* (Matt. 5:17). Jesus did fulfill every part of the law—and He is "the *end* of the law for righteousness to every one that believeth" (Rom. 10:4).

Verse 7: *"But if ye had known what this meaneth, I will have mercy, and not sacrifice, ye would not have condemned the guiltless."*

This point of defense was drawn from a *prophet* (Hosea 6:6). Jesus referred to this same passage in Matthew 9:13, where He told the Pharisees to "go ... and *learn"* the meaning of the words. Here He says, *"But if ye had known what this meaneth ...."*   Thus He pronounced these men ignorant who claimed to be wise in the books of the Old

Testament. These Pharisees did know what the passage was, as far as the *words* were concerned, but they did not know what it was in true meaning. They were in total darkness and ignorance concerning the things of the Spirit, and they refused to allow God to open their minds.

God cannot help any person who has his mind made up concerning a doctrine or a dogma. God cannot change such a person—for God is love, and love never forces, but leads and guides. God will lead a person into light and guide him into truth, but if he has a closed mind, then God cannot help him. These men had made up their minds that this Man Jesus was not their Messiah. They refused to believe anything He said, and they intended to get rid of Him. They refused to acknowledge the miracles that He did, even when some of their own group confessed that no one but God could do such wonders.

"I will have mercy, and not sacrifice." In Hosea 6:6 Jehovah said, "I desired mercy, and not sacrifice; and the knowledge of God more than burnt-offerings." This truth is declared many times in the Word of God. Some of these Scriptures are I Samuel 15:22, Proverbs 21:3, and Hebrews 10:5-8. Also, in Micah 6:6-8 we read:

"Wherewith shall I come before the Lord, and bow myself before the high God? Shall I come before Him with burnt-offerings, with calves of a year old? Will the Lord be pleased with thousands of rams, or with ten thousands of rivers of oil? Shall I give my firstborn for my transgression, the fruit of my body for the sin of my soul? *He hath shewed thee, O man, what is good; and what doth the Lord require of thee, but to do justly, and to love mercy, and to walk humbly with thy God?"*

Notice these words from Isaiah's prophecy:

"To what purpose is the multitude of your sacrifices unto me? saith the Lord: *I am full of the burnt-offerings of rams, and the fat of fed beasts; and I delight not in the blood of bullocks, or of lambs, or of he goats.* When ye come to appear before me, who hath required this at your hand, to tread my courts? Bring no more vain oblations; incense is an abomination unto me; the new moons and sabbaths, the calling of assemblies, I cannot away with; it is iniquity, even the solemn meeting. Your new moons and your appointed feasts my soul hateth: they are a trouble unto me; I am weary to bear them. And when ye spread forth your hands, I will hide mine eyes from you: yea, when ye make many prayers, I will not hear: your hands are full of blood.

"Wash you, make you clean; put away the evil of your doings from before mine eyes; cease to do evil; learn to do well; seek judgment, relieve the oppressed, judge the fatherless, plead for the widow" (Isa. 1:11-17).

God delights in acts of righteousness rather than in one adhering to the letter of the law and observing a ceremony commanded by the law. Remember—"if any man be in Christ, he is a new creation" (II Cor. 5:17). And we are "*created in Christ Jesus unto good works,* which God hath before ordained *that we should walk in them*" (Eph. 2:10). Jesus said, "Let your light so shine before men, *that they may see your good works,* and glorify your Father which is in heaven" (Matt. 5:16). Even giving a cup of cold water in the name of Jesus brings more glory to God than does practicing the letter of the law while doing acts that are not righteous. So Jesus is telling the Pharisees here in Matthew 12:7 that if they had known the true law, they "*would not have condemned the guiltless.*"

In Mark 2:27 we read, "The sabbath was made for man, and not man for the sabbath." God gave the Sabbath for the welfare of man, to promote happiness—and not to bring misery because of ceremonial requirements. The law is not to be so interpreted as to produce hardships and suffering when the things that are necessary for life seem to be unlawful. Man was not made for the Sabbath. God created man first, and later He gave the Sabbath.

Verse 8:   "*For the Son of man is Lord even of the sabbath day.*"

This gives a fourth defense of the disciples, in the form of a reason why they were guiltless.

112

Jesus said clearly, "I am the Lord of the sabbath. I have the right to direct the manner in which my disciples observe this day." This, of course, declared Him divine—and the Pharisees, scribes, and elders did not *believe* that He was divine. Therefore they did not receive this statement, even though it was the truth. Jesus *was*—and He *is*—Lord of the Sabbath. He is *Lord of all!*

What Jesus said to the Pharisees is simply this: "I have the power to change laws if I so desire. I can grant to these men who follow me a dispensation different from the law. What I command or permit my disciples to do is right. I am the Word Incarnate—I am the fulfillment of every jot and tittle of the law." Jesus was God in flesh—and none but God can permit men to do that which is contrary to law. God is above all, and He cannot and will not do anything that is wrong. It was not wrong for the disciples to gather wheat and barley and rub it together in their hands and eat it on the Sabbath day. They were hungry—and they were on a journey for Jesus; therefore what they did was *right,* even though in the sight of the Pharisees it was wrong. According to the Pharisees' interpretation of the law, it was sinful; but it was right in the sight of God, and that is what matters.

Jesus was the greatest Teacher and the greatest Preacher who ever lived. Who today could have used the words He used so effectively on a crowd who claimed to be so strictly religious, adhering to the law in every minor detail? He reminded them that it is recorded in the law how that on the Sabbath day the priests in the temple profaned the Sabbath and yet were blameless. They labored hard and long hours on the Sabbath, but they were not condemned. Instead, they were honored for it, since they had the approval of the temple law. It was lawful for them to do this *because they were priests serving in the temple.* In the case of the disciples of the Lord Jesus Christ, that which *they* did had the sanction of *the temple's Lord. The temple's LORD is FAR GREATER THAN THE TEMPLE!*

There are people today who think it is very sinful to do anything on *Sunday.* Please notice—I said Sunday, not the Sabbath, because the Sabbath is *Saturday.* The Sabbath has never been changed and never will be changed. Christians worship on the first day of the week, and there are those who think that it is extremely wrong to do any kind of labor on Sunday. However, oftentimes the *minister* works harder on *Sunday* than on any other day. In our modern society many types of work have become necessary on Sunday. Policemen and highway troopers must be on their jobs, and there are also men who work at the power plants to produce electricity to light the church building so that the services can be conducted. This type of work is necessary and certainly is not sinful on the Lord's day. We are not to keep "days"; we are to worship Christ and serve Him. Whatever you do—on Sunday, or any other day in the week— if you do it to the glory of God, it is not sin. If all you do is for His glory, you need not worry about those who follow ceremonialism and external observances. If you are dedicated to the Lord and doing what you are doing to glorify Him, the criticism of others will not bother you.

Jesus Heals the Withered Hand on the Sabbath

Verses 9 and 10: *"And when He was departed thence, He went into their synagogue: and, behold, there was a man which had his hand withered. And they asked Him, saying, Is it lawful to heal on the sabbath days? that they might accuse Him."*

(The account of this healing is found also in Mark 3:1-6 and in Luke 6:6-11.)

"And when He was departed thence, He went into their synagogue." We should naturally infer, had we Matthew's Gospel alone, that this incident took place on the same Sabbath as the one mentioned in verses 1 through 8. But Luke 6:6 says it was "on *another* sabbath"—and nothing in Matthew's statement conflicts with this.

In the synagogue *"there was a man which had his hand withered."* (Luke says it was his *right* hand.) The Word of God does not reveal to us exactly what was wrong with the man's hand,

115

but only that it was withered. Some scholars believe that it was a form of palsy.

The Pharisees asked Jesus, *"Is it lawful to heal on the sabbath days?"* Mark and Luke do not record this question, but point out that the Pharisees *"watched* Him, whether He would heal him on the sabbath day." This they did *"that they might accuse Him."* They did not ask Jesus this question for their own instruction, because they felt they knew all there was to know on religious matters. They asked the question on this occasion, as on many others, for the specific purpose of accusing Him and condemning Him.

When the Pharisees brought to Jesus the woman who had been taken in adultery (John 8:3-11), they asked Him, "Now Moses in the law commanded us, that such should be stoned: *but what sayest thou?"* But they said this, "tempting Him, *that they might have to accuse Him."* When they asked Him about the tribute money, they were seeking "to *catch Him in His words"* (Mark 12:13-17). And in Luke 11:53, 54 we read that "the scribes and the Pharisees began to urge Him vehemently, and to provoke Him to speak of many things: *laying wait for Him, and seeking to catch something out of His mouth, that they might accuse Him."*

Verse 11: *"And He said unto them, What man shall there be among you, that shall have one sheep, and if it fall into a pit on the sabbath day, will he not lay hold on it, and lift it out?"*

Mark and Luke tell us that Jesus spoke to the man first and requested him to stand forth in the midst of the group. It seems that Jesus placed him in the most conspicuous place. After first speaking to the man, Jesus asked the people a question: "Is it lawful to do good on the sabbath days?" (Mark 3:4). According to our passage in Matthew, the Jews had asked Jesus if it was lawful to heal on the Sabbath, and Jesus probably in turn asked them if it was lawful to do good on the Sabbath day. But they were silent—"they held their peace" (Mark 3:4).

Jesus then appealed to them and drew an argument from their own conduct in other matters. He was a great illustrator in teaching the people. Here He speaks of a man who has only one sheep and it falls into a pit. On other occasions He spoke of the sower and the seed, the hen and her little chickens. He used illustrations that all could immediately understand. Jesus tells the Jews here that if a man *"shall have one sheep, and if it fall into a pit on the sabbath day,"* he would certainly rescue it. Even though it was the Sabbath day, the man would get a rope or a line and pull the animal from the pit. Common decency teaches a man to do this in the case of an animal—and how much more in the case of his fellow man!

Verse 12: *"How much then is a man better*

*than a sheep?   Wherefore it is lawful to do well
on the sabbath days."*

The argument set forth by Jesus—that a man
who saw his sheep fall into a pit would lift him
out on the Sabbath—proved that it is right to do
good to needy men on the Sabbath day. If a man
would show an act of kindness toward an *animal*
on the Sabbath, how much more important it is
for us to show kindness to a *man*—one who is
created in the image of God.   *"Wherefore it is
lawful to do well on the sabbath days."* The
Jews allowed acts of kindness toward animals on
the Sabbath day; therefore, what He was about
to do was, by their own confession, lawful. How
could anyone ever entertain the idea that it is not
right to help a poor needy creature—man or beast—
on the Sabbath?

The arguments set forth by the Lord Jesus were
so overwhelming that without a doubt many of
the Jews were ashamed that they ever brought up
the subject; however, the hardhearted leaders did
not change their minds about Him. Zeal for externals and hatred of spiritual things, when united,
certainly can—and do—create narrow bigotry.

Verse 13:   *"Then saith He to the man, Stretch
forth thine hand. And he stretched it forth; and
it was restored whole, like as the other."*

Mark reveals to us a fact that many people
refuse to accept. He says, *"And when He had*

looked round about on them WITH ANGER, being grieved for the hardness of their hearts . . ." (Mark 3:5). Notice: ANGER! Jesus was moved exceedingly at their ignorance and hardness of heart. The Lamb of God looked upon these dignified, dedicated-to-religion teachers with anger. What pitiful creatures such men are, giving their lives to religion instead of serving the Lord Jesus Christ. We have hundreds of them today the world over, dedicated mind, spirit, and body, to religion; but they have never been born again, saved by grace, washed in the blood. They are too busy serving religion to allow the Lord to speak to them and to hear Him say, "Come unto me, and I will give you rest." The envy, bitterness, and hatred in the hearts of the religious leaders in our Scripture excited feelings of holy indignation on the part of the Lamb of God.

Then Jesus said to the man with the withered hand, *"Stretch forth thine hand."* This was a remarkable way in which Jesus showed His power. He did not touch the man—He just *spoke* to him. This man could have said to Jesus, "How do you expect me to stretch forth my hand when it is limp? There is no strength in my arm, and I cannot stretch forth my hand." This shows the power of the Word of God. We do not know whether this man had heard Jesus teach before or not. No doubt he had heard much *about* Jesus, and when he saw Him and heard His words, he was convinced in his heart that Jesus was not an ordinary man. Therefore, he obeyed the command to stretch forth his hand. This man had faith in Jesus. If he had not, he would not have attempted to stretch forth his hand.

We have here a picture of salvation. The sinner is strengthless, withered, dead in trespasses and sins—and when we were *"without strength,* in due time Christ died for the ungodly"* (Rom. 5:6). The sinner is just as helpless as this man's withered arm. We believe and are saved when we accept the Word of God as this man accepted the words of Jesus. We will never know this side of heaven the power of the Word of God. There is no way to express the miracle-working power of God's Word. Paul says this to the Hebrew believers:

"For the Word of God is quick, and powerful, and sharper than any twoedged sword, piercing even to the dividing asunder of soul and spirit, and of the joints and marrow, and is a discerner of the thoughts and intents of the heart" (Heb. 4:12).

". . . and it was restored whole, like as the other." A moment ago the man had one good hand and one withered hand; now he had two good hands! Jesus spoke, the man believed—and the miracle was the result.

"Faith cometh by *hearing,* and hearing *by the Word of God"* (Rom. 10:17). Whatever we desire from God we must receive through faith; there is no other channel. I believe in bodily healing, but

I do not believe it is God's will to heal *all* sick people. I know that He can heal *any* disease and can even raise the dead—but I do not believe that it is His will in all cases to heal all people. God allows sickness, and He allows believers to be in the hospital for various reasons; sometimes it could be to win to Christ a person in the room with the sick believer. Whether we understand it or not, *"all things* work together for *good* to them that love God, to them who are the called according to His purpose" (Rom. 8:28).

You remember that earlier Jesus claimed to be Lord of the Sabbath. He proved it by healing this man on the Sabbath day. Jesus had before claimed divine power and divine authority (vv. 6-9). He now proves what He formerly claimed. No man could heal a withered hand except the Man Christ Jesus.

If there is any healing today, it is divine. There is no such thing as a human healer. Thank God for doctors, nurses, and drugs that help the sick; but divine healing comes from God, and *all healing is divine.* God uses men to *pray* for the sick, but man cannot *heal* the sick. *God* must do the healing. I have prayed for many sick people individually in hospitals and in homes, but I have never claimed to be a healer. I have seen people raised up from their death bed. But I do not claim that I prayed the prayer of faith; someone else may have prayed that prayer. Let me repeat: I believe in praying for the sick, and I believe that God can heal; but I do not believe it is God's will to heal every sick person.

We have in these first thirteen verses of Matthew chapter 12 two cases which prove that Jesus is Lord of the Sabbath and that the Lord is greater than a holy day. He permitted the disciples to gather the grains of wheat on the Sabbath day, rub them in their hands and eat them, because they were hungry. This was a case of *necessity.* Now He has performed a *miracle*—and this is an act of *mercy.* Therefore, it is perfectly in harmony with the law of God to perform acts that are necessary on *any* day, and it is also according to God's plan to perform acts of *mercy* on any day.

Even from their own point of view the Pharisees must have found it difficult to call this healing (of the withered hand) breaking the Sabbath. Jesus used no remedy and performed no action. He simply spoke the word—and the man merely stretched forth his hand. These Jews had hoped to make a strong case against the Lord—and being silenced by His arguments and baffled by His actions, they were all the more angry—"filled with madness" (Luke 6:11).

The Plot to Destroy Jesus; His Withdrawal

Verse 14: *"Then the Pharisees went out, and held a council against Him, how they might destroy Him."*

As previously quoted from Luke 6:11, the religious leaders were "filled with madness." After Jesus healed the withered hand, they called a council meeting to decide *"how they might destroy Him."* Mark tells us that the Herodians also took part in the plot. The Herodians were probably a political group who followed Herod Antipas, son of Herod the Great, tetrarch of Galilee. This was the same Herod that imprisoned John the Baptist and had him beheaded because he preached against Herod's adulterous living. This was also the Herod before whom Jesus was arraigned. He was under Roman authority and was a fanatic to enforce Roman power. All the friends of the family of Herod were enemies of the Lord Jesus Christ and were always anxious to join any plot to destroy Him. They remembered, no doubt, the attempts of Herod the Great against Jesus when He was a Babe in Bethlehem and were still irritated and very angry because He escaped from the bloody hands of Herod at that time.

The attempt on His life now on the part of the Pharisees was the result of hatred and envy. They hated Him because great crowds thronged after Him, especially when He performed miracles. They were losing influence over the people—and therefore they were determined in their hearts to kill Him.

If a minister desires to rid his congregation of hypocrites, the way to do it is to preach the Word of God pure and straight. The Word of God is like a fire—and when you build a fire under a man, he will move! Fire either warms or burns. If we are in the right position, the fire warms us; if we are in the wrong position, it *burns* us. These Pharisees could not bear the words of Jesus, for they were like fire, and they were powerful and sharper than a twoedged sword. The Pharisees hated Jesus. He completely baffled them; they could not understand Him, they could not silence Him—so they were determined to slay Him.

Because of the growing popularity of Jesus with the multitudes, it would not be easy to destroy Him; so the Pharisees held a council. They deliberately planned their cruel act of murder upon Jesus. Men in *this* hour still "hold council against Him." All skeptics, liberals, modernists, and haters of true Christianity are working together to discredit the Word of God and destroy the plan of salvation.

Verse 15: *"But when Jesus knew it, He withdrew Himself from thence: and great multitudes followed Him, and He healed them all."*

"Jesus knew it." The secret meeting of the Pharisees was no secret to Jesus, because He was omniscient. Knowing what was in their hearts and minds, He acted accordingly. Jesus was always a little ahead of those who would destroy Him. His "hour" had not come, and His work

was not finished. So *"He withdrew Himself"* from the scene, *"and great multitudes followed Him."* Mark gives the following account:

"But Jesus withdrew Himself with His disciples to the sea: and a great multitude from Galilee followed Him, and from Judaea, and from Jerusalem, and from Idumaea, and from beyond Jordan; and they about Tyre and Sidon, a great multitude, when they had heard what great things He did, came unto Him. And He spake to His disciples, that a small ship should wait on Him because of the multitude, lest they should throng Him" (Mark 3:7-9).

The crowd flocked after Jesus; and since He was merciful, longsuffering, tender, and kind, He could not refuse to bless them and heal them—*"and He healed them all."* Today many modern "healers" send some away still sick, still withered; and they tell the congregation that the individual did not have enough faith. But Jesus did not ask the man with the withered hand how much faith he had. Jesus just said, "Stretch forth thy hand," and the man did. When the multitudes followed Him, He did not heal some and send others away sick. *"HE HEALED THEM ALL!"* If *I* had the gift of healing, I would empty every hospital in America just as rapidly as I could. (Mark 3:11 adds that "unclean spirits, when they saw Him, fell down before Him, and cried, saying, Thou art the Son of God.")

125

Verse 16: *"And charged them that they should not make Him known."*

The Greek word translated *"charge"* is stronger than our English word. It indicates that Jesus would be very much displeased with the people if they should disobey Him and publish the news that He had wrought miracles—for at that time He desired concealment to avoid excitement, contention, and interference from the Jewish rulers. Today it is quite different. He is displeased with *us* if we *fail* to publish the glad tidings and the good news of the Gospel of the grace of God. We are to preach the Gospel to *every creature* and tell *all* that Christ died for our sins according to the Scriptures.

Popularity became a hindrance to the work of Jesus. Many ministers today desire to be popular; Jesus did not. Some men today *court* popularity, but Jesus shunned it. For general reasons why He charged the people *"that they should not make Him known,"* see comments under verse 4 of chapter 8. In the passage beginning with verse 17 of our present chapter, Jesus gives an additional reason: *the fulfillment of prophecy.*

Verses 17 and 18: *"That it might be fulfilled which was spoken by Esaias the prophet, saying, Behold my Servant, whom I have chosen; my Beloved, in whom my soul is well pleased: I will put my Spirit upon Him, and He shall shew judgment to the Gentiles."*

The words we find in verses 18 through 21 are quoted from Isaiah 42:1-4, which reads as follows:

"Behold my Servant, whom I uphold; mine elect, in whom my soul delighteth; I have put my Spirit upon Him: He shall bring forth judgment to the Gentiles. He shall not cry, nor lift up, nor cause His voice to be heard in the street. A bruised reed shall He not break, and the smoking flax shall He not quench: He shall bring forth judgment unto truth. He shall not fail nor be discouraged, till He have set judgment in the earth: and the isles shall wait for His law."

This is the only Gospel which gives us these words recorded by the Prophet Isaiah centuries before. Matthew has already mentioned other prophecies fulfilled in Jesus (Matt. 1:22, 23; 2:15, 17, 18, 23; 4:14-16; and 8:17).

The Jews—and the disciples, at first—expected that the Messiah would be a conqueror. When they saw Him retiring before His enemies, and instead of taking them by force, seeking a place of concealment, it was contrary to all of their previous notions of the Messiah. Matthew by this quotation shows that their conception of Him had been wrong. He reminds them that Isaiah proclaimed centuries before Jesus was born that the Servant of God, beloved and delightsome to Jehovah, would come forth in the fullness of time and declare God. He would reveal the Lord's mind to the nation Israel and then to the Gentile nations. But Jehovah's Servant would not come with noise, clamor, turmoil, and a great outward show. The method of the first coming of Jesus was of another sort altogether. He is coming the *second* time as *the Lion of the tribe of Judah,* but He came the first time as a *Babe* wrapped in swaddling clothes and placed in a manger.

"Behold my Servant, whom I have chosen; my Beloved, in whom my soul is well pleased." The names given the Saviour here are very interesting and exceedingly precious. They are certainly worthy of careful meditation, especially in connection with the passage in Isaiah. Notice: Jesus is the *chosen* One of God. God alone chose Him to come into the world and pay the sin-debt. He ordained Jesus to be His *Servant.* Jesus was both Son and Servant, both God and Man, both divine and human. During our Lord's earthly ministry, God said on two occasions that Jesus was *beloved and well pleasing* to Him (Matt. 3:17; 17:5). Just before Jesus went to Calvary, He prayed, "Father, glorify thy name." Then God the Father said to Him, "I have both glorified it, and will glorify it again" (John 12:28). To any and all who desired to know the truth, there was no excuse for anyone missing the identity of the Messiah.

"I will put my Spirit upon Him"—i. e., in a special and remarkable degree. God, in the divine Spirit, would lie upon Him. At His baptism the Holy Spirit descended upon Jesus and remained

upon Him. In fact, God had revealed to John the Baptist that the One upon whom the Spirit descended and remained was truly the Son of God. God's Servant, ordained of God and empowered by the Spirit, would teach the words of God, and *only* the words of God. Jesus said on many occasions, "I came not to do my will but the will of Him that sent me. The words I speak, they are the words He gave me to speak. The works I do, they are the works that my Father gave me to do."

Jesus, the God-man, took a body of humiliation —one just like ours, except without sin—in order to conquer the world, the flesh, and the devil. His life was a testimony against sin, a judging and a condemning of sin before the eyes of all men with whom He came in contact. The prophecy of Zechariah was fulfilled in Jesus: "Not by might, nor by power, but by my Spirit, saith the Lord of hosts" (Zech. 4:6). And it was by the Spirit that Christ prevailed and the truth went out through His lips to all who would receive it.

Verse 19: *"He shall not strive, nor cry; neither shall any man hear His voice in the streets."*

The meaning here is simply that Jesus would not come as a warrior, shouting and crying out in the streets for the slaughter of the enemy. He did not come to destroy men's lives, He came to save them. He did not come to shout out against them, He came to calmly invite them. The Jews expected

their Messiah to come as a great warrior to lead
them in battle and conquer their foes. On occasion
Jesus did cry out against their sins, and I believe
He raised His voice at times. But Jesus did not
seek publicity or popularity as a great military
leader would. He came to seek and to save the
lost. He came in the form of a servant (Phil. 2:7)
to obey and serve the Father. He came to offer
the Kingdom to the nation Israel, and when they
rejected Him the Kingdom was set aside for a
season and He turned to the Gentiles. (All nations
that are not Jews are Gentiles.)

Verse 20: *"A bruised reed shall He not break,
and smoking flax shall He not quench, till He
send forth judgment unto victory."*

This verse quoted from Isaiah clearly explains
why the Lord Jesus did not smite and destroy His
enemies at that time. Instead of destroying them,
He meekly turned from them. He found the nation
Israel as a bruised reed—they were not stable,
strong, or sturdy. Their worship was so corrupt
that it was a grievous offense unto Jesus. The
religious leaders had perverted the law of God and
had added their own ideas and traditions. Therefore, the worship of Israel at the appearing of
Christ was so corrupt that it was as offensive to
Him as *"smoking flax."* But Jesus had not yet
come to judge Israel. He would not *break the
bruised reed* or *quench the smoking flax* at that

time—but He will at His second coming. In the meantime, the Gospel is preached to all nations, and Jesus is taking out a Gentile bride, the New Testament Church. (Please study Acts 15:12-18.)

Let me add here that Jesus did not have time to argue with the teachers and those who claimed to be the authorities on God's law. He left the "bruised reed" of the religion of the Pharisees to prove its own emptiness and vanity. It was not worth His while to break that bruised reed at that time, and the smoking flax of self-righteousness He passed by as He would filthy rags (Isa. 64:6). He will deal with all this another day, when He comes in mighty power to remove all that is offensive and vile. In the end He will judge those hypocrites who were useless bruised reeds and extinguish the offensive smoking flax. But His first mission was to display the spirit of a Lamb— meek, lowly, tender, and compassionate.

"*. . . till He send forth judgment unto victory.*" In this particular case, *"judgment"* means *the truth of God* or *the Gospel of good news*. The Word shall be victorious; it shall not be vanquished. Jesus commanded His disciples to preach the Gospel to the ends of the earth: "Go ye into all the world, and *preach the Gospel to every creature*" (Mark 16:15). Just before the Day of Pentecost, He commanded the apostles to tarry in Jerusalem until they were endued with power; then they were to preach the Gospel at home and to the uttermost parts of the earth (Luke 24:49; Acts 1:4-8).

It may seem today that believers are losing the battle and the Gospel is being defeated, but this is not so. You can rest assured that the message of the Word of God will be victorious in the end. Not all will be saved, but there will be a number saved which will make up the New Testament Church, the bride of Christ. When that number is completed, the Church will be taken out of this world and judgment then will fall upon His adversaries. Even though Jesus was not the great military leader that the Jews expected to come, He was the greatest Conqueror that ever came into the world—and eventually He will conquer *ALL*. One day all enemies will become His footstool (Heb. 10:12, 13).

Verse 21: *"And in His name shall the Gentiles trust."*

The Hebrew in Isaiah 42:4 is, "And the isles shall wait for His law." The idea, however, is the same. The isles denote the Gentiles, or those who lived outside of Judaea. The meaning is that the Gospel of the grace of God would be proclaimed to the Gentiles and that they would receive the salvation message. Multitudes of the Gentiles *have* believed the Gospel message and have been born into the family of God. The message today is, *"Whosoever will,* let him take the water of life freely" (Rev. 22:17).

In our present day there are those who declare
that we should give first and foremost to Jewish
missions. I fully agree that we should support
Jewish missions and we should preach to the Jews.
The Gospel Hour ministry has supported Jewish
ministries and has given many thousands of dollars
over the years to Jewish work. However, today the
message is to "whosoever will"—no one is *first.*
The nation Israel *had* the first chance. Jesus *came*
to the Jews, to "the lost sheep of the house of
Israel." He told the Syrophenician woman that it
was not "meet" to give the children's bread to
dogs (Matt. 15:21-28). He told His disciples to go
to the Jews and to stay away from the Gentiles
(Matt. 10:5, 6). Finally the nation Israel rejected
their King and the Gospel was sent to the Gentiles:

*"He came unto His own, and His own received
Him not. But as many as received Him, to them
gave He power to become the sons of God,* even to
them that believe on His name" (John 1:11, 12).

But Israel is not completely cut off. (Study
Romans chapter 11.) The "fig tree" is cut down
(Luke 13:6-9)—but only to the ground. The roots
are still alive, and one day they will sprout again
and complete that mission for which Jesus died.

A Demoniac Healed; the Pharisees Blaspheme

You will find the account of this miracle also in
Mark 3:22-30 and in Luke 11:14-23.

I am going to depart here just a bit from the

133

usual full verse-by-verse exposition. Instead, I will give you the verses with a brief comment, and then I am going to give you the teaching in the Word of God concerning the unpardonable sin. I feel this is greatly needed today.

Verse 22: *"Then was brought unto Him one possessed with a devil, blind, and dumb: and He healed him, insomuch that the blind and dumb both spake and saw."*

Someone brought to Jesus a man possessed with a devil. The Greek word can be translated "demon." This man had a demon, and he was blind and dumb. After Jesus healed him, his eyes were opened and he began to speak.

Verse 23: *"And all the people were amazed, and said, Is not this the son of David?"*

All the people were astonished, and they asked a question: *"Is not this the son of David?"* From the standpoint of the flesh, He *was* the Son of David. But notice what happens in the next verse.

Verse 24: *"But when the Pharisees heard it, they said, This fellow doth not cast out devils, but by Beelzebub the prince of the devils."*

The Pharisees, the religious leaders, heard the people asking, *"Is not this the son of David?"* They said, "This fellow Jesus is working miracles; we cannot deny that a great miracle has just been wrought.   *BUT*, He is doing this by Beelzebub, the prince of demons."

Verse 25:   *"And Jesus knew their thoughts, and said unto them, Every kingdom divided against itself is brought to desolation; and every city or house divided against itself shall not stand."*

Jesus was omniscient even though He was in a body of humiliation.   The Pharisees did not need to *speak*, for He knew what they were *thinking*. He said to them, "Every kingdom divided against itself eventually comes to desolation.   Every city or house which is divided will fall, for it cannot stand."   They knew this.   A divided kingdom can never win a battle; a divided home cannot stand; a divided city is destined to destruction.

Verse 26:   *"And if Satan cast out Satan, he is divided against himself; how shall then his kingdom stand?"*

Jesus continued by saying, "If Satan cast out Satan, then it stands to reason that Satan is divided against himself.   Then how shall his kingdom stand?   If I am casting out demons by the power of demons, how can the kingdom of the devil and demons stand?"   We know after two thousand years that the kingdom of the devil is still operating, and it seems stronger than ever.

Verse 27:   *"And if I by Beelzebub cast out*

135

*devils, by whom do your children cast them out?
therefore they shall be your judges."*

Jesus was the greatest Preacher that ever lived,
and He used logic, especially here, that no one
could miss. *"Your children"* (or *sons*) means those
who had been instructed by the Pharisees. *Exor-
cists* (see Acts 19:13) would naturally belong to the
Pharisees—for no *Sadducees* would profess the ex-
pulsion of demons since that party did not believe
in spirits, evil or good. By His answer Jesus
showed that their accusation might as well be
applied to themselves as to Him. Jesus does not
affirm that they cast out demons, but they *pretended* to; and He argues from the point of view of
the blasphemers. He was saying to them, "If your
argument be true—that a man who casts out demons is in league with the devil—then your children have made a covenant with him also. *Therefore they shall be your judges."*

Verse 28: *"But if I cast out devils by the
Spirit of God, then the Kingdom of God is come
unto you."*

Jesus added, "You say I am doing this by the
power of demons; however, if this is not so, and if
I am casting out demons by the Spirit of God,
then the Kingdom of God has come unto you. The
Kingdom that you have been looking for has come,
but you cannot see it because you are too busy
looking for something through which and by which

you can condemn the King. Because I do not measure up to your qualifications, you want to destroy me."

Verse 29: *"Or else how can one enter into a strong man's house, and spoil his goods, except he first bind the strong man? and then he will spoil his house."*

Jesus continued His comparison by saying, "How can anyone enter into a strong man's house and spoil the man's goods unless he is strong enough to bind the man? He must be stronger than the man he is going to rob, if he intends to take what he has. Unless he is stronger and able to bind him, he cannot spoil his house."

Verse 30: *"He that is not with me is against me; and he that gathereth not with me scattereth abroad."*

We do not need any explanation or exegesis on this. Jesus said to the religious leaders—and He is saying the same to you and me—"If you are not with me, you are against me. There is no middle of the road. There is no partial or percentage following me, and following the devil at the same time. You are either gathering people to me or you are driving people from me."

The Unpardonable Sin

Verse 31: *"Wherefore I say unto you, All manner*

of sin and blasphemy shall be forgiven unto men: but the blasphemy against the Holy Ghost shall not be forgiven unto men."

Please note—*"WHEREFORE."* Since what He had just said was true (and they *knew* it was true), He continued speaking to those who had accused Him of casting out demons by Beelzebub, the prince of demons: "I am saying to you that all manner of sin, every different kind of sin and blasphemy, shall be forgiven; but the blasphemy against the third Person of the Trinity, the Holy Spirit, shall not be forgiven."

Verse 32: *"And whosoever speaketh a word against the Son of man, it shall be forgiven him: but whosoever speaketh against the Holy Ghost, it shall not be forgiven him, neither in this world, neither in the world to come."*

Jesus goes even a step further. He says: "You can talk about me, you can call me an illegitimate, you can call me an impostor, and God will forgive you for that. But whosoever—even you Pharisees, scribes, and rulers of the Jews—shall speak against the Holy Ghost, that sin shall not be forgiven in this world nor in the world to come." I cannot imagine how these men must have felt when Jesus finished this discourse on the one sin for which there is absolutely no forgiveness in this world or throughout eternity.

As I read my mail, I have discovered that there

are two things about which the devil torments believers more than anything else. The *first* is *doubting salvation.* A doubter is miserable—for he cannot enjoy his spiritual birthright, nor can he win souls. The *second* is *the unpardonable sin.* Not only do many *letters* come from people who think they have committed the unpardonable sin, but I have received long distance phone calls about this from all over the United States. Some of these calls have been from people who testify that they were born again many years ago, lived a dedicated life for many years, and now the devil tells them they have committed the unpardonable sin. They are frustrated, disturbed, tormented, and they need help.

Probably the most abused subject in the Bible is that of the unpardonable sin. Ministers do not agree concerning this doctrine. I have read sermons by some of the greatest preachers who have ever lived, and these great men of God do not agree on this subject. But the Word of God is clear and understandable. The Holy Spirit is the Teacher, and if we will look at Bible facts without denominational slants or the ideas of men, I believe we can discover what the unpardonable sin is, who can commit it, who will not commit it, and if it can be committed in this dispensation. As we study, we need to follow the admonition of the Apostle Paul: "Let God be true, but every man a liar" (Rom. 3:4).

First, I would like for us to weigh the word "unpardonable." This word is not in the Scripture text, but we do find these words: *"It shall not be forgiven him, neither in this world, neither in the world to come."* Therefore, if there is a sin that shall not be forgiven in this life or in the life to come, then that sin is unpardonable. The word "unpardonable" means "cannot be pardoned—the penalty must be paid." Let me use an illustration here:

Suppose a man is tried and convicted of first-degree murder with no recommendation for mercy, and the judge sentences the man to die in the gas chamber. The lawyers appeal and ask for a new trial, but they are rejected. The man is placed on death row with only a few weeks to live, and the governor refuses to pardon him. Even up to the time that the man steps into the gas chamber, if the governor so desires, he can by a phone call pardon the man who committed a crime that demands the death penalty. But the unpardonable sin *cannot* be forgiven. If God should forgive one who had committed this sin, then He would cease to be God. God *cannot* and *will not* forgive one who has committed the unpardonable sin.

The Word of God speaks of *sin* (singular) and *sins* (plural). Let me point out in the first place that the unpardonable sin (singular) is different from all other sin or sins. This sin is not against God the Father, it is not against the Son, it is not

140

against one's fellow man. The unpardonable sin is against the third Person of the Trinity, the Holy Spirit.

What is sin? The only place to find the right answer is in the Word of God. Even preachers do not agree on the definition of sin. One minister will declare that something is sin, another minister will declare that it is not. But the Bible answers: "Whosoever committeth sin transgresseth also the law: for *sin is the transgression of the law*" (I John 3:4).

What is the law? The law is the revealed will of God in regard to human conduct, including all the Divine commands and precepts as proclaimed through Moses: "For the law was given by Moses" (John 1:17). We are not *under* law, but God's law has not been destroyed or altered. Jesus came into this world in a body of humiliation, and in that body He fulfilled every jot and every tittle of the law. He said, "Think not that I am come to destroy the law, or the prophets: *I am not come to destroy, but to FULFIL*" (Matt. 5:17). God's law still stands, and it will never pass away.

Let me briefly point out the law of God in the Ten Commandments, found in Exodus 20:

"Thou shalt have no other gods before me. . . . Thou shalt not make unto thee any graven image . . . Thou shalt not take the name of the Lord thy God in vain . . . Remember the sabbath day, to keep it holy. . . . Honour thy father and thy mother

. . . Thou shalt not kill. Thou shalt not commit adultery. Thou shalt not steal. Thou shalt not bear false witness against thy neighbour. Thou shalt not covet."

The first four commandments concern one's duties to God; the last six have to do with our fellow man. All kinds of sin except the unpardonable sin are either directly against God or against one's fellow man. Please do not misunderstand me. I know that God is *one* God manifest in *three Persons* — the Father, the Son, and the Holy Spirit. In this study, we are dealing with the Trinity in their separate offices concerning redemption and man's entrance into heaven. This is the Dispensation of Grace, the Dispensation of the Holy Spirit. In this age the Holy Spirit is in the world, convicting, convincing, and drawing men to Christ. The Holy Spirit came on the Day of Pentecost, and He will remain here until the Rapture, when He will be taken out with the Church.

Time and space will not permit us to discuss the various ideas concerning the unpardonable sin, but the most common definition of this sin is *putting off salvation too long*. Some ministers say that the unpardonable sin is rejecting God one time too many, and then one dies and goes out to meet God and is lost forever. However, anyone who knows anything at all about the Word of God knows that there is no repentance after death. Some religions teach a second chance after death, but they do not have any Scripture to substantiate their doctrine.

As long as there is life, there is hope of salvation, unless one has committed the unpardonable sin. I believe it is possible for a man to be saved on his death bed — even one minute before he dies! The thief on the cross was saved there on the cross as he was dying, but I believe that this was his first opportunity to be saved. But I do not believe a person who has had opportunity after opportunity to be saved and has continually rejected Jesus over the years will be saved on his death bed. There are a lot of people who *profess* to be saved when they get real sick, but their lives do not back up their profession when they get well.

The favorite Scripture of those who teach that the unpardonable sin is putting off salvation too long is Genesis 6:3: "And the Lord said, My Spirit shall not always strive with man, for that he also is flesh: yet his days shall be an hundred and twenty years." They say that the Spirit of God strives with a man up to a point, then the Spirit leaves the man; or if he goes out to meet God without being saved, that is the unpardonable sin.

But the warning in Genesis 6:3 was given just before the flood. People were living and acting then as they are now — for I believe we are living in a repetition of Noah's days. They lived as though they would stay here forever, and God warned them that their days were only one hundred and twenty years. God did not mean that man would live to be one hundred and twenty years old, but that it would be one hundred and twenty years until the flood would cover the entire earth. In that day men lived to be eight or nine hundred years old, and *now* the promise is threescore and ten, which is *seventy* (Psalm 90:10). I feel that to interpret Genesis 6:3 as meaning man will live one hundred and twenty years is wrongly dividing the Word. I believe that procrastination is *very dangerous* and often *disastrous*—but it is not the unpardonable sin.

The unpardonable sin is not *breaking any one of the Ten Commandments,* because Jesus *fulfilled* every jot and every tittle of the law. John the Baptist announced Jesus to his disciples in these words: "Behold the Lamb of God, which taketh away the sin of the world" (John 1:29). Jesus came to take away the sin of the world. And we read in John 19:30, *"It is finished."* Since Jesus finished what He came to do, He *did* take away the sin of the world. In the intercessory prayer just before He went to Calvary, He said to the Father, "I have finished the work which thou gavest me to do" (John 17:4). If Jesus finished the work the Father gave Him to do and took away the sin of the world, then the unpardonable sin is a singular sin. There is no sin like it in any way, and the thing that we need to do is see exactly what it is.

Jesus was going about doing good. On this

occasion (here in Matthew 12) He had just healed a man who was possessed with a demon and was blind and dumb. When the man could see and talk, the Pharisees said that Jesus performed the miracle by Beelzebub—and this led to the statement by Jesus that blasphemy against the Holy Spirit would not be forgiven in this world nor in the world to come.

I want us to find out what *blasphemy* is. I quote from Webster's dictionary: "In Jewish law, cursing or reviling God or the king, who was God's representative; in the later usage, pronouncing the forbidden name of God. Indignity offered to God, in words, writing, or signs; also, act of claiming the attributes or prerogatives of Deity. Irreverence toward anything regarded as sacred." We have here the definition according to Jewish law. We also read that to blaspheme is "to speak of or address with impious irreverence, to revile, or to abuse."

Just what did these men do to whom Jesus spoke these scorching words? Jesus healed the boy that was possessed with a demon, and they said He did it by the power of Beelzebub, the prince of demons. They attributed the miracle that Jesus had wrought by the Spirit of God to the power of *demons,* thus speaking irreverently against the Holy Spirit. Jesus said later, "If I cast out demons by the Spirit of God, then the Kingdom of God is come unto you." Jesus *did* cast out demons by

145

the Spirit of God—but they attributed to the prince of demons what Jesus had done by and through the power of the third Person of the Trinity, the Holy Spirit. They blasphemed the name of God's Spirit.

Can this sin be committed in this dispensation? I feel the only possible way to get the right answer is to compare Scripture with Scripture and spiritual things with spiritual things. It is true that Jesus uttered these words before the birth of the Church; however, we must acknowledge that this is the Dispensation of the Holy Spirit. God the Father is sitting on the throne with God the Son seated at His right hand. The Holy Spirit is in the world, seeking and calling out a bride for the Son. The Holy Spirit came on the Day of Pentecost and has been here ever since. In the Old Testament era He came upon men (and at times upon beasts) for a period of time and then departed. But in this dispensation He has remained here and will remain until the close of this age. Therefore, it is only reasonable to believe that God intended for us to know that it is possible to blaspheme the Holy Spirit in this dispensation since He is God's representative on earth today. He is in the world and is convicting men of sin, of righteousness, and of judgment:

"Nevertheless I tell you the truth; It is expedient for you that I go away: for if I go not away, the Comforter will not come unto you; but if I depart, I will send Him unto you. *And when*

He is come, He will reprove the world of sin, and of righteousness, and of judgment: of sin, because they believe not on me; of righteousness, because I go to my Father, and ye see me no more; of judgment, because the prince of this world is judged" (John 16:7-11).

I believe—and I have preached throughout all of my ministry—that *it is possible to commit the unpardonable sin today;* however, I believe there are very few people who have. I believe there are very few people alive today who are guilty of the unpardonable sin. I will tell you a little later how you can know for sure if you have committed this sin.

Who can commit the unpardonable sin? *Any unbeliever* is a candidate to commit this sin. The devil desires to damn every soul that he can. Therefore, any person who is not a child of God is able to commit the unpardonable sin. The devil knows if he can cause you to commit this sin, you cannot be saved—he need not worry about you any more, because you are his property. The devil hates the Godhead—and if he can damn you or me, he is stabbing at God, because we are created in the image of God. All men who are damned are lost forever from the family of God. If the devil can cause you to speak or do something that is blasphemous against the Holy Spirit, then he knows that your destiny is sealed. Therefore I say to any unbeliever who reads these lines, that you are a candidate to commit the unpardonable sin. Since it is possible for you to commit this terrible sin, if you are wise you will come to God and be saved today, yielding your mind, heart, and body to Him. "Be sober, be vigilant; because *your adversary the devil, as a roaring lion, walketh about, seeking whom he may devour*" (I Pet. 5:8).

Who will *not* commit the unpardonable sin? Is there anyone alive who will not or *cannot* commit the unpardonable sin? Yes! Every person who is genuinely born again, genuinely covered by the blood, genuinely saved by grace and, therefore, a child of God, has the assurance that he will never blaspheme the Holy Spirit. I want you to keep in mind that I said *born-again* people—not church members, religionists, professors of religion. Truly born-again, blood-washed, redeemed children of God *will not* commit the unpardonable sin.

Where is my Scripture to prove this point? First of all, Jesus declared that no man can come to Him for salvation unless God the Father draws him: *"No man can come to me, except the Father which hath sent me draw him:* and I will raise him up at the last day" (John 6:44). And how does God draw a sinner to Christ? Through the power of the Holy Spirit, as revealed in the passage quoted from John chapter 16: "Nevertheless I tell you the truth; It is expedient for you that I go away: for if I go not away, *the Comforter* (the Holy Spirit) will not come unto you; but if I depart, I will send Him unto you. And *when He is come, HE will reprove the world of sin,* and of righteousness, and of judgment" (John 16:7, 8).

The Spirit of God draws men to Jesus. The Spirit uses the *Word,* which is the *light,* the *sword,* the *hammer,* the *fire,* the incorruptible *seed,* the *bread,* and the *water.* The Spirit uses the Word to convict men that they need the Saviour, and He draws men to the place of repentance. The Spirit, using the Word of God, leads men to repent because they are commanded in the Bible to do so: "Except ye repent, ye shall all likewise perish" (Luke 13:3).

But the Spirit does not stop when He draws us and convicts us. The Spirit of God *"borns"* us into God's family. In John chapter 3 we read that Nicodemus, a ruler of the Jews, came to Jesus by night and confessed that Jesus was "a Teacher come from God," for no ordinary man could do what He was doing "except God be with him." Jesus told Nicodemus that "except a man be born again, he cannot see the Kingdom of God." When Nicodemus asked how a man could be *born* when he was *old,* Jesus answered, "Verily, verily, I say unto thee, Except a man be born of water and of *the Spirit,* he cannot enter into the Kingdom of God. That which is born of the flesh is flesh; and that which is born of the Spirit is spirit. Marvel not that I said unto thee, Ye must be born again" (John 3:1-7).

So we see that the Spirit of God *draws us* to Christ, the Spirit *"borns" us* into the family of God—and the Spirit of God comes into the believer's heart and *dwells:* "Ye are not in the flesh, but in the Spirit, *if so be that the Spirit of God dwell in you. Now if any man have not the Spirit of Christ, he is none of His. . . .* For as many as are led by the Spirit of God, they are the sons of God. . . . The Spirit (Himself) beareth witness with our spirit, that we are the children of God" (Rom. 8:9, 14, 16). We read in I John 3:24, ". . . And hereby we know that He abideth in us, *by the Spirit which He hath given us."* The promise of the indwelling Spirit is repeated in I John 4:13: *"Hereby know we that we dwell in Him, and He in us, because He hath given us of His Spirit."* We are made *partakers of the divine nature:* "Whereby are given unto us exceeding great and precious promises: that by these ye might be partakers of the divine nature, having escaped the corruption that is in the world through lust" (II Pet. 1:4).

But even this is not all. The Spirit not only draws us, "borns" us, and indwells us, but He *seals us:* ". . . after that ye believed, *ye were sealed with that Holy Spirit of promise,* which is the earnest of our inheritance until the redemption of the purchased possession . . ." (Eph. 1:13, 14). Paul says, "Grieve not *the Holy Spirit of God, whereby ye are sealed unto the day of redemption"* (Eph. 4:30).

Do you think that the Holy Spirit who draws us to God, "borns" us into the family of God, indwells us, and seals us, would lead us to blaspheme Himself? The Bible clearly teaches that "as many as are *LED by the Spirit of God*, they are the sons of God" (Rom. 8:14). The Spirit leads us to glorify Jesus, not to blaspheme any member of the Godhead. Jesus said, *"When He, the Spirit of truth, is come, He will guide you into all truth:* for He shall not speak of Himself; but whatsoever He shall hear, that shall He speak: and He will shew you things to come, *He shall glorify me..."* (John 16:13, 14).

A person who is born again will never commit the unpardonable sin. The Spirit of God witnesses with our spirit that we are the children of God, and we have the witness of the Spirit in our hearts (Rom. 8:16; Heb. 10:15). I am not speaking of the witness as an audible voice, but of the peace and assurance brought by the Spirit of God. We read in I John 5:13, "These things have I written unto you that believe on the name of the Son of God; *that ye may KNOW that ye have ETERNAL LIFE,* and that ye may believe on the name of the Son of God." If you do not have this assurance, bow your head and invite Jesus to come into your heart — and He will save you.

How can a sinner know whether or not he has committed the unpardonable sin? The answer to that question is very clearly stated in the Word of God. No man can come to Jesus for salvation unless the heavenly Father *draws* him (John 6:44), and the Father draws men by and through the power of the Holy Spirit. The Holy Spirit convicts men that they are sinners, convinces them that they need the Saviour, and draws them through the Word to the place of salvation. Therefore, any person who has any *desire* to become a born-again child of God *has not* committed the unpardonable sin. The very desire to become a Christian is planted in a person's heart by the Holy Spirit. If one has committed the unpardonable sin, his heart is as hard as stone and is without emotion, as far as feelings toward God are concerned. Such a person is forever given up and God has ceased to deal with him; therefore, he will have no desire whatsoever to be saved.

Let me sum up what has been said:

1. The religious leaders (in Matthew 12:24) gave the devil credit for what the Spirit of God had done.

2. Jesus informed them that He was casting out demons by the Spirit of God, and not by Beelzebub. If he were in union with Beelzebub, then the kingdom of the devil would fall. It had not fallen —nor has it yet fallen—so we know that Jesus was not working with the devil nor the devil with Him. Jesus said that if He was casting out demons by the Spirit of God, then the Kingdom of God had come to them.

3. Sin is transgressing God's law. Jesus came to take away the sin of the world, and He finished the work He came to do. Therefore, any and all who will ask God to forgive their sin and ask Jesus to come into their heart, will be saved.

4. The unpardonable sin is blasphemy against the Holy Spirit. One who has blasphemed the Holy Spirit will have no desire to be saved. Those who are born again are possessors of the Holy Spirit, and He will never lead a child of God to blaspheme Himself.

Destiny in Words

Verse 33: *"Either make the tree good, and his fruit good; or else make the tree corrupt, and his fruit corrupt: for the tree is known by his fruit."*

A tree is known to be corrupt or good not by its leaves, but by its *fruit*. In the Sermon on the Mount, Jesus said: "Every *good tree* bringeth forth *good fruit;* but a *corrupt tree* bringeth forth *evil fruit*. A good tree cannot bring forth evil fruit, neither can a corrupt tree bring forth good fruit. . . . Wherefore *by their fruits ye shall know them"* (Matt. 7:17-20).

The truth given here is that we judge a man by the words he speaks and the works he does. We cannot say a man is in league with Satan if his works are righteous. If he is one of Satan's workers, his works will be unrighteous. Sweet and

153

bitter water do not proceed from the same fountain, and righteous works cannot proceed from an
evil heart. The Pharisees had just accused Jesus
of casting out demons by Beelzebub, the prince of
demons. Certainly it was a good thing to deliver
a man from blindness and dumbness. No one
could deny that the miracle performed on the man
was indeed good and wonderful, but they accused
Jesus of being corrupt. If He had performed a
righteous deed, He could not be corrupt in His
heart. If the tree is good, the fruit is good; if the
tree is corrupt, the fruit is corrupt. So He said,
"Either make the tree good" and the *fruit good,*
or *"make the tree corrupt"*—because a tree *"is
known by his fruit."*

Jesus told the Pharisees on another occasion:
"Ye are of your father the devil, and the lusts of
your father ye will do. He was a murderer from
the beginning, and abode not in the truth, because
there is no truth in him. When he speaketh a lie,
he speaketh of his own: for he is a liar, and the
father of it" (John 8:44).

Verse 34: *"O generation of vipers, how can ye,
being evil, speak good things? for out of the abundance of the heart the mouth speaketh."*

"O generation of vipers . . . ." Jesus repeats
the words of John the Baptist here (Matt. 3:7). A
viper is a very poisonous kind of serpent, and in
that day and area it was about three feet long

and an inch thick, with a flat head. The viper (or the snake) is always used in the Bible as an emblem of the devil or wickedness. This was strong language and severe—but the loving Saviour did not shrink from the severest rebukes when needed. His words described the character of the men who declared that He was in league with the devil and was performing miracles through Satan's power. In doing this, they sealed their eternal doom; for Jesus clearly informed them that they would not be forgiven in this world nor in the world to come.

"How can ye, being evil, speak good things?" These men were evil, for they were the offspring of Satan. How could they do otherwise than accuse Him of blasphemy when they were of their father the devil? Their hearts were so full of malice and hatred toward Him that it would be impossible for them to say anything good about Him—*"for out of the abundance of the heart the mouth speaketh."* (In Mark 7:21-23 we find catalogued the evil things that proceed from the heart.) These men were evil; therefore, they spoke evil of Jesus. Had they been righteous, they would have uttered words of righteousness about Him. Man looks on the outward appearance, but *God* looks on the *heart*—and it is from a cesspool of iniquity within, that wickedness flows out into the life of a sinful man. The abundance of the heart produces the words uttered by the lips.

Verse 35: *"A good man out of the good treasure of the heart bringeth forth good things: and an evil man out of the evil treasure bringeth forth evil things."*

When the Bible speaks of *"a good man,"* the reference is to a *righteous* man, or a man with a *new heart*. In Ezekiel 36:26 God promised a new heart and a new spirit. In II Corinthians 5:17 we read: "Therefore if any man be in Christ, *he is a NEW CREATURE:* old things are passed away; behold, all things are become *new."* A righteous man *"out of the good treasure of the heart bringeth forth good things";* that is, when one speaks words of righteousness and works deeds of righteousness, that person has a righteous heart. When one works deeds of iniquity and speaks words of blasphemy, that person has a wicked, evil heart.

In John 14:8-12 we read: "Philip saith unto Him, Lord, shew us the Father, and it sufficeth us. Jesus saith unto him, Have I been so long time with you, and yet hast thou not known me, Philip? He that hath seen me hath seen the Father; and how sayest thou then, Shew us the Father? Believest thou not that I am in the Father, and the Father in me? The words that I speak unto you I speak not of myself: but the Father that dwelleth in me, He doeth the works. Believe me that I am in the Father, and the Father in me: or else *believe me for the very works' sake.* Verily, verily, I say unto you, He that believeth on me, the works that I do shall he do also; and greater works than these shall he do; because I go unto my Father."

Anyone—especially those acquainted with the Old Testament Scriptures—who heard the words of Jesus and witnessed His works, should have known that He was the Messiah. John tells us that the officers on one occasion went to arrest Jesus; and when they returned without Him, they confessed the reason they did not bring Him: "Never man spake like this Man" (John 7:46).

In John chapter 9 we read that on the Sabbath day Jesus healed a man who was born blind, and His enemies were very angry. Refusing to believe the man's story, they asked his parents if he was born blind. But the parents were afraid of the religious leaders and told them that the man was of age and for them to ask *him*. Then they questioned him again concerning the miracle, but he said, "I have told you already, and ye did not hear: wherefore would ye hear it again? Will ye also be His disciples?" (v. 27).

"Then they reviled him, and said, Thou art His disciple; but we are Moses' disciples. We know that God spake unto Moses: as for this fellow, we know not from whence He is. The man answered and said unto them, Why herein is a marvellous thing, that ye know not from whence He is, and yet He hath opened mine eyes. Now we know that God heareth not sinners: but if any man be a worshipper of God, and doeth His will, him He

157

heareth. *Since the world began was it not heard THAT ANY MAN OPENED THE EYES OF ONE THAT WAS BORN BLIND.* If this Man were not of God, He could do nothing. They answered and said unto him, Thou wast altogether born in sins, and dost thou teach us? And they cast him out" (John 9:28-34).

A man born blind, who did not profess to know anything about prophecy, taught the Pharisees in wonderful words of reason. No man had ever opened the eyes of one born blind, yet this Man Jesus had opened his eyes; therefore, He must be from God. But the religious leaders refused to receive his testimony and cast him out.

In this day, men are being thrown out of denominations, churches, and schools for believing in the verbal inspiration of the Scriptures, the deity of Christ, and other fundamentals of the faith. Remember, we are either *for* Christ or *against* Him; there is no middle of the road. You are either a child of God or a child of the devil. You either believe the Bible or you deny it—and if you deny any part of it, you deny all of it, because all Scripture is of God: *"ALL Scripture is given by inspiration of God,* and is profitable for doctrine, for reproof, for correction, for instruction in righteousness: that the man of God may be perfect, throughly furnished unto all good works" (II Tim. 3:16, 17).

Verse 36: *"But I say unto you, That every idle*

word that men shall speak, they shall give account thereof in the day of judgment."

"Idle" in the Greek means "vain, thoughtless, useless"; that is, words that do not bring any constructive message, help, or declaration, and would have been better not to have been spoken. The word here could mean *wicked, injurious, false, malicious*—for such were the words the Pharisees had just spoken in verse 24. This passage must not be understood as condemning all light pleasantries of conversation. It simply says that the idlest nothings we ever utter are included within the range of accountability to God. We must therefore see to it that our pleasantries are not untruthful, that they are free from malice and impurity—in a word, that they are innocent and not harmful.

We should certainly weigh the words of Jesus here and take stock of our conversation. Words come from the heart, and one's character is announced by words uttered through his lips. God keeps a record of *"every idle word"* that we speak, and these useless words will face us at the *"judgment."*

This may seem impossible as we think of all the words spoken by all the people in the world in one single day. But in this age of electronics and microfilm, our *government* keeps almost as strict record on every one of us. If *man* can do such a thing, what can Almighty God do? God has a record of every word we have ever spoken, every thought we have ever had, and every deed we have ever done. The only way to get those things that are unrighteous destroyed is to get them under the blood. When one believes on the Lord Jesus Christ and puts his faith in the finished work of the Lamb of God, all sin is put under the blood and God remembers it against us no more.

We should pray with the Psalmist, *"Let the WORDS OF MY MOUTH, and the meditation of my heart, be acceptable in thy sight, O Lord,* my strength, and my Redeemer"* (Psalm 19:14). In another place, David cried out to God, "O Lord, open thou my lips; and my mouth shall shew forth thy praise" (Psalm 51:15).

Verse 37: *"For by thy words thou shalt be justified, and by thy words thou shalt be condemned."*

"By thy words . . . ." The literal translation here reads, *"Out of* thy words," meaning that which proceeds from their words, or a result or consequence of their words. Note that the phrase is repeated: *"Out of thy words* thou shalt be justified, and *out of thy words* thou shalt be condemned." You can rest assured that out of words uttered by a man, one can reckon what he is thinking in his heart. Just as a tree is known by its fruit, man will show in words what he is in his heart.

We are instructed in Matthew 10:32, 33 that if

160

we confess Jesus before men, He will confess us before the Father; but if we deny Him before men, He will deny us before the Father. We confess Him with *words*. Of course, we also confess Him by the things we *do*—our *works* declare whether we are servants of God or servants of the devil. But by words we confess that we are a child of God and that we love God, or by words we confess that we are a child of the devil and we love unrighteousness. In Romans 10:9, 10 we read, "If thou shalt *confess with thy mouth* the Lord Jesus, and shalt believe in thine heart that God hath raised Him from the dead, thou shalt be saved. For with the heart man believeth unto righteousness; and *with the mouth confession is made unto salvation.*" We confess in words that we know Jesus, for we are not ashamed to announce that we are His child. On the other hand, if we are a son of Satan, we confess that also by our words.

Words are *extremely important,* for they reveal character (verses 33-35). Words uttered by us affect those around us, whether we realize it or not. The only sin declared in the Bible to be unpardonable is a sin of *speech* (verses 31 and 32). Words are a mighty force, with great power for either good or evil. Notice the following passage from God's Word:

"My brethren, be not many masters, knowing that we shall receive the greater condemnation. For in many things we offend all. *If any man offend not in word, the same is a perfect man,* and able also to bridle the whole body. Behold, we put bits in the horses' mouths, that they may obey us; and we turn about their whole body. Behold also the ships, which though they be so great, and are driven of fierce winds, yet are they turned about with a very small helm, whithersoever the governor listeth. Even so *the tongue is a little member, and boasteth great things.* Behold, how great a matter a little fire kindleth! And *the tongue is a fire, a world of iniquity: so is the tongue among our members, that it defileth the whole body, and setteth on fire the course of nature; and it is set on fire of hell.*

"For every kind of beasts, and of birds, and of serpents, and of things in the sea, is tamed, and hath been tamed of mankind: *but the tongue can no man tame; it is an unruly evil, full of deadly poison. Therewith bless we God, even the Father; and therewith curse we men, which are made after the similitude of God. Out of the same mouth proceedeth blessing and cursing. My brethren, these things ought not so to be.* Doth a fountain send forth at the same place sweet water and bitter? Can the fig tree, my brethren, bear olive berries? either a vine, figs? So can no fountain both yield salt water and fresh. Who is a wise man and endued with knowledge among you? Let him shew out of a good conversation his works with meekness of wisdom" (James 3:1-13).

The Jews Ask for a Sign; the Sign of the Prophet Jonah

Verse 38: *"Then certain of the scribes and of the Pharisees answered, saying, Master, we would see a sign from thee."*

The terrible denunciation Jesus gave His enemies in the preceding verses fell on deaf ears. Their response was that they wanted *"a sign."* In that day a "sign" commonly referred to a miracle or something extraordinary which proved that God had sent a person. It is very strange that the Jews completely ignored all of the miracles that Jesus had already performed and asked for a sign that would prove to them that God had sent Him. Indeed they were evil and had no spiritual truth in their hearts.

These religious leaders were not interested in the truth; they were not really concerned whether or not Jesus was the Messiah. They were attempting to find something to use to condemn Him. Some may say that perhaps these particular individuals had not *seen* Jesus perform miracles. But if they had not actually seen one of His miracles, certainly they had heard from others about the miracles He had wrought previous to this. In either case—whether they had seen or had not seen them—the Jews were "tempting Him" (Luke 11:16); they were not interested in knowing whether or not He was really their Messiah.

163

(After Jesus came back from the dead, *Thomas* refused to believe He was *alive* and declared that he would not believe unless he put his finger in the prints of the nails in His hands and thrust his hand into the side of Jesus. Jesus appeared later when Thomas was with the other disciples, and after Thomas confessed it was the Lord, Jesus said to him, "Because thou hast seen me, thou hast believed: *blessed are they that have NOT seen, and yet have believed*" — John 20:24-29.)

Luke 11:16 states that "others, tempting Him, sought of Him a sign from heaven." Perhaps the emphasis of the Jews' request should be laid on the words *"from heaven."* It could be that they desired to see thunder and lightning from heaven, as when God called Moses up on the mountain and gave him the law. Seeing Jesus change five loaves and two fishes into enough food to feed five thousand hungry men did not satisfy them. Witnessing the healing of the blind and dumb man was not enough. Raising the little daughter of Jairus was not enough. They demanded more.

Verse 39: *"But He answered and said unto them, An evil and adulterous generation seeketh after a sign; and there shall no sign be given to it, but the sign of the prophet Jonas."*

"An evil and adulterous generation . . . ." Jesus had clearly branded these religionists as vipers or deadly snakes, and now He pronounces them *evil*

and *adulterous*. It is well to keep in mind here that the relation between God and the Jews in the Old Testament is often represented as a marriage, with God as the husband and the nation Israel as His wife. (Please study Isaiah 54:5; Jeremiah 31:32; Ezekiel chapter 16; Hosea chapter 2, and 3:1.) When the nation Israel sinned against God, their apostasy and idolatry are referred to as adultery. This is what Jesus is referring to here. The Jews were unfaithful to the covenant that God made with Abraham and to the commandments that He gave to Moses. They were evil and adulterous in the spiritual sense, because they were certainly unfaithful and untrue to God.

These people were *seeking after a sign*—but Jesus said, *"There shall no sign be given to it...."* Man does not proposition God. These religious leaders demanded a sign from heaven, but Jesus informed them in understandable words that there would be no sign given. They wanted a direct miracle, such as manna falling out of heaven, total darkness over the land, a blazing light, or a gigantic clap of thunder. But Jesus said that He would not perform any such miracle for the satisfaction of a sinful and adulterous people. He did not mean that He would not work any more miracles or that He would not give any more outward evidence that He was "that Prophet" of whom Moses spoke. He meant that He would not give to these people upon their request a direct miracle from heaven.

"*. . . but the sign of the prophet Jonas.*" In the last part of this verse, Jesus reminds the Jews that in the Prophet Jonah they had already had a miracle. Just as Jonah was preserved by God three days and three nights in the belly of the whale and then restored alive, so *He* would be in the tomb three days and three nights, and then He would come out alive. If the Jews were really in earnest, really sincere, they would see this—because Jonah was a type of Christ. His experience in the belly of the whale was a type of the death, burial, and resurrection of Jesus. So Jesus would not cause something spectacular or divine to occur in their presence, but He would give them a sign that should convince them—the sign of Jonah.

Jesus Foretells His Death and Resurrection

Verse 40:   "*For as Jonas was three days and three nights in the whale's belly; so shall the Son of man be three days and three nights in the heart of the earth.*"

"*Jonas was three days and three nights in the whale's belly.*"   This event took place in the Mediterranean Sea somewhere between Joppa and Tarshish. God had called Jonah to preach to the wicked city of Nineveh, but instead of obeying, he went in the other direction—fleeing "from the presence of the Lord." He boarded a ship headed for Tarshish; but the Lord sent "a mighty tempest

in the sea, so that the ship was like to be broken."
Realizing that the storm had come on his account,
Jonah told the ship's crew, "Take me up, and cast
me forth into the sea; so shall the sea be calm
unto you: for I know that for my sake this great
tempest is upon you." Then "they took up Jonah,
and cast him forth into the sea: and the sea
ceased from her raging"—and *the Lord had prepared a great fish* to swallow up Jonah. And
*Jonah was in the belly of the fish three days and
three nights."* (Read the entire story in the book
of Jonah.)

". . . *so shall the Son of man be three days and
three nights in the heart of the earth."* The pres-
ervation of Jonah in the great fish was a sign or a
type of our Lord's entombment and His resurrection from the dead. The experiences of both Jonah
and the Lord were miraculous. The prophet Jonah
typifies Christ as the One sent from God, raised
from the dead and delivering the good news of
salvation to the Gentiles.

I do not suppose there is any passage in all the
Word of God that critics have attacked more than
the account of Jonah in the belly of the whale
three days and three nights. They declare that
whales did not travel in that particular part of
the Mediterranean Sea—and even if they did, the
critics declare that the throat of a whale is entirely
too small to swallow a man. But they forget that
God prepared a great fish (Jonah 1:17).

All who believe in God believe that in the beginning He created the heaven, the earth, and all things that therein are. If God spoke this earth into existence—and He *did*—I do not think it would be very difficult for Him to speak and a great fish appear. I believe this was a special fish, built to order, prepared for this one mission—to swallow Jonah, the backslidden prophet running from God. The argument that the throat of a whale is entirely too small to swallow a man is foolish and silly. The Bible tells us that God prepared a great fish—and if God prepared this fish, his throat could have been large enough to swallow a ship with all the men on board! When we believe the Bible is the Word of God, we put no question marks around anything in the Bible, knowing that *there is NOTHING too hard for God.* If God had anything to do with it, we should have no trouble believing what the record declares.

Some have tried to explain that this was probably a shark or some other kind of fish. I would not waste one line in this commentary trying to explain anything about this fish except to state that *God prepared it*—and since God prepared it, the fish could have been one thousand feet long and his throat could have been one hundred feet in diameter! Jonah could have *walked* in, so far as that is concerned. I have no trouble believing the account of Jonah and the whale.

In my meetings when I preached on this subject,

I used to make this statement: "I do not find it difficult to believe that Jonah was swallowed by a great fish. The thing that I have difficulty understanding is how a fish kept a backslidden preacher on his stomach three days without vomiting!" I think one of the most sickening things on earth is a backslidden preacher, and that is exactly what Jonah was. He was backslidden, running from God—and God brought him back. You can rest assured that when he landed on the beach, he may not have had a diploma from the denominational university, but he had a message and he delivered it!

Please notice—Jesus clearly stated that just as the prophet Jonah spent three days and three nights in the whale's belly, the Son of man would be *three days and three nights in the heart of the earth.* (When we reach the account of the Crucifixion and the Resurrection, we will see that Jesus actually spent three days and three nights in the heart of the earth—not two nights and part of three days, as some teach.)

The Pharisees did not forget the prophecy Jesus proclaimed here and on other occasions. When He was taken down from the cross and placed in the tomb, they visited Pilate and reminded him of what Jesus had said:

"Now the next day, that followed the day of the preparation, the chief priests and Pharisees came together unto Pilate, saying, Sir, *we remember* that that deceiver said, while He was yet alive, *After three days I will rise again.* Command therefore that the sepulchre be made sure until the third day, lest His disciples come by night, and steal Him away, and say unto the people, He is risen from the dead: so the last error shall be worse than the first. Pilate said unto them, Ye have a watch: go your way, make it as sure as you can. So they went, and made the sepulchre sure, sealing the stone, and setting a watch" (Matt. 27:62-66).

You can rest assured that Jesus remained in the tomb as prophesied and *rose again* as prophesied. After the Resurrection the guards went to the chief priests and revealed unto them the thing that had happened: ". . . behold, some of the watch came into the city, and shewed unto the chief priests all the things that were done. And when they were assembled with the elders, and had taken counsel, they gave large money unto the soldiers, saying, Say ye, His disciples came by night, and stole Him away while we slept. And if this come to the governor's ears, we will persuade him, and secure you. So they took the money, and did as they were taught: and this saying is commonly reported among the Jews until this day" (Matt. 28:11-15). (If these guards had really slept and the body had been stolen, they would have been put to death immediately.)

Some may not understand what Jesus meant by *"the heart of the earth."* The Jews used the

word "heart" to denote the *interior* of anything
or to speak of being "in a thing." Of course, the
body of Jesus was in the sepulchre three days and
three nights, but Jesus actually descended into the
lower parts of this earth—far beyond the tomb of
Joseph. While His body was in the tomb His
spirit went into Paradise and announced to the
saints that the sin-debt had been paid, redemption
had been purchased, the victory had been won, and
they would be delivered from the Paradise in the
heart of the earth and carried to the Paradise far
above all heavens. Peter tells us that "He went
and *preached unto the spirits in prison*" (I Pet.
3:19). And in Ephesians 4:8-10 we read: *"When
He ascended up on high, HE LED CAPTIVITY
CAPTIVE, and gave gifts unto men. (NOW THAT
HE ASCENDED, what is it but that HE ALSO
DESCENDED FIRST INTO THE LOWER PARTS
OF THE EARTH? HE THAT DESCENDED IS
THE SAME ALSO THAT ASCENDED UP FAR
ABOVE ALL HEAVENS, that He might fill all
things.)"*

Verse 41: *"The men of Nineveh shall rise in
judgment with this generation, and shall condemn
it: because they repented at the preaching of Jonas;
and, behold, a greater than Jonas is here."*

The city of Nineveh was the capital of Assyria,
located on the banks of the river Tigris to the
northeast of Babylon. It was founded by Asshur:

"Out of that land went forth Asshur, and builded Nineveh, and the city Rehoboth, and Calah" (Gen. 10:11). Nineveh was a great and vast city and a very wicked and ungodly city. There were walls around the city one hundred feet high and ten feet thick, and the city was defended by fifteen hundred towers two hundred feet in height. The last verse in Jonah says there were more than 120,000 people in the great city.

Nineveh *"repented at the preaching of Jonas,"* and it was spared (according to historians) for two hundred years. It was then overthrown by Babylon about six centuries before the birth of Jesus. During the battle when the city fell, the river Tigris overflowed and washed out part of the wall, through which the enemy entered the city, robbed it, and destroyed it completely. The destruction of Nineveh was foretold more than one hundred years before it happened: "But with an overrunning flood He will make an utter end of the place thereof, and darkness shall pursue His enemies" (Nahum 1:8). We also read in Nahum 2:6, "The gates of the rivers shall be opened, and the palace shall be dissolved."

"The men of Nineveh shall rise in judgment with this generation, and shall condemn it." Nineveh repented at the preaching of Jonah, and God spared it. Jesus reminded Israel that the people who repented at the preaching of Jonah would *rise up in judgment* and *condemn them.* The

people of Nineveh were wicked, ignorant heathen; yet they repented at the preaching of just an ordinary prophet—Jonah. These Jews, who professed to be enlightened, the custodians of God's law, *rejected* the Son of God—a far greater than Jonah the prophet. They refused to repent, and they sought to destroy Him instead of receiving His message of warning and His forgiveness of sin. Therefore, *their* condemnation would be much greater than that upon Nineveh, because *a much greater than Jonah* was present with them.

Verse 42: *"The queen of the south shall rise up in the judgment with this generation, and shall condemn it: for she came from the uttermost parts of the earth to hear the wisdom of Solomon; and, behold, a greater than Solomon is here."*

"The queen of the south" was without a doubt the queen of Sheba. Sheba was a city of Arabia and was located south of Judaea. In II Chronicles 9:1-8 we have the account of the queen of Sheba making the journey referred to here:

"And *when the queen of Sheba heard of the fame of Solomon, she came to prove Solomon with hard questions at Jerusalem,* with a very great company, and camels that bare spices, and gold in abundance, and precious stones: and when she was come to Solomon, she communed with him of all that was in her heart. And Solomon told her all her questions: and there was nothing hid

173

from Solomon which he told her not. And when the queen of Sheba had seen the wisdom of Solomon, and the house that he had built, and the meat of his table, and the sitting of his servants, and the attendance of his ministers, and their apparel; his cupbearers also, and their apparel; and his ascent by which he went up into the house of the Lord; there was no more spirit in her.

"And she said to the king, *It was a true report which I heard in mine own land of thine acts, and of thy wisdom:* howbeit I believed not their words, until I came, and mine eyes had seen it: and, behold, the one half of the greatness of thy wisdom was not told me: for thou exceedest the fame that I heard. Happy are thy men, and happy are these thy servants, which stand continually before thee, and hear thy wisdom. Blessed be the Lord thy God, which delighted in thee to set thee on His throne, to be king for the Lord thy God: because thy God loved Israel, to establish them for ever, therefore made He thee king over them, to do judgment and justice."

"From the uttermost parts of the earth" means from the most distant parts of the habitable world then known. (We have a similar expression in Deuteronomy 28:49.) The queen of Sheba came a great distance from a remote country *"to hear the wisdom"* and to see the glory of an earthly king, *Solomon.* But *Israel* would not listen to the wisdom of One *much greater* than Solomon, even

174

though He was present with them making known to them the wonderful words of life. Instead, they rejected their Messiah, and they refused to receive the gift of God, which was salvation by grace through faith in Christ. Therefore, the queen of Sheba will *"rise up" in condemnation* against that generation because they had a much greater opportunity than she had, and yet they rejected their opportunity.

Self-Reformation Is Worthless

Verse 43: *"When the unclean spirit is gone out of a man, he walketh through dry places, seeking rest, and findeth none."*

In verses 43 through 45 Jesus illustrates the worthlessness of self-reformation. The leaders of the Jewish religion had by-passed the Divine and had made clean "the outside of the platter," but the inside was full of filth and uncleanness (Matt. 23:25). They rejected the miracle-working power of Jesus upon the soul and spirit.

Nicodemus, a ruler of the Jews, came to Jesus and confessed that Jesus was a Teacher from God because no man could do the miracles that Jesus was doing except God be with him. Jesus clearly declared to Nicodemus that a man must be *born again* to see and to enter the Kingdom of God. Nicodemus immediately thought of the *natural,* not the supernatural. He asked, "How can a man be born when he is old? Can he enter the second time into his mother's womb, and be born?'' (Read John 3:1-10.) Nicodemus was probably a middle-aged man, a teacher in Israel—and he thought that Jesus was speaking of a second *natural* birth. But Jesus was speaking of a *spiritual* birth, and He replied, ''That which is born of the flesh is flesh; and *that which is born of the Spirit is spirit.*'' In like manner, these Jews (here in Matthew 12) were majoring on the *externals*—holy days, offerings, rituals, and the traditions of their fathers. However, the Word of God says that *obedience* is ''better than sacrifice'' (I Sam. 15:22).

The Pharisees had just accused Jesus of casting out demons by Beelzebub, the prince of demons. Jesus answered their insult by declaring that if the prince of demons cast out his subjects he would virtually be casting out himself, since they were doing his work. Here again Jesus speaks of Satan and his emissaries, using an illustration of a man who is possessed by an unclean spirit:

''When the unclean spirit is gone out of a man . . . .'' Please notice—no one asked the unclean spirit to leave. God did not cast him out. The unclean spirit left of its own free will and desire.

''. . . he walketh through dry places, seeking rest . . . .'' The Jews believed that demons and unclean spirits found their dwelling place in the desert and in tombs—that is, in ''dry places.'' An evil spirit is dissatisfied and cannot rest unless it

occupies a body. From God's Word we know that evil spirits do occupy the bodies of men and women, and at times have temporarily occupied the bodies of animals. Jesus cast a legion of demons out of the man at Gadara, and the demons "besought Him, saying, . . . Suffer us to go away into the herd of swine" (Matt. 8:31)—and Jesus allowed them to go. Here in Matthew chapter 12 this unclean spirit left the man and walked through dry places looking for rest, *"and findeth none."* That is, he searched for rest outside of the man from whom he departed, but he did not find any rest. Evidently the demon did not seek to enter another body, since he knew he could return to "his own house." The Lord did not cast this demon out, as He did the ones in Matthew 8 who had to find refuge in the swine.

Verse 44: *"Then he saith, I will return into my house from whence I came out; and when he is come, he findeth it empty, swept, and garnished."*

"Then he saith, I will return into my house from whence I came out." I agree with the Bible scholars that Jesus is speaking primarily to Israel here. But according to II Timothy 3:16,17, *"ALL SCRIPTURE is given by inspiration of God,* and is *profitable* for doctrine, for reproof, for correction, for instruction in righteousness: that the man of God may be perfect, throughly furnished unto all good works."* Therefore, there is a tremendous

lesson here in this passage for you and me. The unclean spirit had a conversation with himself and decided that since he had sought rest and could find none, he would return to his house. Please notice the words *"my house."* "House" here denotes the man whom he had possessed or occupied.

There are some denominations which use this Scripture to uphold their doctrine of falling from grace or losing one's salvation. They say that this is a picture of a man who has been saved, then he loses his salvation and is seven times worse than he was before he was saved. However, this has nothing to do with a born-again, blood-washed, saved-by-grace, redeemed child of God. The evil spirit said, "I will return into *MY HOUSE."* The house belonged to the evil spirit before he left, he left of his own free will and accord, and the house still belonged to him. This could not be the picture of a genuine Christian.

"When he is come, he findeth it EMPTY . . . ." The evil spirit returned into his own house, and he found it empty. The empty house could not represent the heart of a *believer,* because when a sinner is saved *Jesus* comes into that heart in the Person of the Holy Spirit. Jesus said, "If a man love me, he will keep my words: and my Father will love him, and *we will come unto him, and MAKE OUR ABODE WITH HIM"* (John 14:23). The Apostle Paul speaks of *"Christ in you,* the

178

hope of glory" (Col. 1:27), and in Ephesians 3:17 he prays that *"Christ may DWELL IN YOUR HEARTS by faith."* So the "house" of a Christian is *not empty!*

Here is what happened: This unclean spirit left the man whom he occupied, and he left of his own free will. He walked, he sought rest, but he did not find any rest; and while he was out, the man reformed. He *"swept"* the house, he cleaned the house; he redecorated, he painted, he *"garnished"* the house. The house (the man) was thoroughly remodeled (reformed) and empty when the evil spirit returned; therefore he re-entered it.

Verse 45: *"Then goeth he, and taketh with himself seven other spirits more wicked than himself, and they enter in and dwell there: and the last state of that man is worse than the first. Even so shall it be also unto this wicked generation."*

Notice: the evil spirit re-entered his own house, and he took with him *"seven other spirits more wicked than himself"* — so all eight entered the house and *lived* there. They did not just *visit,* they *remained; "and the last state of that man,"* of course, was *"worse than the first."* You can watch it in your community or in your church: if a person makes a *false profession,* he will try to clean up his life. For awhile he will succeed in his efforts, but it will not last. Usually after a short period of time that person is much more wicked than he was before he reformed.

God does not "garnish" the spirit or the soul; *He creates within us a NEW HEART and a NEW SPIRIT:* "A *new heart* also will I give you, and a *new spirit* will I put within you: and I will take away the stony heart out of your flesh, and I will give you an heart of flesh" (Ezek. 36:26). *He makes us a NEW PERSON in Christ:* "Therefore if any man be in Christ, *he is a new creature:* old things are passed away; behold, *all things are become NEW"* (II Cor. 5:17).

God does not remodel us, He does not repair us, He does not overhaul us as we would an automobile or a house. God puts within us a new heart, a new spirit—and we are "new creatures" when we are born again. Born-again persons possess the Holy Spirit, a divine nature, and they are led by the Spirit in the paths of righteousness. "As many as are led by the Spirit of God, they are the sons of God," and they do not fulfill the lusts of the flesh because the Spirit leads each believer.

"Even so shall it be also unto this wicked generation." I confess readily that these words were spoken directly to the Jews that lived in that day, and we know that it happened as Jesus prophesied it would. But not only does this apply to the Jews and the nation that crucified the Messiah; it applies to people today.

180

As already stated, this passage does not picture a sinner who comes to Jesus, the devil is cast out, and then later the devil returns and takes over the heart of the man and makes him worse than he was before he was saved. This is definitely *not* the picture of a saved man, for this man was never saved. This man never possessed the Holy Spirit, the divine nature of Christ in his heart. He never had a new heart, he only had a "swept and garnished" heart. If the Scripture read, "And he said, I will return to the house that used to be my house; and when he came, he found a new house," then I would agree that the Scripture would be speaking of a born-again Christian. But the evil spirit returned to his *own* house. It was not a new house, but an empty one that had been completely remodeled, garnished, and beautified. Do not ever accuse God of saving a sinner and leaving his heart empty. God puts within the heart the Holy Spirit, and the Christian is not empty, but is a possessor of divine nature.

I go a step further and declare emphatically and without apology that an evil spirit cannot get into the heart of a Christian. An evil spirit may enter the mind of a Christian and temporarily occupy the *flesh* of a Christian, but an evil spirit cannot enter the heart. When God saves a man, He *seals* him—and Satan cannot break the seal of Almighty God. Paul urges believers to *"grieve not THE HOLY SPIRIT OF GOD, WHEREBY YE ARE*

SEALED unto the day of redemption" (Eph. 4:30). And he points out that a Christian is hid in Christ: "For ye are dead, *and YOUR LIFE IS HID WITH CHRIST IN GOD"* (Col. 3:3).

To suggest that Satan can break the seal of God on a believer's heart and re-enter that heart after he has been cast out by the power of God, is to say that Satan is more powerful than God. To say that Satan can recapture the heart of a born-again, redeemed believer is to say that Satan can enter *God* and steal away a child of God who is hid with Christ in God! Paul declares that we *"sit together in heavenly places IN CHRIST JE-SUS"* (Eph. 2:6).

This is not fatalism; it is Bible doctrine. Not all church members are born-again believers, and not all professing Christians are born again. *Only God* knows for sure who are born-again believers. We believe that certain people are born again—for they have the *fruits,* and we sincerely believe that they have been saved—but only God knows for sure. *You* know whether or not *you* are saved, but you cannot positively declare that someone else is. You cannot know the heart of any person except yourself—and the only reason you know your own heart is because the Holy Spirit is there and He bears witness with your spirit that you are a child of God: "The Spirit itself beareth witness with our spirit, that we are the children of God" (Rom. 8:16).

I John 5:10-13 speaks of the witness which we have in our hearts:

"He that believeth on the Son of God hath the witness in himself: he that believeth not God hath made Him a liar; because he believeth not the record that God gave of His Son. And this is the record, that God hath given to us eternal life, and this life is in His Son. He that hath the Son hath life; and he that hath not the Son of God hath not life. These things have I written unto you that believe on the name of the Son of God; that ye may know that ye have eternal life, and that ye may believe on the name of the Son of God."

Our King and His Earthly Relatives; Jesus Makes Known a New Relationship

Verse 46: *"While He yet talked to the people, behold, His mother and His brethren stood without, desiring to speak with Him."*

Israel, His "kinsmen according to the flesh," rejected Jesus. (In Romans 9:3 the Apostle Paul said, "I could wish that myself were accursed from Christ for *my brethren, my kinsmen according to the flesh."*) Jesus announces here (in verses 46 through 50) the beginning of a new family, the family of faith, which includes all—not just the elect nation, as in the Old Testament era, but Jews, Gentiles, rich, poor, bond, and free.

(In connection with our present passage, please

study Mark 3:31-35 and Luke 8:19-21.) While Jesus *"yet talked to the people,"* Mary and the brethren of Jesus came *"to speak with Him."* It was certainly sad enough that the leading men among His own nation Israel rejected Him and blasphemed Him, but this was not all the suffering Christ endured. From other Scriptures we learn that He endured cruel opposition from His nearest kindred. Paul tells us to *"consider Him that endured such contradiction of sinners against Himself,* lest ye be wearied and faint in your minds" (Heb. 12:3). Some of His nearest kindred misunderstood Him for a long time. In John 7:3-5 we read: "His brethren therefore said unto Him, Depart hence, and go into Judaea, that thy disciples also may see the works that thou doest. For there is no man that doeth any thing in secret, and he himself seeketh to be known openly. If thou do these things, shew thyself to the world. *For neither did His brethren believe in Him."* This was a definite fulfillment of the words in Psalm 69:8 — *"I am become a stranger unto my brethren, and an alien unto my mother's children."*

There is a difference of opinion among Bible teachers as to who the persons referred to here as *"brethren"* were. Some suppose that they were the children of Mary, the mother of Jesus; and others say that they were the children of Mary, the wife of Cleophas (or Alphaeus). In the latter case, they would have been His *cousins,* called "brethren"

184

according to the customs of the Jews in that day—
for at times they did refer to all relatives as brethren. However, the natural and very obvious meaning here is that they were the children of Mary,
the mother of Jesus. In Mark 6:3 we read: "Is
not this the carpenter, the son of Mary, the brother
of James, and Joses, and of Juda, and Simon? and
are not His sisters here with us? And they were
offended at Him." No one has any reason to
suggest anything else. The persons desiring to see
Jesus were His brothers—born of the same Mary
of whom Jesus was born. She was a *virgin* when
Jesus was born, but I believe there were children
born of Mary and Joseph later, regardless of what
some may teach.

On the occasion we are studying (in Matthew 12)
the mother and brethren of Jesus *"stood without."*
(One commentator says that they stood without,
desiring to *speak* with Him, when they should have
been standing *within,* desiring to *hear* Him.) The
purpose for their coming we learn from Mark
3:20, 21. Combining that account with this one in
Matthew, we see that Jesus and the twelve apostles
came into a house, and there was such a crowd
present that they did not even have room to eat.
It was at this time that Mark records that "when
His friends heard of it, they went out to lay hold
on Him: for they said, He is beside Himself."
"Friends" here does not mean the *apostles,* for
they were with Him in the house. As His mother

and His brothers finally reached the house and desired to speak with Jesus, it is natural to understand that *they* are meant by the phrase vaguely rendered "friends." They could not get in because of the crowd; therefore they sent in the message to Jesus.

Verses 47 and 48: *"Then one said unto Him, Behold, thy mother and thy brethren stand without, desiring to speak with thee. But He answered and said unto him that told Him, Who is my mother? and who are my brethren?"*

The messenger who reached Jesus and delivered the message that His mother and brethren stood without desiring to speak with Him no doubt thought that Jesus would consider the claims of His mother and brethren as paramount and would at once go forth to them. But instead, Jesus asked, *"Who is my mother? and who are my brethren?"*

Let me point out that there was no want of love, respect, and deep affection on the part of Jesus for His mother. He loved her and revered her, and He proved it throughout His whole earthly life. In Luke 2:51 we read, "And He went down with them, and came to Nazareth, and was subject unto them: but His mother kept all these sayings in her heart." Even in His suffering on the cross, His concern for His mother is apparent: "Now there stood by the cross of Jesus His mother, and His mother's sister, Mary the wife of Cleophas, and Mary Magdalene. *When Jesus therefore saw His mother, and the disciple standing by, whom He loved, He saith unto His mother, Woman, behold thy son! Then saith He to the disciple, Behold thy mother! And from that hour that disciple took her unto his own home"* (John 19: 25-27). Jesus asked the question, "Who is my mother? and who are my brethren?" to focus the attention of His audience on the answer He was about to give.

Verse 49: *"And He stretched forth His hand toward His disciples, and said, Behold my mother and my brethren!"*

Jesus always answered the questions He asked, and He answered this one. He stretched His hands toward His disciples and said that *these* were His mother and brothers. He came for *all* men—and though He was born of a woman, He who is the second Adam, taking our entire humanity on Him, is not on that account more nearly united to her (Mary) than to all those who are united to Him by the Spirit. Nor was Jesus bound to regard the call of earthly relations so much as the welfare of those whom He came to teach and to *save*.

Verse 50: *"For whosoever shall do the will of my Father which is in heaven, the same is my brother, and sister, and mother."*

The new family of faith is made up of whosoever

believeth on Jesus unto salvation—Jew, Gentile, rich, poor, bond or free, slave or slavemaster. Any and all who *do the will of God* are His brothers and His sisters and His mother. Notice, He states it in such a way that He declares that all who believe, all who receive salvation are His brother, sister, and mother. There is no difference in the love He has for any one mother, brother, or sister. It matters not; they are all one, and He loves them more dearly than a mother could love her child or a child could love his mother. All born-again believers are members of the body of Christ: "For we are members of His body, of His flesh, and of His bones" (Eph. 5:30).

And in Galatians 3:26-28 we read: *"Ye are all the children of God by faith in Christ Jesus.* For as many of you as have been baptized into Christ have put on Christ. There is neither Jew nor Greek, there is neither bond nor free, there is neither male nor female: *for ye are all one in Christ Jesus."*

Chapter XIII

1. The same day went Jesus out of the house, and sat by the sea side.

2. And great multitudes were gathered together unto him, so that he went into a ship, and sat; and the whole multitude stood on the shore.

3. And he spake many things unto them in parables, saying, Behold, a sower went forth to sow;

4. And when he sowed, some seeds fell by the way side, and the fowls came and devoured them up:

5. Some fell upon stony places, where they had not much earth: and forthwith they sprung up, because they had no deepness of earth:

6. And when the sun was up, they were scorched; and because they had no root, they withered away.

7. And some fell among thorns; and the thorns sprung up, and choked them:

8. But other fell into good ground, and brought forth fruit, some an hundredfold, some sixtyfold, some thirtyfold.

9. Who hath ears to hear, let him hear.

10. And the disciples came, and said unto him, Why speakest thou unto them in parables?

11. He answered and said unto them, Because it is given unto you to know the mysteries of the kingdom of heaven, but to them it is not given.

12. For whosoever hath, to him shall be given, and he

shall have more abundance: but whosoever hath not, from him shall be taken away even that he hath.

13. Therefore speak I to them in parables: because they seeing see not; and hearing they hear not, neither do they understand.

14. And in them is fulfilled the prophecy of Esaias, which saith, By hearing ye shall hear, and shall not understand; and seeing ye shall see, and shall not perceive:

15. For this people's heart is waxed gross, and their ears are dull of hearing, and their eyes they have closed; lest at any time they should see with their eyes and hear with their ears, and should understand with their heart, and should be converted, and I should heal them.

16. But blessed are your eyes, for they see: and your ears, for they hear.

17. For verily I say unto you, That many prophets and righteous men have desired to see those things which ye see, and have not seen them; and to hear those things which ye hear, and have not heard them.

18. Hear ye therefore the parable of the sower.

19. When any one heareth the word of the kingdom, and understandeth it not, then cometh the wicked one, and catcheth away that which was sown in his heart. This is he which received seed by the way side.

20. But he that received the seed into stony places, the same is he that heareth the word, and anon with joy receiveth it;

21. Yet hath he not root in himself, but dureth for a while: for when tribulation or persecution ariseth because of the word, by and by he is offended.

22. He also that received seed among the thorns is he that heareth the word; and the care of this world, and the deceitfulness of riches, choke the word, and he becometh unfruitful.

23. But he that received seed into the good ground is he

that heareth the word, and understandeth it; which also beareth fruit, and bringeth forth, some an hundredfold, some sixty, some thirty.

24. Another parable put he forth unto them, saying, The kingdom of heaven is likened unto a man which sowed good seed in his field:

25. But while men slept, his enemy came and sowed tares among the wheat, and went his way.

26. But when the blade was sprung up, and brought forth fruit, then appeared the tares also.

27. So the servants of the householder came and said unto him, Sir, didst not thou sow good seed in thy field? from whence then hath it tares?

28. He said unto them, An enemy hath done this. The servants said unto him, Wilt thou then that we go and gather them up?

29. But he said, Nay; lest while ye gather up the tares, ye root up also the wheat with them.

30. Let both grow together until the harvest: and in the time of harvest I will say to the reapers, Gather ye together first the tares, and bind them in bundles to burn them: but gather the wheat into my barn.

31. Another parable put he forth unto them, saying, The kingdom of heaven is like to a grain of mustard seed, which a man took, and sowed in his field:

32. Which indeed is the least of all seeds: but when it is grown, it is the greatest among herbs, and becometh a tree, so that the birds of the air come and lodge in the branches thereof.

33. Another parable spake he unto them; The kingdom of heaven is like unto leaven, which a woman took, and hid in three measures of meal, till the whole was leavened.

34. All these things spake Jesus unto the multitude in parables; and without a parable spake he not unto them:

35. That it might be fulfilled which was spoken by the

prophet, saying, I will open my mouth in parables; I will utter things which have been kept secret from the foundation of the world.

36. Then Jesus sent the multitude away, and went into the house: and his disciples came unto him, saying, Declare unto us the parable of the tares of the field.

37. He answered and said unto them, He that soweth the good seed is the Son of man;

38. The field is the world; the good seed are the children of the kingdom; but the tares are the children of the wicked one;

39. The enemy that sowed them is the devil; the harvest is the end of the world; and the reapers are the angels.

40. As therefore the tares are gathered and burned in the fire; so shall it be in the end of this world.

41. The Son of man shall send forth his angels, and they shall gather out of his kingdom all things that offend, and them which do iniquity;

42. And shall cast them into a furnace of fire: there shall be wailing and gnashing of teeth.

43. Then shall the righteous shine forth as the sun in the kingdom of their Father. Who hath ears to hear, let him hear.

44. Again, the kingdom of heaven is like unto treasure hid in a field; the which when a man hath found, he hideth, and for joy thereof goeth and selleth all that he hath, and buyeth that field.

45. Again, the kingdom of heaven is like unto a merchant man, seeking goodly pearls:

46. Who, when he had found one pearl of great price, went and sold all that he had, and bought it.

47. Again, the kingdom of heaven is like unto a net, that was cast into the sea, and gathered of every kind:

48. Which, when it was full, they drew to shore, and

sat down, and gathered the good into vessels, but cast the bad away.

49. So shall it be at the end of the world: the angels shall come forth, and sever the wicked from among the just,

50. And shall cast them into the furnace of fire: there shall be wailing and gnashing of teeth.

51. Jesus saith unto them, Have ye understood all these things? They say unto him, Yea, Lord.

52. Then said he unto them, Therefore every scribe which is instructed unto the kingdom of heaven is like unto a man that is an householder, which bringeth forth out of his treasure things new and old.

53. And it came to pass, that when Jesus had finished these parables, he departed thence.

54. And when he was come into his own country, he taught them in their synagogue, insomuch that they were astonished, and said, Whence hath this man this wisdom, and these mighty works?

55. Is not this the carpenter's son? is not his mother called Mary? and his brethren, James, and Joses, and Simon, and Judas?

56. And his sisters, are they not all with us? Whence then hath this man all these things?

57. And they were offended in him. But Jesus said unto them, A prophet is not without honour, save in his own country, and in his own house.

58. And he did not many mighty works there because of their unbelief.

Jesus Teaches by Parables

Verse 1: *"The same day went Jesus out of the house, and sat by the sea side."*

As we closed the last chapter, Jesus was informed

that His mother and brethren were outside and desired to speak with Him. We also saw that Jesus used the occasion to make a most affecting declaration of His love for His disciples—for *all* who do the will of His Father in Heaven. He then departed from the house where He was and freely went His way.

"The same day went Jesus out of the house." This statement is full of significance. It is a prophetic suggestion of His final break with Israel. (No word of God is void of power or empty of meaning.) It was on *that day* when Jesus took His place among His people as the One greater than David, greater than Solomon, greater than Jonah, and as the Lord of the Sabbath. It was His rightful place; He was *all* or He was *nothing.* He said to the rich young ruler (in Mark 10:18), *"Why callest thou me good? There is none good but one, that is, GOD."* In other words, if Jesus was good, He was *God*—and if He was not God, He was not *good.* His own received Him not— they rejected Him, they desired to put Him to death; therefore, *"the same day went Jesus out of the house."* Where did He go? Insofar as "His own" were concerned, He had no place to go.

It is very notable that Jesus *"sat by the sea side"* (the Sea of Galilee), for the sea in Scripture is a type of the restless Gentile nations. (Please study Daniel 7:2, 3, 17 and Revelation 17:1-15.) When Jesus went out of the house and sat by the seaside, *in a figure* He turned His face to the Gentiles, to take out of them a people for His name.

How calm and serene was the behavior of the Lord Jesus. He was very *man* as truly as He was very *God;* therefore it must have been a great relief for Him to get away from the controversies that He had encountered and to sit down and commune with nature. He sat by the seashore— but very shortly He was not alone, for a great multitude gathered.

Verse 2: *"And great multitudes were gathered together unto Him, so that He went into a ship, and sat; and the whole multitude stood on the shore."*

"And great multitudes were gathered together unto Him." Great multitudes longed to hear the words of Jesus and to see His miracles. Many of them—maybe most of them—were concerned about the spectacular miracles He performed, rather than about the power of the Man. The multitude pressed upon Him eagerly, and there were so many gathered that there was a danger that He would be pushed out into the sea—and it was at that moment that Jesus chose a fishing vessel for His pulpit: *"He went into a ship, and sat."* I am sure that whoever took care of the vessel swung it out by its cable or anchor a little distance from the shore, giving Jesus opportunity to speak to the great multitude that was gathered on the beach.

Seven Parables That Set Forth the Mysteries of the Kingdom of Heaven

Verse 3: *"And He spake many things unto them in parables, saying, Behold, a sower went forth to sow."*

"And He spake many things unto them in parables." The first thing we should do here is find out exactly what a parable is and why Jesus chose to teach in parables. We are mainly concerned with the parables of the Lord Jesus and the meaning as He applied them in His teachings. The revised edition of the *Smith-Peloubet Dictionary* (copyrighted in 1884) has the clearest and most complete definition of a parable that I have been able to find. According to that dictionary, the word "parable" in the Greek is *parabole,* which signifies "placing beside or together; a comparison." Therefore, a parable is literally placing one thing beside another or comparing one thing with another. It is generally used of a somewhat lengthy utterance or narrative drawn from nature or human circumstance, the object of which is to set forth a *spiritual lesson.*

Let me point out here that *the parables given by Jesus were not FABLES.* According to Webster's Dictionary, a *fable* is "a fictitious story meant to teach a moral lesson; the characters are usually animals." The *parable* is constructed to set forth a truth—spiritually and heavenly. This the fable, with all of its value, is not. The fable is essentially of the earth and never lifts itself above the earth. It never has a higher aim than to instill the rule of discreet morality, caution, or foresight. The fable just reaches that pitch of morality which the world will understand and approve. But it has no place in Scripture.

A parable is not a MYTH. In mythology, the *truth* and that which is only the *vehicle* of truth are blended together—so that it is difficult to separate the one from the other. In a parable, however, it is clearly understood that what is being told has not actually occurred, though it *could* have occurred and it *may* occur.

A parable *differs* from an *allegory*. This it does in *form* rather than in *essence*. An allegory gives the description of one thing under the image of another, the qualities and properties of the first being attributed to the last, and the two blend together, instead of being kept quite distinct. The allegory is self-interpreting, and the persons in it are invested with the attributes of those represented in the allegory—as in John 15:1-8, where Jesus said, "*I (Jesus)* am the true *vine, . . . ye* are the *branches* ...." In a parable, the course of action related and understood run parallel, but the persons in the parable are strictly confined to their own natural places and actions which are in their relation and succession typical of higher things, therefore setting forth a comparison, a similitude, or an illustration.

197

A parable is a serious narration that is within the limits of probability, with a course of action pointing to some great moral or spiritual truth. It derives its force from real analogies impressed by the Lord Jesus Christ, by whom and for whom all things were created. He gave these parables to impress upon man the seriousness and the simplicity of spiritual truths. He who taught in parables, the Lord Jesus, "needed not that any testify of man: for He knew what was in man" (John 2:25). He *made* man, and since He was omniscient, He knew the very thoughts and intents of the hearts of all men. He alone dare teach by parables. Man cannot see the inner spring out of which flow the laws of eternal truths and justice which the parable is framed to elucidate. *Our* parables would be in danger of perverting the truth instead of making simple, clear, and understandable the deep truths of spiritual things.

The parables given by Jesus were adapted to different classes of hearers all at one time. Each person, regardless of his social standing or who he might be, understood the teaching according to his measure of understanding. In verse 12 of this chapter we learn that the parables given by Jesus had double force. They were revealing and at the same time concealing. Some people had an ear to hear, while others closed their ears and eyes and refused to see or hear. To those who were ready to hear, the parables revealed spiritual truth;

from those who closed their ears and eyes was taken away even the opportunity they had.

In His teaching and preaching Jesus used methods of instruction that were natural to men in general and familiar to the Jews in particular. From the rhetorical point of view, the illustrations given by the Lord Jesus in the parables are marked by explicit simplicity, unusual elegance, and profound wisdom. The parables also served to put truths at first but imperfectly understood, into a compact form in which they could be easily remembered, until they should afterward be understood more thoroughly. In addition, they enabled Him to declare truths that likely would cause offense, in such a form that the enquiring soul could understand, while the enemies of our Lord would not see their point. Thus while He was instructing some in His vast audience, He was not, in respect to others, "casting pearls before swine."

The parables given by Jesus were like the pillar of cloud and fire in the days of Moses. The cloud was dark to the Egyptians and confounded them, but it had a silver lining to the Israelites, to lead and comfort them. We might say, also, that a parable is like the shell of a walnut—within is good fruit for the diligent, but those who are slothful cannot partake of the fruit.

In interpreting the parables, we have the guidance of the Lord Jesus Christ. He fully interpreted the parables of the sower and of the wheat and tares; and to a degree, He interpreted the parable of the net. In our interpretation of the parables we must make sure of understanding the language used by our Lord in the parable itself and the various allusions to physical phenomenon or social usage. We must ascertain what subject the Lord Jesus designs to illustrate in each parable. At times Jesus Himself stated the subject or the design He wished to illustrate, either before or after the parable.

As we study the parables, we must also consider in what light each presents the subject set forth. In this respect it is important to regard the parable as a whole, just as we do any other illustration. We should not begin by attempting to assign the meaning of some particular item without considering the general meaning of the entire parable. You can rest assured that Jesus, the greatest Teacher of all teachers, used in His parables illustrations of common-sense principles and subjects easily understood. If you will study the parables and the sermons of our Lord, you will see readily that He taught down to earth where men could understand what He was teaching.

There is today a tendency on the part of some teachers to go to the extreme in the interpretation of a parable by attempting to give a very definite spiritual meaning to every little detail, and many times this cannot be. We should not strain any portion of Scripture to prove a denominational point or a conviction on our part; we are to *study* and *rightly divide* the Word.

As Jesus gave these parables, there is a filling out of the story (or added words) to make sense as He gave the narration. As we read the interpretation given by the Lord of the parables of the sower and of the wheat and tares, we will see that He did go into much detail; therefore, we must not strip the parable to a bare trunk, divested of all its foliage. In some parables, the resemblance (or the analogy) is more complete than in others, and the points of contact in some are much more numerous than the points of contact in others. So I repeat, we must be very cautious as we interpret the parables given by Jesus. We must not strain any point or detail of the parable to prove our own ideas concerning matters mentioned in the parables. In general, the details of a parable must never be pressed into teaching what is contrary to the truth of the Scriptures as a whole. We must always apply the rule of the Bible—comparing Scripture with Scripture, spiritual things with spiritual things.

We will find the explanation Jesus gave His disciples for speaking in parables in verses 11 through 17 of this chapter. It was God's judicial hand upon Israel because of their deliberate rejection of the Lord Jesus Christ. Israel refused the light already given to them by God; therefore further light was denied them. This is the spiritual law of divine revelation. God reveals truth only so far as we *obey* truth. When we rebel against truth already known to us, we not only receive no new truth or new light, but we lose that which we already have. This does not mean that a person will lose his salvation if he is born again. It simply means that until we act upon the light given to us by God, He will not reveal any deeper truth or greater light on spiritual matters than He has already revealed. This is borne out in verse 12 of this chapter.

This thirteenth chapter of Matthew contains seven parables in which the rejected Messiah sets forth the condition of the Kingdom of Heaven after its rejection by the elect nation Israel until the return of the King to sit on the throne of David in Jerusalem. The number "seven" in the Bible stands for completeness, and the parables that set forth the mysteries of the Kingdom give a complete view of the present dispensation, extending from our Lord's personal ministry following His rejection to His personal return at the end of the age.

The sevenfold preview of this dispensation in this chapter differs from the message concerning the *seven churches* contained in the Revelation. In Matthew, we have in view the whole Kingdom; in Revelation, the picture is confined to the churches. In both places we have revealed an awful condition of apostasy and false profession. In

Matthew, we are not only looking at the churches, but our minds are also occupied in the whole realm of profession. There is much religion and religious profession that is entirely outside of the churches. Even in cases where men have no connection whatsoever with the churches, there is much talk of religion, Christian civilization, Christian nation, Christian government—but they are Christian *only in name.* What we most commonly call "Christendom" is what we are beholding in these parables in the thirteenth chapter of Matthew; it includes everything called Christian.

As we study the parables given by Jesus, we should compare the accounts given in the Gospels of Mark and Luke in order to get a complete picture of what Jesus taught about the Kingdom of Heaven. The Sermon on the Mount in chapters 5 through 7 of Matthew dealt with the same theme. The parables may be regarded as an illustrative appendix to the marvelous, matchless, unusual Sermon on the Mount. In the Sermon on the Mount, the Lord dealt with the Kingdom abstractly and impersonally. In the parables, Jesus uses figures that are familiar to His listeners, to illustrate how the Gospel affects various classes under various conditions. In the Sermon on the Mount, Jesus was primarily retrospective; however, in His parables, Jesus is almost entirely prospective. He unfolds the manner in which the Kingdom will progress and the nature of the consummation of the

Kingdom. This is why the Sermon on the Mount and the parables of the Lord Jesus should be studied together and compared by the student who desires to reap a rewarding harvest of spiritual truth and strength.

These seven parables are divided into two groups —one group of four, and the other group of three. The first four show man's failure. Four is the number of the earth or the world. The last three show God's thoughts and purposes perfectly worked out. Three is the number of the Trinity or the Godhead. God's program and plan cannot fail. God foreordained all things before the foundation of the world, and all hell cannot stop His program. However, this does not alter the free will or the responsibility of man. God is omniscient, omnipotent, and omnipresent; therefore, He knows all from the beginning, simply because He is God.

In the first parable Jesus gave, He said, *"A sower went forth to sow."* The parable of the sower is also found in Mark 4:3-9 and Luke 8:5-8. This parable and the one of the wicked husbandmen (Matt. 21:33-45) are the only parables that Matthew, Mark, and Luke all three record.

The figure given here of the sower marks a new beginning. For one to labor in the vineyard of God (Isaiah 5:1-7) is one thing; however, for one to go forth sowing seed in the field is altogether another thing. Later in this chapter the Lord Jesus interprets the parable. He does not leave the interpretation to man, but He interprets it Himself because it is extremely important.

Verse 4: *"And when he sowed, some seeds fell by the way side, and the fowls came and devoured them up."*

"Some seeds fell by the way side." In that day, roads passed through cultivated fields. (Please notice Matthew 12:1.) As the sower sowed, the grain that he was sowing fell not only on the plowed ground but also on the road path, where the ground was smooth and hard. Seeds falling on the roadbed would lie exposed on the hard surface; therefore, when the birds saw the seeds, they would devour them. Luke 8:5 also tells us that these seeds were *trodden under foot.* In the Bible lands, it is still very common to see large flocks of birds following a man in the field sowing grain, and picking up the grains that are left exposed.

Verses 5 and 6: *"Some fell upon stony places, where they had not much earth: and forthwith they sprung up, because they had no deepness of earth: and when the sun was up, they were scorched; and because they had no root, they withered away."*

"Some (seeds) fell upon stony places"—that is, rocky ground. Palestine is a rocky country. There are stones everywhere—little and big—and one wonders just how in the days of our Lord, the

poor farmer could till the ground with the limited tools with which he had to work. But even stony ground will produce good wheat if the seeds can be plowed under so that the fowls will not pick them up. In this parable, many of the seeds in the rocky ground found just enough dirt and moisture to sprout, and the little green shoots came forth—but the hot sun soon killed the young plants. Since the rocks were so plentiful, the little grain could not send roots deep enough into the ground to obtain moisture. Luke says that "some fell upon a rock; and as soon as it was sprung up, it withered away, because it lacked moisture" (Luke 8:6). Therefore, when the hot sun beat down upon it and the dry weather came, the stocks withered and died. Many died before they grew at all; others lived for a time and then died.

Verse 7: *"And some fell among thorns; and the thorns sprung up, and choked them."*

Not only did some of the seed fall upon the hard places in the roadbed and in the stony places where they could not get enough moisture to survive and produce a harvest, but other seed *"fell among thorns."* There are many thorn bushes in Palestine. (Remember, the soldiers made a crown of thorns and placed it on the head of Jesus before He was crucified. It was not difficult for them to find thorn bushes from which they could easily and very quickly make a crown of thorns.) Some of the seed fell among the thorns, the thorns choked out the tender plants, and they failed to produce.

Verse 8: *"But other fell into good ground, and brought forth fruit, some an hundredfold, some sixtyfold, some thirtyfold."*

Some seed fell upon *"good ground,"* were covered by the earth, and the moisture caused them to sprout and come forth. The roots went deep into the soil, the moisture fed the plants, and, of course, the plants produced.

Please notice that even though these seed fell upon good ground and were not hindered by rocks or thorns, even under the very best of conditions, the seed brought forth various quantities—*some thirtyfold, some sixty, some one hundred.* The yield depended primarily upon the fertility or the richness of the soil. When a farmer reaped thirtyfold, he certainly reaped a good crop; but if one grain produced *one hundred* other grains, that was a *bountiful* crop. Some of the ground around Palestine was extremely rich, and men reaped heavy crops. (Please notice Genesis 26:12.)

In this parable of the sower and the seed, we see a type of all of the rest of the parables of Jesus, and He also gives to us the reason why He taught in parables. As we look back to that memorial day when Jesus began to speak in parables, we see the plain of Gennesaret and a little fishing boat just off shore in the blue waters of the beautiful Sea of Galilee. We see a great multitude standing on the beach around the area where the boat is just off shore. Jesus could see up on the hillside, because the ground continues to elevate away from the edge of the Sea of Galilee. As He looked up over the hills of Palestine, it could be that He saw a man sowing seed, with birds flying behind him picking up the seeds that were not covered with the earth. Jesus used that simple, understandable illustration to point out that He had come to sow seed—not wheat and barley, but the incorruptible seed of the Word of the living God.

In this parable of the sower and the seed we have three constituent elements: (1) the sower, (2) the seed, (3) the soils. It is most interesting to note that in some of the other parables there are sets of threes—three types of response in the parable of the talents, three travelers on the Jericho road, three kinds of soil, and three rates of growth. In other parables we have *twos*—the two sons, the two debtors, and the Pharisee and the publican.

The sower in this first parable is not to be taken lightly, because he is not incidental to the parable. Without him there would be no sowing, and without the sowing there would be no fruit. The word "sower" is generic, representing not a certain individual as such, but a class or a company of persons. The language here implies any

208

typical sower. We must not overlook the fact that the Lord Jesus directs our attention to the sower in His interpretation of the parable, in verse 18.

As we study the parable we notice that scarcely anything is revealed about the sower beyond the fact that he actually sowed the seed. The emphasis in this parable is upon the seed, the various kinds of soil, the obstacles to growth and production, and the fruit produced. The personality of the sower or the method he used to sow is secondary; the seed and the fruit are primary.

In the Old Testament *God likens Himself unto a sower:* "Behold, the days come, saith the Lord, that *I will sow* the house of Israel and the house of Judah with the seed of man, and with the seed of beast" (Jer. 31:27). God sows in the natural realm and also in the spiritual realm. He performs His sowing alone and is untiring and not discouraged in this task. God knows that even though many seed fall by the wayside, many are devoured by the fowls, and many wither—ultimately there will be a great harvest.

The Lord Jesus Christ is also a sower. In the second parable given in this chapter, Jesus announces Himself as "the sower." He came into this world to declare God, to speak words of soberness and truth, words of "spirit and life." He came to sow this earth with the incorruptible seed of truth that men might be born of this seed and become sons of God. There had been many before

Him that had paraded as sowers, sowing beside the road and on all kinds of fields and soil; however, their seed was not incorruptible because they were tainted with tradition, dogma, man-made doctrine. Then Jesus came, the Word of the living God in flesh (John 1:14).

The Holy Spirit, the third Person of the Trinity, is also a sower. God sows, the Son sows, the Spirit sows. The Holy Spirit inspires every born-again believer to sow seeds of the good news of the Gospel, and He also waters the seed sown. Every breath of the Spirit is divine. He bears the Word home to the heart, and the entrance of the Word brings light and life. The Lord Jesus Christ returned to the Father's side, but the Holy Spirit came on the day of Pentecost — and speaking through the one hundred and twenty in the upper room, He declared the words of salvation to all the devout Jews dwelling in Jerusalem from every nation (Acts 2:5). They went back to their own homes and villages and announced the good news that the Redeemer had paid the price and brought salvation down to man.

Every born-again believer should be a sower. In a sense, every born-again believer *is* a sower, whether he realizes it or not. Those who are born again automatically display the love of God — some thirtyfold, some sixtyfold, and some one hundred-fold. However, we should not only show forth the love of God in our faces and in our lives, but we

should sow the good seed of the Word of God by
distributing good sound Gospel literature, writing
letters to the unsaved, and in many other ways.
Jesus commanded His disciples to go into all the
world and *sow the seed:* "Go ye therefore, and
teach all nations, baptizing them in the name of
the Father, and of the Son, and of the Holy Ghost:
teaching them to observe all things whatsoever I
have commanded you: and, lo, I am with you
alway, even unto the end of the world" (Matt.
28:19, 20). We also read in Mark 16:20, "And *they
went forth, and preached every where,* the Lord
working with them, and confirming the Word
with signs following."

What Jesus began to teach, His apostles continued to teach. (We read in Acts 1:1, "The former
treatise have I made, O Theophilus, of all that
Jesus BEGAN both to do and teach.") The *Apostle
Paul* was a great sower of the seed of the Gospel
which is the power of God unto salvation. To the
believers at Corinth he wrote, ". . . ye seek a proof
of *Christ speaking in me . . .*" (II Cor. 13:3). Paul
thought of his entire ministry as that of sowing
spiritual seed. He said, *"If we have sown unto
you spiritual things,* is it a great thing if we shall
reap your carnal things?" (I Cor. 9:11). From the
very time of his conversion, when he met the Lord
Jesus face to face just outside the city wall of
Damascus, Paul knew that he was a chosen vessel
to sow the precious seed of the Gospel of the grace

of God to Jews and Gentiles. The Lord said unto Ananias on that day, "Go thy way: *for he (Paul) is a chosen vessel unto me, to bear my name before the Gentiles, and kings, and the children of Israel*" (Acts 9:15). And later, in his testimony before Agrippa, Paul related the words Jesus spoke to him on the Damascus road:

"*. . . I have appeared unto thee for this purpose, to make thee a minister and a witness both of these things which thou hast seen, and of those things in the which I will appear unto thee;* delivering thee from the people, and from *the Gentiles, unto whom now I send thee, to open their eyes, and to turn them from darkness to light, and from the power of Satan unto God, that they may receive forgiveness of sins, and inheritance among them which are sanctified by faith that is in me*" (Acts 26:16-18).

It is a grand and glorious privilege to sow the seed of the Gospel, but it is also a *command*. It is a responsibility on the part of every believer. There are few today who are faithfully sowing the seed. Jesus exhorts us to pray that the Lord of the harvest will send forth laborers (sowers) into the fields. That is one glorious thing about Christianity—all can be laborers, sowers, workers. The young, the old, the rich, the poor, the educated, the uneducated—*anyone* can tell this glorious Gospel message and point the poor lost sinner to the Saviour. The Psalmist said, "*He that goeth forth*

212

*and weepeth, bearing precious seed, shall doubtless
come again with rejoicing, bringing his sheaves
with him"* (Psalm 126:6). If we give just a cup of
cold water in the name of Jesus, we will not lose
our reward. God does not look upon the number
of seed sown, but upon the faithfulness with which
we sow the seed.

Let me point out further that the responsibility
of the sower is to *sow*. After sowing, his power is
ended; that is, he cannot make the seed grow. If
he sows the seed faithfully, that is all he can do.
It is not left up to us to convict men of sin and
cause them to receive the Word; it is up to us to
faithfully *present* the Word. The sower is to *sow*,
then leave the results with God. The Holy Spirit
is the One who bears the seed home to the heart,
opens the heart, and moves the heart to receive
the Word.   If we are diligent and faithfully distribute the seed, then the rest is up to the Holy
Spirit and the power of the Word. Mark expresses
it in this way:

*"And He said, So is the Kingdom of God, as if
a man should cast seed into the ground; and should
sleep, and rise night and day, and the seed should
spring and grow up, he knoweth not how.* For
the earth bringeth forth fruit of herself; first the
blade, then the ear, after that the full corn in the
ear.   But when the fruit is brought forth, immediately he putteth in the sickle, because the
harvest is come"* (Mark 4:26-29).

The "seed" is "the Word of the Kingdom" (Matt. 13:19), or "the Word of God" (Luke 8:11). So we see that the seed is definitely God's Word. And *all* of the seed must be sown—we cannot sow just the part of the Word that we enjoy sowing. The whole counsel of God must be presented to men. Paul "preaching the Kingdom of God" was equivalent to Paul *testifying* of "the Gospel of the grace of God" (Acts 20:24, 25). We read that Paul was continually "teaching those things which concern the Lord Jesus Christ" (Acts 28:31). The Word is the seed—the Word from beginning to the end, all of it, not just the part that we enjoy or that causes men to rejoice. We need to preach it *all;* we need to sow all of the seed.

The seed (the Word, the Gospel, the message of salvation) *is incorruptible:* "Seeing ye have purified your souls in obeying the truth through the Spirit unto unfeigned love of the brethren, see that ye love one another with a pure heart fervently: *being born again, not of corruptible seed, but of incorruptible, by the Word of God, which liveth and abideth for ever.* For all flesh is as grass, and all the glory of man as the flower of grass. The grass withereth, and the flower thereof falleth away: but *the Word of the Lord endureth for ever.* And this is the Word which by the Gospel is preached unto you" (I Pet. 1:22-25).

The seed is powerful: Paul said, "For I am not ashamed of the Gospel of Christ: for *it is the* power of God unto salvation to every one that believeth; to the Jew first, and also to the Greek" (Rom. 1:16). (Even our faith to *believe* comes from the Word: "So then *faith cometh by hearing, and hearing by the Word of God*"—Rom. 10:17.) And we read in Hebrews 4:12: "For *the Word of God is quick, and powerful,* and sharper than any two-edged sword, piercing even to the dividing asunder of soul and spirit, and of the joints and marrow, and is a discerner of the thoughts and intents of the heart."

The seed is divine: God said, "For as the rain cometh down, and the snow from heaven, and returneth not thither, but watereth the earth, and maketh it bring forth and bud, that it may give seed to the sower, and bread to the eater: *so shall MY WORD be that goeth forth out of my mouth:* it shall not return unto me void, but it shall accomplish that which I please, and it shall prosper in the thing whereto I sent it" (Isa. 55:10, 11).

The seed is everlasting: "The grass withereth, the flower fadeth: but *the Word of our God shall stand for ever*" (Isa. 40:8).

The seed is engrafted, therefore able to save the soul: "Every good gift and every perfect gift is from above, and cometh down from the Father of lights, with whom is no variableness, neither shadow of turning. Of His own will begat He us with the Word of truth, that we should be a kind of firstfruits of His creatures. . . . Wherefore lay apart

215

all filthiness and superfluity of naughtiness, and receive with meekness *the engrafted Word, which is able to save your souls"* (James 1:17-21).

The seed is life: Jesus said, "It is the Spirit that quickeneth; the flesh profiteth nothing: *the words that I speak unto you, they are spirit, and they are life"* (John 6:63).

The seed is God: "In the beginning was the Word, and the Word was with God, and *the Word was God. . . .* And the Word was made flesh, and dwelt among us, (and we beheld His glory, the glory as of the only begotten of the Father,) full of grace and truth" (John 1:1, 14).

Jesus came not only to *sow* the seed—He Himself *is* the seed. The *written* Word of God testifies of Him who came as the *living* Word of God, who was in the beginning with God. Jesus said, *"Search the Scriptures;* for in them ye think ye have eternal life: and *they are they which testify of me"* (John 5:39). All who receive the seed of the written Word *live,* because they have life through Christ who is the *living* Word. He is *Truth;* and when they receive the Word, they receive not only *words,* they receive a *Personality*—and they have life through His name. John said: "Many other signs truly did Jesus in the presence of His disciples, which are not written in this book: but these are written, that ye might believe that Jesus is the Christ, the Son of God; and that believing *ye might have life through His name"* (John 20:30, 31).

Christ dwells in the believer: "To whom God would make known what is the riches of the glory of this mystery among the Gentiles; which is *Christ in you,* the hope of glory" (Col. 1:27). And believers are also made partakers of divine nature: "Whereby are given unto us exceeding great and precious promises: that by these *ye might be partakers of the divine nature,* having escaped the corruption that is in the world through lust" (II Pet. 1:4).

When we sow the seed of the Word, the seed we sow is not only *from* Christ, the seed *is* Christ, as stated before. It is not inconsistent when we speak of Christ as the seed, and yet He is referred to also as the Sower. He preached the Saviour, and He was the Saviour whom He preached:

"And He came to Nazareth, where He had been brought up: and, as His custom was, He went into the synagogue on the sabbath day, and stood up for to read. And there was delivered unto Him the book of the prophet Esaias. And when He had opened the book, He found the place where it was written, *The Spirit of the Lord is upon me, because He hath anointed me to preach the Gospel to the poor; He hath sent me to heal the brokenhearted, to preach deliverance to the captives, and recovering of sight to the blind, to set at liberty them that are bruised, to preach the acceptable year of the Lord.* And He closed the book, and He gave it again to the minister, and sat down.

And the eyes of all them that were in the synagogue were fastened on Him. And He began to say unto them, *This day is this Scripture fulfilled in your ears"* (Luke 4:16-21).

Verse 9: *"Who hath ears to hear, let him hear."*

The statement here suggests to the disciples that they were to pay very close attention to what Jesus was about to say. He was about to convey to them spiritual instruction that was very important. Not all would understand this instruction; therefore He wanted them to listen carefully and attentively to what He was about to say.

Reasons for Speaking in Parables

Verse 10: *"And the disciples came, and said unto Him, Why speakest thou unto them in parables?"*

There is a possibility that the crowd complained to the disciples that they could not understand what Jesus was saying. Being perplexed themselves, naturally they could not answer the people, and they inquired of the Teacher just what He was attempting to teach by speaking in parables. Mark tells us that Jesus was alone when they asked Him the question. Both Mark and Luke make it plain that the disciples did not understand what Jesus meant by the parable of the sower (Mark 4:13; Luke 8:9).

"Why speakest thou unto them in parables?"
Notice that "parables" is plural, while as far as
we know only one parable had been spoken on
this occasion. But the plural might be used as
designating the method of instructing in general.

We need not suppose that Jesus meant to give
what follows as the only reason for employing
parables. However, we can see a special fitness in
His dwelling on this reason upon the present
occasion, for it was the day on which the scribes
had blasphemously accused Him of being in league
with Beelzebub (Matt. 12:24). Jesus was now surrounded by a great crowd that beyond any shadow
of doubt were very excited. The enthusiasm of the
crowd was no secret to Jesus, and He knew that
it was superficial and shortlived. Not very long
after this Jesus had to dispel illusions among
fanatical followers by the searching discourse on
the Bread of Life, recorded in John 6:26-66. At the
end of this discourse we read: "From that time
many of His disciples went back, and walked no
more with Him" (v. 66). It appears that Jesus in
these parables is commencing this work of warning
and discrimination.

Jesus was not deceived by the great crowds that
gathered. They apparently were attentive, but
most of the people were not listening from the
heart or listening to discover whether or not He
was the true Messiah. They were excited simply
because the crowds were following Jesus. He had

performed miracles, and they wanted to get into the trend of things and be a part of the mass emotionalism that was present with the crowds. In this parable especially, Jesus warns of the perils which threaten the seed as it is sown even by His true disciples. Also, in these parables—particularly the one of the sower, the one of the mustard seed, and the one concerning the leaven—we find consolation for Jesus Himself, as He clearly refers to the comparatively small number of true converts He was thus far making. In John 6:37, He cried out, "Him that cometh to me I will in no wise cast out." But very few were coming with sincere hearts. They were following Him for the loaves and fishes and for the excitement, but not for the true spiritual blessing that He had come into the world to give.

Verse 11: *"He answered and said unto them, Because it is given unto you to know the mysteries of the Kingdom of Heaven, but to them it is not given."*

The usual reason for Jesus using parables was to make truth clear and understandable. He used parables to arrest the attention of His listeners and to impress spiritual truth so deeply upon their memory that they would not forget it. But in this particular case, the Lord Jesus was fulfilling the sentence which had long before been passed upon the apostate nation of Israel from whom He received such mean and unworthy treatment. The nation was doomed to have the light of the Gospel taken away and to remain willfully in spiritual darkness. To His twelve apostles Jesus would explain why He spoke in parables, but not to the mass of unbelieving apostates who rejected Him as their Messiah. To anyone in the multitude who sincerely desired to know whether or not Jesus was the true Messiah, He would make Himself known. But those who rejected Him as Messiah even while listening to the parables He gave, would be hearing, and yet hear not. They would be seeing, and yet perceive not. To hear the spoken words of Jesus is not necessarily to hear with the ear of faith. Faith comes by hearing, but the hearing must be from the heart.

"To know the mysteries of the Kingdom" is a gift given to man by God's grace. To His disciples Jesus said, *"It is given unto you."* Then He added, *"but to them it is not given."* (These are solemn words that no one dare utter except the Anointed of Jehovah.) The natural man does not receive the things of the Spirit of God. No man has ever been willing to serve God until God puts within him the will to serve. Man is not born again of the will of the flesh or the will of man, but he is born of *God:* "As many as received Him, to them gave He power to become the sons of God, even to them that believe on His name: *which were born, not of blood, nor of the will of*

the flesh, nor of the will of man, but of God"
(John 1:12, 13). I reiterate: even the faith to receive the gift of God must come by hearing God's
Word: "So then faith cometh by hearing, and
hearing by the Word of God" (Rom. 10:17). In
John 5:24 we read, "Verily, verily, I say unto you,
He that *heareth my Word*, and believeth on Him
that sent me, hath everlasting life, and shall not
come into condemnation; but is passed from death
unto life."

A *mystery* in the Word of God is a truth previously hidden but now divinely revealed or made
known, but in which a supernatural element still
remains. We read several times in the New Testament about the mysteries of God or the mysteries
of spiritual things. The outstanding mysteries
mentioned are:

The mysteries of the Kingdom of Heaven:

In Matthew 13:3-50 we have seven parables that
reveal unto us—as far as it is God's will for us to
know at this time—the mysteries of the Kingdom
of Heaven.

*The mystery of Israel's blindness during the Dis-
pensation of Grace:*

"For I would not, brethren, that ye should be
ignorant of *this mystery*, lest ye should be wise in
your own conceits; *that blindness in part is happened to Israel, until the fulness of the Gentiles*

be come in" (Rom. 11:25). (Please study the entire eleventh chapter of Romans.) It is true that the nation is blinded now, but one day the eyes of their understanding will be opened. Zechariah tells us that when they see Jesus they will ask Him where He received the scars in His hands and feet. He will reply, "In the house of my friends" (Zech. 13:6). Then they will recognize Him as their Messiah and will crown Him King, and He will sit on the throne of David in Jerusalem.

The mystery of the translation of the living saints at the end of the Dispensation of Grace:

We know this as the Rapture of the Church. Paul said, "Behold, I shew you *a mystery: We shall not all sleep, but we shall all be changed, in a moment, in the twinkling of an eye, at the last trump:* for the trumpet shall sound, and the dead shall be raised incorruptible, and we shall be changed" (I Cor. 15:51,52). This will be the time when all living believers will be taken out of this world in the twinkling of an eye. Saints who have departed this life will join their resurrection bodies, and together with the living saints they will be caught up in the clouds to meet Jesus in the air. (Study also I Thessalonians 4:13-18.)

The mystery of the New Testament Church as one body made up of all born-again believers—both Jew and Gentile:

This mystery was revealed to the Apostle Paul. In Ephesians 3:3-6 he said, "... by revelation (God) made known unto me *the mystery* ... which in other ages was not made known unto the sons of men, as it is now revealed unto His holy apostles and prophets by the Spirit; *that the Gentiles should be fellowheirs, and of the same body, and partakers of His promise in Christ by the Gospel.*" Please study carefully Romans 16:25, 26; Ephesians 3:1-11; 6:19; and Colossians 4:3.

The mystery of the Church as the Bride of Christ:

God also revealed this to the Apostle Paul. In Ephesians 5:28-32 he wrote: "So ought men to love their wives as their own bodies. He that loveth his wife loveth himself. For no man ever yet hated his own flesh; but nourisheth and cherisheth it, even as the Lord the Church: for we are members of His body, of His flesh, and of His bones. For this cause shall a man leave his father and mother, and shall be joined unto his wife, and they two shall be one flesh. *This is a great mystery: but I speak concerning Christ and the Church.*"

The mystery of the living Christ abiding within the believer:

Each and every believer is a partaker of divine nature (II Pet. 1:4). Paul speaks of this mystery in Colossians 1:26, 27: "Even *the mystery which hath been hid from ages and from generations, but now is made manifest to His saints:* to whom God would make known what is the riches of the glory of this mystery among the Gentiles; *which is Christ in you,* the hope of glory." We also read in Galatians 2:20, "I am crucified with Christ: nevertheless I live; yet not I, but *Christ liveth in me:* and the life which I now live in the flesh I live by the faith of the Son of God, who loved me, and gave Himself for me."

The mystery of God—even Christ:

Christ is the incarnate fullness of the Godhead embodied. In Colossians 2:2-9 we read: "That their hearts might be comforted, being knit together in love, and unto all riches of the full assurance of understanding, to the acknowledgement of *the mystery of God, and of the Father, and of Christ; in whom are hid all the treasures of wisdom and knowledge....* Beware lest any man spoil you through philosophy and vain deceit, after the tradition of men, after the rudiments of the world, and not after Christ. For *in Him dwelleth all the fulness of the Godhead bodily."* Christ is He in whom all the divine wisdom for man subsists: "But we speak the wisdom of God in a mystery, even the hidden wisdom, which God ordained before the world unto our glory" (I Cor. 2:7).

The mystery of the process by which godlikeness is restored to man:

225

"And without controversy great is *the mystery of godliness:* God was manifest in the flesh, justified in the Spirit, seen of angels, preached unto the Gentiles, believed on in the world, received up into glory" (I Tim. 3:16).

The mystery of iniquity:

"For *the mystery of iniquity* doth already work: only He who now letteth will let, until He be taken out of the way" (II Thess. 2:7). There is a day coming when a man will walk upon this earth who will be the devil incarnate just as truly as Jesus the Man was God incarnate. The devil will visit this earth again in the person of a man who will indeed be a superman. (Please study II Thessalonians 2:1-12.)

The mystery of the seven stars:

"*The mystery of the seven stars* which thou sawest in my right hand, and the seven golden candlesticks. *The seven stars are the angels of the seven churches:* and the seven candlesticks which thou sawest are the seven churches" (Rev. 1:20).

The mystery of Babylon:

"And upon her forehead was a name written, *MYSTERY, BABYLON THE GREAT,* THE MOTHER OF HARLOTS AND ABOMINATIONS OF THE EARTH. And I saw the woman drunken with the blood of the saints, and with the blood of the martyrs of Jesus: and when I saw her, I wondered with great admiration. And the angel said unto me, Wherefore didst thou marvel? I will tell thee *the mystery of the woman,* and of the beast that carrieth her, which hath the seven heads and ten horns" (Rev. 17:5-7). (Please study all of Revelation chapter 17.)

The word "mystery" (or "mysteries") is found here in Matthew 13:11, in Mark 4:11, and in Luke 8:10, but nowhere else in the four Gospels nor in Acts. As we have seen, it is found several times in the epistles of Paul and in Revelation.

Verse 12: *"For whosoever hath, to him shall be given, and he shall have more abundance: but whosoever hath not, from him shall be taken away even that he hath."*

Those who had received the truth given to them by Jesus would come to greater light and greater truth. Those who willfully rejected the truth and would not walk in the light would become more confused, more bewildered; and totally rejecting Him would close the door of opportunity to know Him. Whosoever receives the truth, *"to him shall be given"* more light, *"and he shall have more abundance."* Jesus came that we might have life and have it abundantly (John 10:10). But when one rejects the light and refuses to receive by faith the truth set forth by Jesus, then from that person *"shall be taken away"* even the very *oppor-*

tunity to come to the light and the knowledge of salvation.

I do not know how many times nor how long God allows one to reject the Gospel. But each time one rejects the truth, the next time it is a little easier to do so. Each time one refuses light, the next time it is a little easier to refuse light. For those who desire and choose to walk in darkness, the darkness will become even greater.

One of the great Bible teachers of many years ago made a very thorough study and found that after people reach twenty-five years of age, only one out of 10,000 is born again; after thirty-five years of age, one out of 50,000; after forty-five years of age, one out of 200,000; after sixty-five years of age, one out of 500,000; and after seventy-five years of age, only one out of 700,000 is converted. I might add that after more than a quarter of a century of evangelistic meetings across America and on the foreign mission field, I can testify that this is true. The longer one puts off salvation, the easier it is for him to put it off. The devil has never asked any man to sign a contract to spend eternity in hell. All he wants is one moment at a time, one day, one altar call. The devil knows if he can lead a man to procrastinate that eventually he will plunge that soul into the lake of fire.

The sun that melts the ice and changes it to water also bakes the mud and changes it into brick. The light of the sun that warms the earth and gives to us the light in which we walk, would *blind* us if we looked at it the wrong way. Just so, the Gospel softens hearts when received, but hardens hearts when rejected. The Gospel brings light when received, but darkness when rejected. A little later in this same chapter we read concerning Israel, "For this people's heart is waxed gross, and their ears are dull of hearing, and their eyes they have closed; lest at any time they should see with their eyes and hear with their ears, and should understand with their heart, and should be converted, and I should heal them" (Matt. 13:15).

In John 3:19-21 Jesus explains why men are condemned: "And *this is the condemnation, that light is come into the world, and men loved darkness rather than light,* because their deeds were evil. For every one that doeth evil hateth the light, neither cometh to the light, lest his deeds should be reproved. But he that doeth truth cometh to the light, that his deeds may be made manifest, that they are wrought in God." Men are condemned because they refuse to receive the light and walk in the light. Later in the Gospel of John, Jesus clearly declared to all, "I AM THE LIGHT OF THE WORLD" (John 8:12).

Verse 13: *"Therefore speak I to them in parables: because they seeing see not; and hearing they hear not, neither do they understand."*

Since Jesus was omniscient, He knew the hearts

of the people and He knew that if He spoke to them in naked spiritual truth, they would reject completely every word He said. It would be utterly impossible for them to conceive true Bible doctrine; therefore, He clothed the deep things of God in parabolical language, using illustrations that they could understand. If Jesus had given them naked truth, they probably would not have listened at all but would have walked away. However, since He gave them parables, they did at least listen; but the plainer His teaching, the more simple He made it, the more they were puzzled by it. These people had become so spiritually and morally diseased that the only thing that would attract them was spectacular miracles—and even then they accused Him of doing them by the power of the prince of demons. He gave them simple truth—but they did not want it, they did not like it, they had no perception, they could not understand it, they refused to attempt to understand it.

As it was in that day, so it is today. The only possible way for man to deal with God is *by faith*. Jesus said to His disciples, *"Have faith in God"* (Mark 11:22). Paul declared that *without* faith it is impossible to *please* God (Heb. 11:6). Men are still attempting to figure out why the world is here. They marvel at the universe and are still probing to find the answer to the question as to how it came into existence. The *Bible* answers: "In the beginning *GOD CREATED the heaven and the earth"* (Gen. 1:1). If men would only believe and accept this by faith, they would no longer search in their laboratories attempting to find the answer. *All* of the answers are recorded in the Word of God; and regardless of what men may think or say, the Word is *forever settled in heaven.* The entrance of the Word brings light, and apart from the Word of God, it is impossible for men to understand the things of God.

Verses 14 and 15: *"And in them is fulfilled the prophecy of Esaias, which saith, By hearing ye shall hear, and shall not understand; and seeing ye shall see, and shall not perceive: for this people's heart is waxed gross, and their ears are dull of hearing, and their eyes they have closed; lest at any time they should see with their eyes and hear with their ears, and should understand with their heart, and should be converted, and I should heal them."*

The Old Testament Scripture quoted here is found in Isaiah 6:9, 10: "And He said, Go, and tell this people, Hear ye indeed, but understand not; and see ye indeed, but perceive not. Make the heart of this people fat, and make their ears heavy, and shut their eyes; lest they see with their eyes, and hear with their ears, and understand with their heart, and convert, and be healed."

As we study the New Testament, we find that the marvelous, enlightening sixth chapter of Isaiah is quoted frequently. How clearly the prophet Isaiah sets forth the doom of the nation Israel, guilty of every sin in the devil's catalog. Those who refused to see the light and *walk* in the light are *punished:* *"THIS is the condemnation — that light is come into the world, and men loved darkness rather than light, because their deeds were evil"* (John 3:19). The penalty for sin has always been the same. God told Adam that the day he ate of the forbidden fruit, he would *die* (Gen. 2:17). Paul tells us that the wages of sin is *death* (Rom. 6:23). James declares that when sin is finished, it brings forth *death* (James 1:15). Sin and death are synonymous.

How sad it is when men trifle with the Word of God. They twist the Word, bend it, add to it, and take from it to prove their religious doctrines and personal ideas. But the Word of God is forever settled in heaven; the Word of God cannot be broken — and when man attempts to make the Word of God teach what he believes, he is on extremely dangerous ground. (Please study Isaiah 6; Acts 28:26-28; Mark 4:12; and Luke 8:10.)

God has always in the past (and will continue to do so) punished men by that which is the natural result of their misconduct and their own violation of the natural laws of God. God has established certain laws, and if man breaks these laws, he will suffer for it.

". . . this people's heart is waxed gross . . . ."

Isaiah's expression, "make the heart fat," gives us the picture of a heart enveloped in fat. Such a heart is less sensitive and less lively in movement, resulting in dullness of senses and an inability to act quickly or to think deeply. It represents a dull heart and an insensible mind. The heart, especially in the Old Testament Scriptures, is represented as the seat of intelligence, sensibility, and will. Therefore, these people were "fat" as to their intellect and their understanding. We know that anyone who is overly fat is sluggish—and these people were very sluggish in their thinking, in their seeing, and in every detail of their lives.

The people had grown "fat" from prosperity, and they were "fat" religiously, having added to, taken from, rearranged, and changed the law of God. Their *ears* were heavy and *"dull of hearing"* because of their fatness, and *"their eyes they (had) closed."* The Hebrew in Isaiah means that they had *smeared over* their eyes. All this they did— and by doing so, they increased their inability to receive the things of God. Jesus said that they searched the Scriptures, thinking they would find eternal life—but the Scriptures testified of Him (John 5:39). He was the Life; He was the Truth; He was the Way; He was the Door. But they would not come to Him. They searched and searched—but they could not see, because they had a closed mind.

". . . lest at any time . . . ." This phrase means

233

"lest perhaps." Since Jesus was omniscient and knew all men and what they would do at all times, He knew that Israel would reject Him and nail Him to a cross. Let me emphasize that this has nothing to do with the free will of man. God knows all things about all people at all times, *simply because He is God.* These people had deadened their own ability to feel—they had closed their eyes willingly. Sin had rendered them heartless, deaf, blind; and they could not and would not accept spiritual truth. Therefore, they had locked the door of salvation to themselves as a nation.

"... *lest at any time they should see with their eyes and hear with their ears, and should understand with their heart, and should be converted, and I should heal them.*" This last part of verse 15 does not give any ground for the doctrine of fatalism—or that some are elected to be saved and others are elected to be damned. Jesus is not teaching such a false doctrine here, nor does He teach it anywhere. The blame for Israel's condition rests upon themselves because of their hardheartedness, their unreadiness to hear, and their blindness. They rejected Jesus, judged Him, condemned Him, and demanded His death. Because of their actions, they could not and they would not be healed. Paul says, "If our Gospel be hid, it is hid to them that are lost: in whom *the god of this world hath blinded the minds of them which believe not, lest the light of the glorious Gospel of*

Christ, who is the image of God, should shine unto them" (II Cor. 4:3, 4).

Verse 16: *"But blessed are your eyes, for they see: and your ears, for they hear."*

"Blessed are your eyes." The pronoun *"your"* is very emphatic here. Because of the insensibility on the part of the chosen nation of Israel, Jesus contrasts the better condition of His disciples. Jesus had chosen these disciples, and they had accepted His invitation to follow Him. These men were *blessed* (or happy) because *they did see, they did hear.* Day by day they were witnessing mighty miracles and they were hearing wonderful words of life. As stated in our next verse, they were seeing what many prophets and righteous men desired to see but failed to see.

Here, as in Matthew 12:28, Jesus distinctly intimates that He is their promised Messiah. Seeing and hearing are here to be understood both of the senses and of the spirit. The disciples saw the miracles and they heard the words of Jesus and understood at least enough to appreciate their spiritual meaning. After Jesus had given the discourse on the Bread of Life (recorded in John chapter 6), many of His followers turned and walked with Him no more. Then we read: "Then said Jesus unto the twelve, Will ye also go away? Then Simon Peter answered Him, Lord, to whom shall we go? *Thou hast the words of eternal life.*

And we believe and are sure that thou art that Christ, the Son of the living God" (John 6:67-69).

Verse 17: *"For verily I say unto you, That many prophets and righteous men have desired to see those things which ye see, and have not seen them; and to hear those things which ye hear, and have not heard them."*

In II Peter 1:19-21 we read: "We have also a more sure word of prophecy; whereunto ye do well that ye take heed, as unto a light that shineth in a dark place, until the day dawn, and the day star arise in your hearts: knowing this first, that *no prophecy of the Scripture is of any private interpretation. For the prophecy came not in old time by the will of man: but holy men of God spake as they were moved by the Holy Ghost."* The Old Testament prophets penned down the things that God gave to them by the Spirit. These prophets saw in one vision the rejected and crucified King and also His glory as the King sitting on the throne of David. However, they did not understand what they saw:

"Of which salvation the prophets have inquired and searched diligently, who prophesied of the grace that should come unto you: *searching* what, or what manner of time the Spirit of Christ which was in them did signify, when it testified beforehand *the sufferings of Christ, and the glory that should follow.* Unto whom it was revealed, that

not unto themselves, but unto us they did minister the things, which are now reported unto you by them that have preached the Gospel unto you with the Holy Ghost sent down from heaven; *which things the angels desire to look into"* (I Pet. 1: 10-12).

Jesus is now making known this truth in the parables He is giving to His disciples—and to all who have an ear to hear. The Old Testament prophet did not see the interval of time between the sufferings and the glory of the Lord. That interval of time we know is occupied with "the mysteries of the Kingdom of Heaven" which are revealed in the seven parables here in Matthew 13.

Interpretation of the Parable of the Sower

Verse 18: *"Hear ye therefore the parable of the sower."*

Please study Mark 4:14-20 and Luke 8:11-15 in connection with the interpretation given here by Jesus of the parable of the sower. His explanation of this parable (and also of the parable of the tares) furnishes us a perfect model for interpreting all His parables in general. Keep in mind that our Lord spoke with authority, and not as the scribes (Matt. 7:29).

"Hear ye . . . ." The Greek puts very strong emphasis on the word *"ye,"* which distinguishes the disciples from the masses of the Jews—those

who rejected the teachings of Jesus and to whom
He gave no explanation. "Ye" points primarily to
the twelve, and probably to others who were sincerely interested and were listening.

"Hear ye *therefore*" presents this as a consequence of the divine principles just before laid
down by Jesus.   The idea of the parable of the
sower and the seed as a whole is that just as the
same grain yielded variously according to the soil
which received the seed, the same is true concerning the Word of God.   The preached Word produces various effects, according to the way the
hearers receive the Word.

Of course, no analogy between physical and
spiritual things can ever be perfect. We know that
the soil in the parable was not responsible for its
condition.   The hard soil was not responsible for
the many feet that trampled it; the rocky soil was
not responsible for the rocks being there; the thorny
ground was not responsible for the thorns.   However, *men ARE accountable* for how they hear the
Word.   They will be held accountable for hearing
the Word improperly, and they will be held accountable to God for what they could have heard
but refused to hear.   Men will be judged *not only*
for what they *did,* but for what they *could have
done but did not do.*   Men should hear the admonition of the Lord: "*TAKE HEED therefore
HOW YE HEAR*" (Luke 8:18).

Verse 19:   "*When any one heareth the Word of*

the Kingdom, and understandeth it not, then cometh the wicked one, and catcheth away that which was sown in his heart. This is he which received seed by the way side."

"The Word of the Kingdom" in Luke 8:11 is called "the Word of God," while Mark 4:14 simply reads "the Word." (We read about "the *Gospel* of the Kingdom" in Matthew 4:23; 9:35; and 24:14.) This "Word of the Kingdom" means especially our Lord's own teaching; and so when He said, *"When any one heareth... and understandeth it not"* the reference is immediately to His own hearers at that time. However, it is still true that anyone who hears the Word of God and closes the eyes of his understanding, refusing to allow the Spirit to reveal the things of God to him, will give an account to God for rejecting the Word. This is just as true today as in the days when Jesus walked here upon this earth and spoke to men face to face.

"Understandeth it not" in the Greek reads, "does not take it in." If the truth heard is not taken into the heart, then "the fowls of the air" (the demons or evil spirits) will take away the Word. When one rejects the truth and keeps on rejecting it, finally God will say as He did in Hosea 4:17, "Ephraim is joined to idols: *let him alone."* Truth that is not understood or not taken into the heart cannot do a person any good.

The people here were hardened into indifference,

and some of them into malicious opposition to Jesus. They had already made up their minds that they would not receive Him; therefore they refused to accept or take in His wonderful words of life. His words, according to His own testimony, are spirit and life (John 6:63). His words are the power of God unto salvation (Rom. 1:16). His words are the incorruptible seed that brings the new birth (I Pet. 1:23). His words are able to save the soul (James 1:18, 21).

The plan of salvation is so practical that one will not truly understand it unless he is willing and ready to *receive* it. Concerning other things, one must *know* in order to love; but in Christianity, one must *love* in order to *know*. Whenever through inattention, lack of spiritual sympathy, unwillingness to receive, or opposition, men fail to understand the Word, it cannot benefit them.

In John 6:53 Jesus said, "Verily, verily, I say unto you, Except ye eat the flesh of the Son of man, and drink His blood, *ye have no life in you.*" (Please study all of John chapter 6.) Jesus did not mean to literally tear His flesh from His bones and eat it, and drink His blood. He meant to *appropriate,* to assimilate, to take into one's heart *His words*. They are the bread of life, the water of life, the incorruptible seed — so when we take the Word into our heart we are actually taking into our heart the divine nature of Jesus Himself (II Pet. 1:4; Col. 1:27).

". . . then cometh the wicked one . . . ." The wicked one is, of course, the devil. Mark's account reads, *"Satan cometh immediately"* (Mark 4:15), and Luke says, *"Then cometh the devil"* (Luke 8:12). There is a real, live, personal devil, a living being. He comes *"and catcheth away . . . ."* The Greek here is very strong. It does not say that he casually removes the Word, but he "SNATCHETH AWAY." It gives the idea of a sudden and violent seizing and carrying off of a thing.

". . . that which was sown in his heart." The individual hears the Word and admits in his mind that what the minister is preaching is reasonable and he will seriously consider in his heart embracing that which he has heard. But because the heart is hardened and the seed cannot penetrate, the wicked one violently rushes in and snatches the Word away.

When one hears the Word and refuses to receive it, the Word for a moment rests upon the surface of the mind and then the evil influences of Satan and his subordinates catch it away. Often the whole impression made upon someone's mind by a sermon delivered by God's preacher is destroyed in an instant when the service is over by an idle joke or a trifling statement by another individual. The person may have listened to the Word and may be under conviction, beginning to think of salvation; but idle conversation may take away the conviction that the Word of God has brought.

"This is he which received seed by the way side." The man was not an opposer or an enemy. He *received* the seed—but on ground that was not ready; that is, the ground was hard. When the seed fell, the enemy saw it immediately—and the devil is afraid to allow truth to remain in a man's mind too long, even though the ground is hard. One thing the devil fears is truth. Jesus is Truth, the Word is truth—and the devil fears Jesus and the Word. The seed remained for a short time, and then "the fowls of the air" swept down and devoured it. The seed was not sown in a prepared heart; it was not received with all the heart. It was not allowed to renew the heart, and therefore it did not take root and bring forth life eternal.

There are many hearers like this today. We preach to them, they listen, they seem to receive the message—but in vain. They seem to learn as they listen, but then they *un*learn by allowing the devil to take the message away. They seem to receive, but then they immediately reject what they seem to have received.

Verse 20: *"But he that received the seed into stony places, the same is he that heareth the Word, and anon with joy receiveth it."*

Here the sower is the same, the seed is the same, but the result is somewhat different. In the case of the man who received seed into stony places, there was not enough soil for the seed to take root. According to Mark's account, "immediately it sprang up, because it had no depth of earth." Then the sun beat down upon the seed, and "it was scorched; and because it had no root, it withered away" (Mark 4:5, 6). The sun beat down upon the seed, and instead of making it sprout and come forth into life, it burned it so that it did not grow, but withered instead.

"He . . . heareth the Word, and anon with joy receiveth it." This person is attentive, easily persuaded, and seemingly happy to accept the message. He seems eager, enthusiastic, and demonstrative. On the surface this looks like a genuine conversion—but the "soil" was not there. It is often the case that superficial and transient religious impressions produce a speedier and more boisterous "joy" than those which are deep and genuine.

Verse 21: *"Yet hath he not root in himself, but dureth for a while: for when tribulation or persecution ariseth because of the Word, by and by he is offended."*

". . . but dureth for a while." We do not have any grounds to determine the length of time a person of this type "endures." Sometimes when one seemingly makes a sincere profession or becomes extremely interested in the things of God, *immediately* the enemy attacks and persecution begins. Sometimes it may be a longer period of

time before trouble starts. When things begin to get difficult and *"persecution ariseth,"* then the real believer is made known. The person who *seemingly* accepted the Lord Jesus Christ—through church membership, baptism, and even good works —is rootless, and therefore dries up. His profession withers, his church attendance drops off, his good works fade away, and people wonder what happened. The thing that happened is that *the person was never genuinely born again.* It is true that he heard the Word, he seemingly received the Word with joy, and he continues thus for awhile—but *"by and by he is offended."* Everything about this person's profession is on the surface and unreal. Jesus said, "The *flesh* profiteth *nothing"* (John 6:63). It is from the *heart* that we *believe unto righteousness,* and with the mouth confession is made unto salvation (Rom. 10:10).

Verse 22: *"He also that received seed among the thorns is he that heareth the Word; and the care of this world, and the deceitfulness of riches, choke the Word, and he becometh unfruitful."*

We have here the third illustration concerning the sower and the seed. A person receives the seed, and the seed goes deep into the ground. The plant springs up, and everything here is as in the genuine profession of faith—with one exception: this particular plant does not bear fruit. It *"becometh unfruitful."* The stalk is beautiful and everything points to fruit bearing, but there is no fruit. The seed is sown in productive ground—but *thorns* are there, and their roots overwhelm the plant and it bears no fruit. In the case of this person, his will is never surrendered to God. He tries to hold on to the world and to spiritual things at the same time, and this always ends in evil conquering and good being defeated. Jesus said, "No man can serve two masters: for either he will hate the one, and love the other; or else he will hold to the one, and despise the other. *Ye cannot serve God and mammon*" (Matt. 6:24).

"*. . . the care of this world, and the deceitfulness of riches . . . .*" This class of hearers is not confined to the rich. Luke names three things which prevent fruitbearing in this case—*cares, riches,* and *pleasures:* "And that which fell among thorns are they, which, when they have heard, go forth, and are choked with cares and riches and pleasures of this life, and bring no fruit to perfection" (Luke 8:14). Mark 4:19 adds, "and the lusts of other things." If we would seek first the Kingdom of God (Matt. 6:33), then all these "other things" would be added, and we would indeed be rich.

Riches in Scripture are not riches *absolutely* (as possessed), but riches *relatively,* as estimated by the desire and the value of riches. We must remember that riches often as grievously deceive those who *vainly seek,* as they do those who actually *obtain* them. Riches deceive men in many ways—as to the means of acquiring them, making things look honest that are not so; as to the reasons they are desired; as to the objects for which their use is intended, etc. Some professed Christians imagine they are in the pursuit of riches simply that later on they will be able to do great things for God, when the true reason is that they love wealth.

It is interesting to notice that there is in these three classes of hearers studied thus far, a threefold progress denoted. First we note a progression of *time*. The first hearer receives a hindrance immediately—that is, very shortly after the sower sows the seed. The seed never comes up. In the second case, soon after the seed has sprung up, the hindrance is seen. In the third case, when the seed has entered the earth, sprung up, and the stalk has grown to the point where there should be fruit, then the hindrance appears and prevents fruitfulness.

Secondly, there is a threefold degree of progress *from bad to better*—but never to perfection. The first group understand not; the second group understand and feel; the third group understand, feel, and in some degree, practice.

Thirdly, even though it appears that there are three steps upward from bad to better, the truth of the matter is that the steps are *from bad to worse*. The first group (those who do not understand at all—they do not receive the Word, and immediately it is taken away) are not in *as severe a spiritual state* as the *second* group (those who feel it, receive it with joy, but then turn their back on the Word). They recognize the opportunity of salvation and they seem to experience a bit of the joy outwardly—and then they fall away. Again, less awful is the spiritual state of the first two than those in the *third* group, who apparently understand, feel, and even "practice religion"— but all the time the heart is not pure and righteous, because their profession is outward only and no more than filthy rags in the sight of God: "We are all as an unclean thing, and *all our righteousnesses are as filthy rags;* and we all do fade as a leaf; and our iniquities, like the wind, have taken us away" (Isa. 64:6).

The Bible clearly teaches that it is better for one never to know the way of life than to know and then turn from the Word of God. In the true sense, the heathen who has never heard the name of Jesus will fare better at the judgment than those who live in America or in other lands where the Gospel is preached daily. We will be judged for the opportunities rejected—that is, that which we could have had if we would have only listened to and obeyed the Word.

Let me point you to the rich young ruler (Mark 10:17-22) in this class of hearers. Notice that he evidently had heard about Jesus and about His wonderful miracles; and upon hearing, he came running to Jesus: ". . . there came one running, and kneeled to Him, and asked Him, Good Master, what shall I do that I may inherit eternal life?" (When we see one running to the altar, falling upon his knees, and crying out to God, then certainly we feel that such a person is definitely interested, under conviction, and desires to be born again.) Jesus answered this young man by telling him that if He was good, He was *God;* and if He was not God, then He was not *good.* Jesus knew that this young man did not believe that He was God in the flesh. He knew exactly the condemning sin of unbelief that held this young man's heart prisoner.

Jesus gave him six commandments; but you will notice that they are all the commandments which have to do with one's fellow man—concerning adultery, murder, stealing, lying, defrauding, and honoring one's father and mother. The young man said to Jesus, "All these have I observed from my youth." Jesus looked at him, loved him, and said to him, "One thing thou lackest: go thy way, sell whatsoever thou hast, and give to the poor, and thou shalt have treasure in heaven: and come, take up the cross, and follow me." When the young man heard that statement, he turned away grieved; for he had great possessions, and he loved his riches. So you see, his seemingly enthusiastic desire to be a follower of Jesus soon faded and he went away grieved—not because he could not have done what Jesus requested him to do, but because he loved the things of this life more than he loved the things of God.

There are many of this group among us today. They hear the Word, they are affected by it—and some go forward, weep, pray, join the church, and are baptized. For awhile they seem to be growing—then they become unfruitful. They begin to grow cold; they miss Sunday school, church, prayer meeting—and then finally they disappear. Such a person professes, joins the church, puts on a religious show, and there are signs of true conversion; but there is no genuine faith in the heart. The "leaf" is beautiful, but finally it begins to wither; the "stalk" is beautiful, and there is even the *appearance* of an ear that bears fruit—but there is no fruit in the ear. Weeds begin to grow, thorns begin to come forth, and finally this person disappears.

Verse 23:   *"But he that received seed into the good ground is he that heareth the Word, and understandeth it; which also beareth fruit, and bringeth forth, some an hundredfold, some sixty, some thirty."*

This seed falls into *"good ground,"* and this represents the man who *hears* the Word, *understands* the Word—and the result is *fruit*. But we must not understand this fourth class of hearers to be a select, specially called company, excluding the other three classes—not by any means. The "soil" is not good by nature: "The *natural* man *receiveth not* the things of the Spirit of God" (I Cor. 2:14). The Word and the Spirit must prepare the soil. This is borne out in Acts 16:13-18, where we find the record of Paul's first opportunity to witness in Europe. He first attended a Bible class; and when he had given one lesson, Lydia was converted and became a believer. Then we read that a fortune teller followed Paul and Silas for "many days," and they preached the Gospel to her. Not one time, but *many* times she heard, and finally she was converted.

One cannot be saved apart from hearing the Gospel, and how quickly one *receives* it depends a great deal upon the background of that person and the opportunities he (or his parents or grand-parents) had to hear the Gospel. In the case of the heathen, many times the missionary toils un-tiringly for years before there is one genuine con-vert. The reason is that these people have lived in darkness and have hearts that are as hard as rocks. However, in this country we may go into a city for revival meetings and have many converts be-cause someone has faithfully sown the seed before us and the people have been exposed to the Gos-pel; therefore, it does not take nearly so long for the seed to take root.

So this fourth class of hearers is not a select, elect group that are chosen over and above all other people. The Word of God prepares the heart, the *Spirit* prepares the heart—and then finally the seed falls into the prepared ground and sprouts up to bring forth fruit.

All men are sinners by nature, born in sin, shapen in iniquity. David said, "Behold, I was *shapen in iniquity;* and *in sin did my mother conceive me*" (Psalm 51:5). There is *no difference*, for we have *all* sinned and come short of the glory of God: "What then? are we better than they? No, in no wise: for we have before proved both Jews and Gentiles, that they are *all* under sin; as it is written, *There is none righteous, no, NOT ONE:* there is none that understandeth, there is none that seeketh after God. They are all gone out of the way, they are together become unprofitable; *there is none that doeth good, no, NOT ONE*" (Rom. 3:9-12).

". . . *and bringeth forth, some an hundredfold, some sixty, some thirty.*" You will notice that there are three degrees of fruit bearing—one hundredfold, sixtyfold, and thirtyfold. There is always fruit if a person is truly born again—not always the same in abundance, but *always fruit.* I can assure you that the thirtyfold fruit was just as wholesome as the sixtyfold. There is no such thing as a born-again believer who does not bring forth *some* fruit displaying righteousness in the heart. God is not so much interested in the *amount,* although we should do all the good that we can. We should win all the souls that we can, give all that we can to the work of the Lord; but it is not the amount that counts—it is the sincerity of the heart.

We are clearly taught in the Word that if we are faithful in a few things, God will make us ruler over many things. A cup of cold water given faithfully, if that is all the individual can give, is as much in God's sight as a million dollars given by a wealthy person. God does not measure as man does. We look on the outward appearance; God looks upon the *heart*. So if you cannot bear a hundredfold, then bear sixty.

Many people who are faithful soul winners do not win as many souls as some other person, for various reasons. God does not call every individual into full-time Christian service, but we are laborers together—one plants, another waters, God gives the increase. In the case of my ministry, millions of people through the years have had a definite part— for the equipment that I use and the money that I have spent have been donated by God's people. Had it not been for the faithfulness of those who give, then my ministry could never have been possible. I have tried to be faithful to the Word and to faithfully sow the seed, but I could not have sown the seed in so many places if it had not been for the faithfulness of those who have supported me down through the years.

God's Word says, "To him that knoweth to do good, and doeth it not, to him it is sin" (James

4:17). Therefore we should do all that we can, and we should not excuse ourselves from doing what can be done. I repeat: It is not the *amount* of "fruit" which is important in God's sight—it is the faithfulness with which we discharge our duties and buy up our opportunities.

There will definitely be degrees of rewards in heaven, but this will not be because of the amount of fruit. It will be the kind of stewardship and the faithfulness of the heart that will count. Paul describes it in these words:

"For other foundation can no man lay than that is laid, which is Jesus Christ. Now if any man build upon this foundation gold, silver, precious stones, wood, hay, stubble; *every man's work shall be made manifest:* for the day shall declare it, because it shall be revealed by fire; and *the fire shall try every man's work OF WHAT SORT it is.* If any man's work abide which he hath built thereupon, he shall receive a reward. If any man's work shall be burned, he shall suffer loss: but he himself shall be saved; yet so as by fire" (I Cor. 3:11-15).

Another solemn warning is given to us in II Corinthians 5:10: *"For we must all appear before the judgment seat of Christ;* that every one may receive the things done in his body, according to that he hath done, whether it be good or bad."

Listen to the words of the Apostle Paul as he rebukes the believers in Corinth: "Who then is

Paul, and who is Apollos, but ministers by whom ye believed, even as the Lord gave to every man? *I have planted, Apollos watered; but GOD GAVE THE INCREASE.* So then neither is he that planteth any thing, neither he that watereth; but God that giveth the increase. Now he that planteth and he that watereth are one: and *every man shall receive his own reward ACCORDING TO HIS OWN LABOUR*" (I Cor. 3:5-8).

How wonderful it is to be a child of God; how glorious it is to be a soul winner. What a marvelous opportunity we have to sow the good seed that brings forth a harvest. God help you and me to be faithful in sowing the seed—and God help us to *leave the results to the Lord Jesus!* We can preach, testify, witness, and warn; but we cannot convict, draw, or save. The Word of God is quick, and powerful, and sharper than any twoedged sword. The Word of God cuts as we preach, and the Holy Spirit convicts men of sin, of righteousness, and of judgment, and draws them to the place of salvation. It is up to us to receive from the Lord the light, the bread, the meat, and then to faithfully distribute that which He gives to us. It is glorious that all believers are laborers together with God. We are God's workmen, we are His servants; and we are to labor according to the grace of God given us. We are to be as wise as serpents, as harmless as doves, doing always all things to the glory of God. When we do anything to bring glory or honor to our own name, then we have failed God and we will certainly lose our reward. We are *saved* by *grace*—salvation is the free gift of God; but we will be *rewarded* for our *faithful stewardship.*

You can rest assured that the fruits of grace in believers are the same *quality* but not always the same *quantity.* That which yields a lesser harvest is still called "good ground," for it produces a real crop. In Matthew 25:14-23, the servant to whom was given two talents was just as faithful as the one who received *five* talents. The other was given more talents, but both received the same commendation—"good and faithful servant." That is the thing which counts with God—*faithfulness.* It is no wonder that Jesus said to His faithful followers in Mark 11:22, "Have faith in God."

The Second Mystery:
The Parable of the Tares Among the Wheat

Verse 24: *"Another parable put He forth unto them, saying, The Kingdom of Heaven is likened unto a man which sowed good seed in his field."*

This parable of the tares and the wheat is given by Matthew only. We have the illustration here in verses 24 through 30, and the interpretation is given in verses 37 through 43.

"Another parable put He forth unto them"—or *set before* them. This is an image derived from

255

setting *food* before persons, as the word is used in Mark 8:6, Acts 16:34, and I Corinthians 10:27. *"Them"* means not just the twelve disciples, but the people in general.

"The Kingdom of Heaven . . . ." In Matthew 3:2 we heard John the Baptist cry out, "Repent ye: for the Kingdom of Heaven is at hand." This phrase "Kingdom of Heaven," literally "of the heavens," is a phrase that is peculiar to the Gospel of Matthew and it signifies the Messianic earthly rule of Jesus, the Son of David. It is called the Kingdom of the Heavens because it is the rule of the heavens over the earth. In the model prayer given by our Lord we read, "Thy will be done in earth, as it is in heaven" (Matt. 6:10).

The phrase "the Kingdom of Heaven" is derived from the book of Daniel, where it is defined. (Please study Daniel 2:34-36, 44 and 7:23-27.) Daniel defined the Kingdom of Heaven as the kingdom "which the God of heaven" will set up after the destruction of the Gentile powers by the "stone cut out without hands." It is the Kingdom God gave to David's seed by a perpetual covenant which cannot be broken. (Please study II Samuel 7:7-16.) The Kingdom was confirmed to Jesus Christ, the Son of David, through the angel Gabriel in Luke 1:32, 33.

We find three aspects of the Kingdom in Matthew's Gospel:

First, John announced the Kingdom of Heaven

as *"at hand."* This was from the beginning of
the ministry of John the Baptist to the rejection
of the King and the announcement of the new
brotherhood in Matthew 12:46-50.

Second, we have the *"mysteries of the Kingdom"* described in the seven parables we are now
studying, which are to be fulfilled during this
present age. To these are to be added the parables
of the Kingdom of Heaven which were spoken
after Matthew 13, which have to do with the sphere
of Christian profession during this dispensation.
However, it is impossible to separate each and
every word and symbol in these parables or to
draw a line and dogmatically say, *"This* is for this
Day of Grace, and *that* is for the Millennium."

The third aspect is the prophetic one—when the
Kingdom is set up after the second coming of the
Lord Jesus Christ, the time when He sits on the
throne of His father David and reigns for one
thousand glorious years. This is known as the
Millennium. (Please study Matthew 24:29 through
25:46, and Acts 15:14-17.)

It is important to keep in mind that there is a
distinct difference between the Kingdom of Heaven
and the *Kingdom of God.* The *Kingdom of Heaven*
will be a *literal kingdom* right here upon this
earth. But the *Kingdom of God* is a *spiritual* kingdom. When the Pharisees demanded that Jesus
tell them when the Kingdom of God would come,
He replied, "The Kingdom of God cometh not

with observation: neither shall they say, Lo here! or, lo there! for, behold, *the Kingdom of God is WITHIN you*" (Luke 17:20, 21).

". . . *is likened unto a man which sowed good seed in his field.*" The sower here is the Lord Jesus, who sows only good seed in His fields. In this parable, which we find interpreted in verses 36 through 43, the *"good seed"* is not "the Word," as in the first parable in this chapter. In that parable the seed is definitely the Word of God that falls on different kinds of ground; but here the seed is *that which the Word has produced*—the children of the Kingdom. In I Peter 1:23 we see that *we are "born again,* not of corruptible seed, but of incorruptible, *by the Word of God,* which liveth and abideth for ever." The seed is sown or scattered here and there in the *"field,"* which is "the world" (verse 38). The "world" is not only the geographical world, but also the world of *mankind.*

Verse 25: *"But while men slept, his enemy came and sowed tares among the wheat, and went his way."*

"While men slept" speaks of the *night,* when there was no one to observe the enemy sowing his seed. There is no reference to any particular group of men negligently sleeping, only that *"his enemy"* selected the most opportune time for secretly doing his evil job.

Chapter 13:25

". . . came and sowed tares among the wheat."
The word rendered *"tares"* has been the subject
of much discussion, but it is pretty generally agreed
that it denotes *darnel.* This is a plant of the same
family as wheat and is not readily distinguished
from wheat, especially in the early stages. Bible
scholars tell us that it is quite difficult to distinguish between wheat and tares until the head
of the grain appears, and then there is a difference.

This is true in the Christian realm—it is very
difficult in some cases to tell believers from unbelievers. It is not difficult to distinguish a true
Christian from those living openly in deep sin, but
there are many people who live clean upright lives
who are not genuinely born again. In fact, some
unbelievers live cleaner lives than some believers,
particularly concerning things that are referred to
as "little sins" and acts that are described as
"not harmful." When we look into the mirror of
the Word of God, we find quite a different definition of sin than we do from the lips of men. Paul
put it in these words dictated by the Holy Spirit:
"Whatsoever is NOT OF FAITH is SIN" (Rom.
14:23). We also read in James 4:17 that *"to him
that knoweth to do good, and doeth it not, to
him it is SIN."* "Whether therefore ye eat, or
drink, or whatsoever ye do, *do ALL to the glory
of God"* (I Cor. 10:31).

I have personally had the opportunity of viewing
the wheat fields in Palestine, and the missionary

259

with us pointed out that tares appear among the wheat even today. There is a very interesting thing about tares. As already pointed out, the grain resembles wheat; however, it is *smaller* and *black*—and the blackness, to me, is a perfect symbol of *sin*. I was told that if one eats bread made from wheat that has tares mixed in, it will make him dizzy; therefore, the grains were not just *useless* for human food, but *noxious*. This fact adds to the point of the parable of our Lord given here.

Some Bible scholars have suggested that the tares were merely degenerate wheat—that is, inferior, or a low grade. But this is not true. A tare is definitely a different grain. There is no mixture of wheat and tares in the seed, for each is separate. This doctrine that tares could be degenerate wheat and by cultivation probably could be brought back to true wheat is very pleasing to the ears of some teachers. It corresponds to the teaching that wicked men are fallen and may be restored with proper training and environment. But this is not true. Man must be born again and become a new creation in Christ before he can enter the Kingdom of God (John 3:1-7; II Cor. 5:17).

"Among the wheat" in the original Greek is very, very strong. The expression signifies that the enemy sowed the tares not just in one little section of the field, but in the *midst* of the wheat. That is, the tares were sown throughout the field in every part, making it impossible to separate

the wheat from the tares without destroying the wheat.

When the "wheat" of God is sown in the world, this is the place where Satan's activity begins. Where you find the children of the Kingdom, you will find among them those who *profess* to be God's children but who are actually *Satan's* children. They are so much like the children of God that only God can know for sure who they are, and only God's angels who are called at "the end of the world" can separate them from the children of God.

Satan is a master deceiver. So great is his power of deception that the "tares" often really suppose themselves to be the children of the Kingdom. In Matthew 7:21-23 we learned that many will say in the day of judgment that they had *prophesied,* and *worked,* and *given* in the name of the Lord—but Jesus will profess that *He never knew them!* If it were possible, Satan would deceive the very elect of God, but the marvelous words of Peter give us assurance that Satan cannot deceive and lead astray those who are truly saved: "Wherefore also it is contained in the Scripture, Behold, I lay in Sion a chief corner stone, elect, precious: and *he that believeth on Him shall not be confounded*" (I Pet. 2:6).

From this chapter on to the end of Matthew, we see this mingled condition set forth; and as long as Jesus tarries, there will be children of God and children of Satan living on this earth. We must mix and mingle with the children of the wicked one. We must rub shoulders with them, but we do not have to partake of their wickedness. There are many other Scriptures that clearly teach the existence of this mingled condition until Jesus comes to take believers unto Himself. (Please study Matthew 22:11-14; 25:1-30; Luke 18:10-14; and Hebrews 6:4-9.)

This parable of the wheat and tares is not given to describe the world, but those who profess to be in the Kingdom. "The field" is the world, "the good seed" are the children of the Kingdom, but "the tares" are "the children of the wicked one" (Matt. 13:38). Jesus plainly calls the religious leaders children of Satan in John 8:38-44:

"I speak that which I have seen with my Father: and ye do that which ye have seen with your father. They answered and said unto Him, Abraham is our father. Jesus saith unto them, If ye were Abraham's children, ye would do the works of Abraham. But now ye seek to kill me, a Man that hath told you the truth, which I have heard of God: this did not Abraham. *Ye do the deeds of your father.* Then said they to Him, We be not born of fornication; we have one Father, even God.

"Jesus said unto them, If God were your Father, ye would love me: for I proceeded forth and came from God; neither came I of myself, but He sent me. Why do ye not understand my speech? even because ye cannot hear my word. *YE ARE OF YOUR FATHER THE DEVIL,* and the lusts of your father ye will do. He was a murderer from the beginning, and abode not in the truth, because there is no truth in him. When he speaketh a lie, he speaketh of his own: for he is a liar, and the father of it.''

Again in Matthew chapter 23 Jesus condemns those who pretended to be what they were not:

"The scribes and the Pharisees sit in Moses' seat: All therefore whatsoever they bid you observe, that observe and do; *but do not ye after their works: for they say, and do not.* For they bind heavy burdens and grievous to be borne, and lay them on men's shoulders; but they themselves will not move them with one of their fingers. But *all their works they do for to be seen of men:* . . .

"Woe unto you, scribes and Pharisees, *hypocrites!* for ye shut up the Kingdom of Heaven against men: for ye neither go in yourselves, neither suffer ye them that are entering to go in. Woe unto you, scribes and Pharisees, hypocrites! for ye devour widows' houses, and *for a pretence make long prayer:* therefore ye shall receive the greater damnation. Woe unto you, scribes and Pharisees, hypocrites! for ye compass sea and land to make one proselyte, and when he is made, ye make him twofold more the child of hell than yourselves. . . .

"Woe unto you, scribes and Pharisees, *hypocrites!*

for ye make clean the OUTSIDE of the cup and of the platter, but WITHIN they are full of extortion and excess. Thou blind Pharisee, cleanse first that which is within the cup and platter, that the outside of them may be clean also. Woe unto you, scribes and Pharisees, hypocrites! for *ye are like unto whited sepulchres, which indeed appear beautiful outward, but are within full of dead men's bones, and of all uncleanness. Even so ye also OUTWARDLY APPEAR RIGHTEOUS unto men, BUT WITHIN YE ARE FULL OF HYPOCRISY AND INIQUITY"* (Matt. 23:2-28 in part).

". . . and went his way." When the enemy had completed his dastardly work in the nighttime while men slept and no one was watching, he departed from the area so no one would know what he had done.

The words *"his way"* bring to my mind two of the saddest words ever spoken about a man. This man is Judas Iscariot, one of the twelve. Luke tells us that the Passover feast was very near, and the chief priests and scribes sought how they might destroy Jesus—but they were afraid of the people. The masses of common people looked upon Jesus as a prophet, and the religious leaders feared them. We read: "Then entered Satan into Judas surnamed Iscariot, being of the number of the twelve. And *he went HIS WAY*, and communed with the chief priests and captains, how he might betray Him unto them" (Luke 22:3, 4). The chief rulers of Israel were glad, and they promised to give him money. Then Judas sought opportunity to betray Jesus into their hands "in the absence of the multitude." Judas wanted to deliver Jesus when He was alone—which signifies the same principle as here in our parable, where the enemy sowed the tares in the night.

I personally believe that Judas was Satan incarnate, in that he was the representative of Satan right in the midst of the twelve apostles, just as we see the tares right in the midst of the wheat. Judas Iscariot was the treasurer of the disciple band—he carried the money. He was respected by all, and he went in and out among them throughout the ministry of Jesus until that fateful night when he betrayed the Lord for thirty pieces of silver. Judas went "HIS WAY." Any man who travels the journey of "his way" is following in the footsteps of the devil, and the end is disappointment, disaster, and eternal destruction.

Verse 26: *"But when the blade was sprung up, and brought forth fruit, then appeared the tares also."*

"The blade" is the same word translated "grass" in Matthew 6:30 and 14:19. The stock began to grow and mature and *"brought forth fruit."* This does not speak of the ripe grain at the time of harvest, but of the head or the fruit of the wheat as it began to mature. *"Then appeared the tares*

also"—and the owner could detect at that point which was wheat and which was tares because, although the heads are similar, there are marks of difference that cannot be missed by those who know the grain.

Verse 27: *"So the servants of the householder came and said unto him, Sir, didst not thou sow good seed in thy field? from whence then hath it tares?"*

The word for *"householder"* is translated "master of the house" in Matthew 10:25. When the servants discovered the tares among the wheat they came to their master and told him. *"Sir"* was simply a title of respect used by all servants and slaves when addressing their owner or employer.

"Didst not thou sow good seed in thy field?" The servants came to their master, "the householder," and asked him if he knew whether or not the seed he sowed was pure seed, not mixed with other seeds. They asked it in a way that would not accuse their master of being negligent. The last part of the verse tells us that they had no doubt in their minds that the master had failed to sow good seed. They said, *"From whence then hath it tares?"* If he had sowed good seed, how did the tares get there?

Verse 28: *"He said unto them, An enemy hath done this. The servants said unto him, Wilt thou then that we go and gather them up?"*

"An enemy hath done this." The master knew exactly what had happened. He had sowed good wheat, but one who was his enemy was attempting to ruin his harvest by mixing bad seed with his good seed. The servants asked their master, *"Wilt thou then that we go and gather them up?"* The servants desired to go into the field and pull the tares up by the roots and take them out of the field and destroy them.

Verse 29: *"But he said, Nay; lest while ye gather up the tares, ye root up also the wheat with them."*

This master was an authority on farming because he knew exactly what would happen if the workers should begin to remove the tares from his field. The roots of the wheat and tares intermingle; therefore he knew that while they were removing the tares, they would be destroying the wheat. This is a picture of life. We cannot exist in this world without mixing and mingling with unbelievers. We must go into their shops, buy their products, work alongside them, and in many other ways deal with them. But when the end comes, the Lord God will do the separating.

Verse 30: *"Let both grow together until the harvest: and in the time of harvest I will say to the reapers, Gather ye together first the tares, and bind them in bundles to burn them: but gather the wheat into my barn."*

"Let both grow together until the harvest."
The owner of the field instructed his servants to
let the wheat and the tares grow together until
they were fully ripe and the harvest time had
come. At that time he would say to the reapers,
*"Gather ye together first the tares, and bind them
in bundles to burn them: but gather the wheat
into my barn."* The gathering of the tares into
bundles for burning, mentioned here by Jesus,
does not signify that the householder would instruct the servants to burn them *at that moment.*
If they were going to be burned at that time, there
would be no point in binding them in bundles.

Satan is not bound today—but he does have
limits. God permits him to go only so far, and
then He stops him. One day he will be *completely*
bound for one thousand years (Rev. 20:1-3), and he
will not be able to operate at all. Later he will be
cast into the lake of fire burning with brimstone.

These bundles of tares are bound, and they will
be burned at the judgment. In verse 40 of this
chapter, we are clearly instructed that the burnings
will occur at the end of this age: "As therefore
the tares are gathered and burned in the fire; *so
shall it be in the end of this world."*

During this age Jesus is taking out a Gentile
bride, the New Testament Church; and when it is
complete, He will remove it from the earth (John
14:3; I Thess. 4:14-18). Then all hell will break
loose right here upon this earth.

Before leaving this parable, let me sum up what I have said. The parable of the wheat and the tares definitely shows to us the reality of hypocrisy in Christendom, which will extend until the end of this Dispensation of Grace. Through this parable we learn that this dispensation is to end without a converted world. Postmillennialists would have us believe that the preaching of the Gospel will convert the world and bring in the Kingdom, but the Bible does not teach any such doctrine. We see clearly that the tares do not grow into wheat at the end, but are gathered up, set aside, and burned. As believers, we will be terribly depressed, disheartened, and disappointed if we expect the conversion of the world before the return of the Lord Jesus the second time. The Bible does not teach it, so we need not look for it. We are told, instead, that "evil men and seducers shall wax *worse and worse*" (II Tim. 3:13).

The Third Mystery:
The Parable of the Grain of Mustard Seed

Verse 31: *"Another parable put He forth unto them, saying, The Kingdom of Heaven is like to a grain of mustard seed, which a man took, and sowed in his field."*

"Another parable put He forth unto them . . . ." When Jesus spoke in parables, He always made it clear that He was doing so. We have discussed

269

previously the statement *"put He forth"*—which simply means that He "set before them," or in more simple words, He *gave* them, another parable.

It is interesting to compare these first parables in Matthew 13, each of which concerns the growth of seeds. First we have the sower who sows the seed, then we have the tares and the wheat growing together side by side, and now we have reached the mustard seed. In this parable, Jesus likens the Kingdom of Heaven *"to a grain of mustard seed, which a man took, and sowed in his field."*

Verse 32: *"Which indeed is the least of all seeds: but when it is grown, it is the greatest among herbs, and becometh a tree, so that the birds of the air come and lodge in the branches thereof."*

This parable prefigures the rapid but unsubstantial growth of the mystery form of the Kingdom from an insignificant beginning to a great and noble place in this earth. The figure here of fowls of the air finding shelter in the branches of the mustard tree is taken from the prophecy of Daniel. The passage in Daniel 4:4-14 shows us how insecure such a refuge is. There is only one safe and secure place for mankind—and that is hid with Christ in God, united to the body of Christ through the miracle of the birth of the Spirit. We may be hiding in the "limbs" of many things, and our hiding place may appear to be secure; but it is not. (Please study John 3:1-7, I Corinthians 12:12-27, Ephesians 4:30, and Colossians 3:3.)

"When it is grown, it is the greatest among herbs, and becometh a tree." We think of a mustard plant as a low plant, but in the hot countries of the east, it sometimes grows eight to ten feet high. Historians agree that in the days of our Lord, the mustard plant grew as high as twelve feet; therefore the thought in this verse is not an exaggeration at all. The plant Jesus is speaking of here is definitely in the herb family, for He tells us that *"it is the greatest among herbs."* This particular plant of which He speaks is likened unto a *tree,* for it was large enough and the branches were strong enough for birds to make their habitation there.

We do not have an interpretation of this parable given by our Lord, but the application is plain from the nature of the case. It represents the growth of Christianity in the world from a very small beginning to its now vast dimensions.

In the parable of the *sower,* the fowls of the air devoured some of the seed, but they did not destroy all. Some of the seed did take root. Here in this parable, the mustard seed has grown into a very large plant and now the fowls seek and find rest in its branches. The devil and his host of demons (the fowls of the air) failed to uproot Christianity in the beginning, and they are now opposing it and doing all the damage they can to it in a more subtle way. Satan and his emissaries are found in the very midst of the visible church, and today it is very popular to "get religion" and join a fashionable church.

Satan is wise, cunning, and subtle, as you will see if you will study his approach to Eve in the Garden of Eden. He is not satisfied to stand on the sideline—he puts his own representatives in the forefront. Some of the most popular and most outstanding religious leaders of this age are "fowls of the air"—they are demon "birds." The true Church has always been cursed by these birds of the air—demons dwelling in the bodies of false leaders and teachers. According to II Corinthians 11:13-15, the devil has ordained ministers, and they are preaching his evil doctrine. Do not ever forget that Satan can take on the form of an angel of light just as easily as he can take on the form of a roaring lion; therefore it is no great thing if the devil's preachers and teachers fashion themselves as preachers of righteousness.

". . . lodge in the branches thereof." Notice that these birds do not just casually *visit* the mustard tree. They are comfortable there; they are not disturbed; they are not driven off. Such is true in Christendom. There are false teachers in places of authority who are very comfortable there—and they are never disturbed or driven away.

Additional Comment

The parable of the mustard tree and the parable of the leaven (which follows) both begin with the same phrase—"The Kingdom of Heaven"; therefore their teaching does not contradict the teaching of the parable of the wheat and the tares. This is true of all of the Kingdom of Heaven parables. However, some preachers and teachers use these two parables to teach postmillennial doctrine—that is, that the Church will grow and expand until it is universal and will usher in the Kingdom. They teach that the gradual growth of the Church will finally eliminate evil and bring in universal righteousness. But this is not sound doctrine. The Church was not put here to convert the world, but to *make disciples* of *all nations* (Matt. 28:19, 20). This has been in progress since Pentecost.

Keep in mind that the Kingdom of Heaven is not identical with the New Testament Church. The Church is the body of Christ; He is the head and the foundation of the body (I Cor. 3:11; Eph. 5:23-32; Col. 1:18). It is impossible to rightly divide the Word (II Tim. 2:15) and make the Church and the Kingdom of Heaven one and the same. The Kingdom of Heaven in this dispensation is *Christendom*, including both the visible church and the true Church, the body of Christ.

The mustard tree, with so small a beginning, grew into a virtual monstrosity that attracted all kinds of fowls. They came, they liked what they saw, they lodged in its branches. Let us acknowledge it! *Christendom* has grown today into a giant organization (mustard tree). Religion is "big business," and a lot of unsaved men are lodging in its "branches"—for business reasons, social reasons, and political reasons.

BUT in the midst of the great TRUNK and LIMBS of the mustard tree of religion you will find that little mustard seed, THE GENUINE Church, made up of true believers. They are *in* the world but not *of* the world (John 17:11, 14-16). God's people are referred to as a *"little flock"* (Luke 12:32). *"Many* are called, but *few* are chosen" (Matt. 22:14). (When God called *Israel,* His elect nation, He did not call them because they were a great nation, or great in number. Read Deuteronomy 7:6, 7.)

According to the parable of the mustard tree, the Kingdom of Heaven would become a huge worldly system rooted into the earth, but bearing the name Christian. "Fowls" of all kinds are attracted to the visible system today because of its wealth, power, and advantage in many walks of life. And this giant system furnishes shelter for many agents of the ruler of darkness of this age. We know these agents as modernists, liberals, and other titles.

In Revelation chapters 2 and 3 we have a picture of the complete history of the professing church throughout the Church Age. The closing description is not of a little log cabin in the hills where a few faithful believers gather to pray, but of a mammoth edifice, so to speak, where the members boast of their riches and their goods, and announce to God that they have need of nothing. However, the God of heaven makes it known to them that they are wretched, miserable, poor, blind, and naked. He then spews them out of His mouth (Rev. 3:14-22). However, before God spews out this nauseating system, we read in Revelation 3:7-13 that He takes out the true Church, made up of blood-washed believers. (Note particularly verse 10.)

In interpreting these parables—especially the seven in chapter 13—it must be clearly understood that they cannot be minutely chopped up and placed in the Dispensation of the Church or in the Millennium. We are prone to strain spiritual points to prove our religious fancies or denominational slants.

The Fourth Mystery:
The Parable of the Leaven

Verse 33: *"Another parable spake He unto them; The Kingdom of Heaven is like unto leaven, which a woman took, and hid in three measures of meal, till the whole was leavened."*

Bible scholars do not agree on the interpretation of this parable. Many expositors use it to illustrate the final victory of the Gospel in this Dispensation of Grace. They say the leaven is a symbol of the Gospel of the grace of God, the woman is a symbol of the Church, and the three measures of meal are the world. They teach that eventually the Gospel will permeate the whole human race, the world will be converted, and the Kingdom will be ushered in. However, this is a false interpretation. To teach that the world will be converted in this dispensation is clearly contradicted by the Lord Jesus in His interpretation of the parables of the wheat and tares and of the net and fishes. In those parables, the Lord presents a picture of the converted in an unconverted world—He pictures both good and bad fish in the very Kingdom net itself.

This parable of the leaven is the fourth in order of the seven recorded in Matthew 13, and it sustains a relationship both intimate and logical to the three preceding parables. In the parable of the sower, we are shown how the Gospel would be received after the ascension of the Lord back to heaven. Jesus clearly sets forth how the extension of the Kingdom will occur—it will be by *sowing seed*, not by mingling leaven with the seed. We saw the sower sowing seed on four different types of ground. Only one-fourth of the ground brought forth fruit to perfection, and that was in varying degrees. We have no hint whatsoever of the conversion of the world through the preaching of the

Gospel. Since we are almost two thousand years on this side of that parable, we know that the Gospel has not filled the earth; but on the contrary, mankind is more wicked and ungodly than when they crucified the Lord Jesus Christ. So the parable of the sower shows us that the Gospel will have a limited reception during the absence of the King.

In the second parable, the enemy sows tares and hides them among the good seed at night, in order to corrupt the harvest. When the wheat comes forth, the tares also come forth. The tares closely resemble wheat, and the owner orders the reapers not to gather the tares out of the wheat but to allow them to grow together in the same field until the harvest time, which is the end of the age. Anyone who teaches anything else is knowingly and maliciously contradicting the words of the Lord Jesus Christ, for He plainly interpreted this parable for us. If Jesus had taught that all the world would be converted before His second coming, He would have pictured a field of pure grain, *all wheat*—certainly not a mixture of wheat and tares. Instead, He uses a figure which in the strongest terms declares that the children of the Kingdom and the children of the devil will dwell side by side in this world until He returns the second time.

In the parable of the mustard seed, we have pictured the growth of Christendom as a whole—

not just the true Church—from a very small beginning, until it mushrooms into a huge organization. The birds are used in the parable of the *sower* to indicate the presence and the power of the wicked one, the devil. Is it right to use one interpretation concerning the birds in the parable of the sower and another concerning the birds in the parable of the mustard seed? If the birds were wicked when they devoured the seed, they were the same birds finding shelter in the mustard tree. The professing church today offers shelter to all kinds of "birds," because the church has become a big business operation instead of operating under the power of the Spirit of God.

Since the first three parables clearly set forth that good and evil, saints and sinners, sons of God and sons of the devil, righteousness and corruption, will be here until the end of the age, do we have any right to interpret *this* parable in direct opposition? Does it seem reasonable that this fourth parable would reverse the whole course of the previous teachings of Jesus and announce to us the universal reception of the Gospel and the conversion of mankind?

In this parable Jesus said, *"The Kingdom of Heaven is like unto leaven."* The interpretation of *"leaven"* as a symbol of the Gospel certainly does extreme violence to the unvarying symbolic meaning of leaven throughout the entire Bible. The definition of leaven is "a species of corruption produced by fermentation and tends to putrefaction." Leaven is in its nature a corrupting substance, and it ruins that with which it is mixed. It was recognized as such a corrupting influence that it was required by Almighty God to be put away from everything which typified Christ in the offerings of the Old Testament.

The children of Israel were commanded to put away leaven during their observance of the Passover: "Seven days shall ye eat unleavened bread; even the first day *ye shall put away leaven out of your houses;* for whosoever eateth leavened bread from the first day until the seventh day, that soul shall be cut off from Israel" (Ex. 12:15).

Leaven must not come in contact with the offering of blood, but must be carefully and entirely kept away: "Thou shalt not offer the blood of my sacrifice with leaven . . ." (Ex. 34:25).

Leaven must also be excluded from the meat-offering: "No meat-offering, which ye shall bring unto the Lord, shall be made with leaven . . ." (Lev. 2:11). God commanded the children of Israel to put away leaven because the meat-offering was holy: ". . . eat it without leaven beside the altar: for it is most holy" (Lev. 10:12).

The Lord Jesus clearly stamps the symbol of corruption and evil on the word *leaven* by using it to describe the evil doctrines taught by His enemies: "Then Jesus said unto them, Take heed and beware of *the leaven of the Pharisees and of the Sadducees.* . . . Then understood they how that He bade them not beware of the leaven of bread, but of *the doctrine of the Pharisees and of the Sadducees"* (Matt. 16:6, 12).

These Pharisees and Sadducees were the religious leaders when Jesus came into the world to die on the cross; they had a *form* of godliness, but they denied the power thereof. They believed in the letter of the law, but they did not believe in the spirit of light. Jesus told His disciples, "Beware ye of the leaven of the Pharisees, which is *hypocrisy"* (Luke 12:1). The leaven of the Pharisees was false doctrine, denying the power of God; therefore, their services were no more than rituals. Jesus warned His disciples to beware of these men. The *Sadducees* believed neither in angels nor in spirits; they denied the resurrection. Their religion was materialism—and we still have some of their kind with us today.

The Lord Jesus also used the word "leaven" to warn His followers against the character of King Herod. He said, "Beware . . . of the leaven of Herod" (Mark 8:15). Since the actions of Herod are represented by leaven and since he was a very evil man, we dare not say that leaven is the pure Gospel of the grace of God.

The Apostle Paul speaks of leaven as setting forth corrupt doctrine: "This persuasion cometh not of Him that calleth you. A little leaven leaveneth the whole lump" (Gal. 5:8, 9). Here "persuasion" and its influence are compared by the Apostle Paul to the work of leaven. This persuasion of which he speaks was the doctrine of the Judaizing teachers who came into Galatia and taught the Christians that Gentiles must be circumcised after the manner of the Law of Moses and walk under the law as a rule of life if they were saved. The "little leaven" among the Galatians was the doctrine of legalism; therefore, legalism, ritualism, materialism—all corrupting doctrines—are typified by leaven.

Paul also uses leaven to portray vain boasting of the flesh: "Your glorying is not good. Know ye not that a little leaven leaveneth the whole lump?" (I Cor. 5:6). Glorying in one's self or what one accomplishes is compared in the Word of God to the working of leaven. Leaven causes dough to rise or puff up, and Paul told the Corinthians, "Ye are puffed up" (I Cor. 5:2). Since leaven typified vain glorying in the Corinthian church, it certainly could not typify that which is produced by the precious Gospel of Christ.

Paul further uses leaven to emphasize his warning against the works of the flesh. In Romans 7 we learn that Paul had no confidence in the flesh. Writing to the believers in Corinth, he spoke of "the leaven of malice and wickedness" (I Cor. 5:8). We know that malice and wickedness are not of the Lord nor of the Spirit. (Study Galatians 5:22,23, where Paul lists the fruit of the Spirit.)

In the Scriptures we have looked at, it is clearly set forth that leaven is used UNIFORMLY to signify either corrupt and false doctrine or the energy and the lusts of the flesh—wickedness, malice, vain glory, worldliness, hypocrisy, etc.

As born-again believers we are before God in the character of His risen Son, the Lord Jesus Christ. We are seated in the heavenlies with Him —for God "hath raised us up together, and made us sit together in heavenly places in Christ Jesus" (Eph. 2:6). We are hid in Him, as revealed in Colossians 3:3: "For ye are dead, and your life is hid with Christ in God." We *possess* Him (in the Person of the Holy Spirit): "To whom God would make known what is the riches of the glory of this mystery among the Gentiles; which is *Christ in you,* the hope of glory" (Col. 1:27). And we have received a new nature, according to II Peter 1:4: "Whereby are given unto us exceeding great and precious promises: that by these ye might be partakers of the divine nature, having escaped the corruption that is in the world through lust."

When God the Father looks upon us, He sees no sin, because He sees us in the Son. Positionally, we are now seated *in the Son* at the right hand of God. However, as we walk upon this earth, our bodies will at times become contaminated and we will need cleansing. The blood of Jesus Christ cleanses us from all sin (I John 1:7). This verse does not teach that the blood *has cleansed* (past tense), or that it *will cleanse* (future tense).   But the blood of Jesus *cleanseth* us—day by day, moment by moment, as we trust in the finished work of Jesus.   As little children we are invited to *confess* our sins; and He, the sinless One, cleanses us (I John 2:1, 2).

We are commanded to walk in the steps of our Lord and do all that we do to the glory of God; but even when we do our very best at all times, we fall short of the glory of God because we are in the flesh.   We still possess the *weakness* of the flesh, and the only possible way that we can overcome the flesh is *in Christ.*   The reason so many religionists and church members are living defeated lives in the world is that they have never been born again.

In the light of God's uniform and unvarying testimony about leaven, let us now examine I Corinthians 5:6-8: "Your glorying is not good.   Know ye not that *a little leaven leaveneth the whole lump?   Purge out therefore the old leaven,* that ye may be a new lump, as ye are unleavened.   For even Christ our Passover is sacrificed for us: therefore let us keep the feast, not with old leaven, neither with *the leaven of malice and wickedness;* but with the unleavened bread of sincerity and truth."   Let me point out three things in this passage: First, the *"old leaven";* second, the *"new lump";* and third, *"ye are unleavened."*

The *"old leaven"* is that which corrupts man

283

and manifests itself in evil habits, practices, and tendencies already described; therefore, it is man's fleshly and sinful nature.

The *"new lump"* is a nature in which is no sinful, corrupt, depraved flesh. This speaks of the new nature received when we are born again and placed in Christ, therefore being in union with the risen, living Lord (Col. 3:3; II Pet. 1:4; Rom. 8:9; John 3:5).

"Ye are unleavened" is the standing or the character of the Church of the living Christ: ". . . AS HE IS, SO ARE WE IN THIS WORLD" (I John 4:17). In Jude 24 the Church is described as being presented *"FAULTLESS before the presence of His glory."* Since these Corinthian believers stood before God in the perfection of Christ, Paul urges them to remove the old leaven, to cast off the works of the flesh and to stop all vain glorying. As leaven was forbidden and strictly excluded from the Passover, there must be no toleration whatsoever of the working of leaven (or the working of the flesh) in connection with the anti-type.

As the nation Israel kept the Passover feast in reality, so the Church must keep the feast in spirit and in practice. Keeping the feast is confessing the judgment of death and appropriating the benefits of the judgment of death, the sacrifice of the Lamb of God on the cross, which took away sin and made righteousness possible. The believer is to "reckon" the flesh put to death judicially in the death of our Saviour the Lord Jesus Christ. Even though we know that we will have a battle with the flesh as long as we live in this body, we are commanded, "Likewise reckon ye also yourselves to be dead indeed unto sin, but alive unto God through Jesus Christ our Lord. Let not sin therefore reign in your mortal body, that ye should obey it in the lusts thereof" (Rom. 6:11, 12).

Please study carefully Romans 7, and then joyfully read *Romans 8.* When a believer recognizes his spiritual birthright in Christ—dead unto sin but alive unto God—he will enjoy his Christian life more than he ever has before. When he recognizes that he is "risen with Christ," who abides in his heart, he will have joy that is "unspeakable and full of glory" (I Pet. 1:8).

"*. . . which a woman took and hid . . . .*" Please notice that the woman (in our verse in Matthew) *hides* the leaven in the lump. This reveals to us clearly that the leaven in this verse could not refer to the Gospel which we are to tell forth to all mankind. The *Gospel* is not to be *hidden* but to be made known openly. Jesus told the disciples, "What I tell you in darkness, that speak ye in light: and what ye hear in the ear, *that preach ye upon the housetops*" (Matt. 10:27). And just before He went back to heaven, He told them, "*Go ye into ALL THE WORLD, and preach the Gospel to EVERY CREATURE*" (Mark 16:15).

This certainly does not sound like hiding the Gospel, but rather making it known.

The *"three measures of meal,"* or the lump which is leavened, does not set forth the world, but the visible church. At first the true Church was made up of one hundred twenty members who met in the upper room and were all baptized into the body of Christ by one Spirit. But before long, unbelievers crept into the assembly—we read of Ananias and Sapphira and others. The few came down out of the upper room and stepped into a world filled with unrighteousness and sin— a world that is controlled by the prince of the power of the air. As the true believer travels this journey on earth, he will not only rub shoulders with brothers and sisters in Christ, but with sons and daughters of the devil.

Allow me to sum up what we have studied. The definition of leaven given in the Scriptures that we have read and studied points to corruptness of doctrine, fleshly practices, and evil. The three measures of meal typifies the professing Church in this age. With this in mind, it is evident that we have in the parable the prophetic truth set forth that the time will come (and it is upon us now) when Christendom will be filled with evils, corrupt doctrine, and fleshly energy. To all born-again, spiritually-minded believers, we find in the truth set forth in this parable, an exhortation to face the presence of leaven in our midst and then cast it off and cast out the works of the flesh and walk before God in newness of life.

The time is at hand for the appearing of the Lord Jesus Christ, and as we see "the day approaching" we ought to be careful what we do, where we go, how we live—and certainly by all means, we should be careful what minister and church we support. God deliver us from supporting the enemies of true Christianity and from giving comfort to those who preach error instead of the pure Gospel. Let us hear the solemn warning in II John 7-11 and heed its admonition:

"Many deceivers are entered into the world, who confess not that Jesus Christ is come in the flesh. This is a deceiver and an antichrist. Look to yourselves, that we lose not those things which we have wrought, but that we receive a full reward. Whosoever transgresseth, and abideth not in the doctrine of Christ, hath not God. He that abideth in the doctrine of Christ, he hath both the Father and the Son. *If there come any unto you, and bring not this doctrine, receive him not into your house, neither bid him God speed: for he that biddeth him God speed is partaker of his evil deeds.*"

Verse 34: *"All these things spake Jesus unto the multitude in parables; and without a parable spake He not unto them."*

"Spake He not" in the Greek reads "spoke He

287

nothing." On other occasions we know that Jesus did speak to the people without using parables. Therefore, this statement undoubtedly means that *on this particular occasion* He spoke only in parables, and not one thing did He speak to the crowd that was not in parables.

Verse 35: *"That it might be fulfilled which was spoken by the prophet, saying, I will open my mouth in parables; I will utter things which have been kept secret from the foundation of the world."*

"That it might be fulfilled . . . ." Here again, as many other times, Matthew points out the fulfillment in Jesus of an Old Testament prophecy. This expression requires us to understand a real fulfillment of a real prophecy brought about in the course of the providence of Almighty God. Even though we cannot understand or explain the sovereignty of God, He knows the end in the beginning and all things that will happen from eternity to eternity.

"By the prophet" literally reads *"through* the prophet." The quotation here is from Psalm 78:2. Many of the Psalms are prophetic—and the Psalmist David is expressly called a prophet in Acts 2:29, 30: "Men and brethren, let me freely speak unto you of the patriarch David, that he is both dead and buried, and his sepulchre is with us unto this day. Therefore *being a prophet,* and knowing that God had sworn with an oath to him, that of

the fruit of his loins, according to the flesh, He would raise up Christ to sit on his throne." The heading of Psalm 78 indicates the author to be *Asaph.* He is called a *seer* in II Chronicles 29:30, which is equivalent to a *prophet* (I Sam. 9:9). The Psalm from which Matthew quotes here gives us the history of Israel and points out its lessons.

"... *I will open my mouth in parables; I will utter things which have been kept secret from the foundation of the world."* The Greek for *"I will utter"* reads literally "to pour out copious speech." The statement *"from the foundation of the world"* was a phrase the Hebrews had which usually signi- fied "from antiquity," thus applying in the Psalm- ist's use to the early history of the nation of Israel. Matthew states it is a part of the divine purpose of God for the Lord Jesus to speak in parables and to use this method of instruction.

The Parable of the Wheat and Tares Explained

Verse 36: *"Then Jesus sent the multitude away, and went into the house: and His disciples came unto Him, saying, Declare unto us the parable of the tares of the field."*

Jesus sent the multitude away and went into the house, followed by His disciples. They came to Him and made a request: *"Declare unto us the parable of the tares of the field."* The Lord Jesus explained this parable in such a clear, under-

289

standable manner that it is almost unnecessary to comment on these next few verses.

Verse 37: *"He answered and said unto them, He that soweth the good seed is the Son of man."*

The One who sowed the good seed is the Son of man; the *Son of man* is the *Son of God,* the Lord Jesus Christ. The Son of man came preaching that men should repent, believe, and receive. He declared that He was the bread that came down from heaven, and whosoever would eat of this living bread would never die (John chapter 6).

Verse 38: *"The field is the world; the good seed are the children of the Kingdom; but the tares are the children of the wicked one."*

"The field is the world." Jesus sowed the good seed all over the areas where He traveled while He was here upon this earth. When He departed back to heaven, He left the business of sowing the good seed of the Gospel in the hands of the disciples and others who would receive Him as personal Saviour. Today it is the plan and program of God for believers to spread the Gospel to all the world —yea, to every creature. The seed was to be carried over all the world—not to just one little particular nation or group of people.

". . . the good seed are the children of the Kingdom." We are born into the family of God through the incorruptible seed, the Word of God. "Faith

cometh by hearing, and hearing by the Word of God" (Rom. 10:17). Jesus said, "He that heareth *my Word,* and believeth on Him that sent me, hath everlasting life" (John 5:24). Jesus spread forth the incorruptible seed of the Word, and it brought forth children into the Kingdom of God. The Saviour toiled, ministered, served, and gave His life a ransom for all who would believe—and the children of the Kingdom are the fruit of the labors of the Lord Jesus.

"*. . . the tares are the children of the wicked one.*" In the midst of the children of the Kingdom, the wicked one sowed tares; and these are the children of the devil—hypocrites, unbelievers, skeptics, and mockers. They are in the world and even in the *visible church*—the local assembly. The devil can use a hypocrite in the church to a much greater advantage than he can a person who lives in sin and does not profess to be a Christian.

Verse 39: *"The enemy that sowed them is the devil; the harvest is the end of the world; and the reapers are the angels."*

"*The enemy that sowed them is the devil.*" As we have mentioned before, Satan is the enemy who sowed the tares among the good seed. The devil has always been an opposer of God's children, and he is constantly attempting to corrupt the Church and destroy its usefulness during this age.

". . . the harvest is the end of the world." The wheat and the tares are to grow together until the harvest, with no attempt being made to separate them. Just so, the children of the Kingdom and the children of the devil must remain together until the end of the age, and then they will be separated. The Church will be raptured out of the world, after which God will deal with wickedness in final judgment. *"The end of the world"* is the period which includes both stages of the second coming of Christ, when the righteous and the wicked will be separated in the process of God's dealing with men. The righteous will enter into the joys of the Lord, and the wicked will be cast into the lake of fire and brimstone.

". . . the reapers are the angels." We see in verse 41 that these angels are *"His* angels" and obey His commands. Peter speaks concerning Christ, "Who is gone into heaven, and is on the right hand of God; *angels and authorities and powers being made subject unto Him"* (I Pet. 3:22).

Verse 40: *"As therefore the tares are gathered and burned in the fire; so shall it be in the end of this world."*

The angels will be instructed to gather first the tares and bind them in bundles to burn. But the wheat (the sons of God) will be gathered into "my barn" (verse 30)—the tares are *burned* and the wheat is *housed.* The Psalmist declares that the righteous shall "behold and see the reward of the wicked" (Psalm 91:8).

Verse 41:   *"The Son of man shall send forth His angels, and they shall gather out of His Kingdom all things that offend, and them which do iniquity."*

Jesus, the Son of man, will *"send forth His angels,"* and they will gather the wicked out of the Kingdom and cast them into the lake of fire. "The ungodly shall not stand in the judgment, nor sinners in the congregation of the righteous" (Psalm 1:5). Those who have already died will also be separated and the wicked cast into the furnace of fire, as we find described in Daniel 12:2: "And many of them that sleep in the dust of the earth shall awake, some to everlasting life, and some to shame and everlasting contempt."

As we look at the visible church today, we see hypocrites and unrighteous men. We see those who live in open sin, and those who make fun of and mock believers who live above reproach and refuse to compromise with the world. But we should rejoice and be exceedingly glad, because we have the assurance here in this verse that not too many days hence the wicked will be separated from the righteous and throughout eternity we will not see any hypocrites or unrighteous men. There will be no one to mock and make fun in that Pearly White City. "And there shall in no wise

enter into it any thing that defileth, neither whatsoever worketh abomination, or maketh a lie: but
they which are written in the Lamb's book of life"
(Rev. 21:27).

Verse 42: *"And shall cast them into a furnace
of fire: there shall be wailing and gnashing of
teeth."*

All who have refused to believe on Jesus will be
gathered out and cast into the lake of fire, where
there shall be weeping, wailing, and gnashing of
teeth. What *terrible suffering* hell must be! The
word *"cast"* is much stronger in the original,
denoting *flinging.* The wicked will be literally
FLUNG into hell. David said, "The wicked shall
be *turned* into hell, and all the nations that forget
God" (Psalm 9:17).

The *"furnace of fire"* denotes the fierceness of
the torment that awaits the wicked. The *"wailing
and gnashing of teeth"* is a very graphic way of
expressing the despair of a man who is in pain
and torment beyond description.

Some argue that this is not *real* fire—but if
Jesus is not speaking of real fire, then whatever
He is speaking of is *more horrible* and *painful* than
literal fire. Can you imagine being thrown into
a furnace burning with fire? Can you imagine the
intense suffering, pain, anguish, misery, and woe
of being tossed into a lake of leaping flames? The
Bible teaches us that the place where the wicked

will be tormented forever and ever is a lake burning with fire and brimstone.

If you argue that this is not literal fire, you still cannot deny that it is certain that Jesus meant to make clear to us that the wicked will suffer *terrible anguish* because of their rejection of Him. The *real* is always more glorious or more terrible than the *symbol*—so if literal fire is only a *symbol* of what hell is, then hell is *much worse* than fire as we know it.

Jesus was the first in the New Testament to use the words "hell fire" (Matt. 5:22). Would you accuse Jesus of talking about hell fire if it does not exist? Would you accuse the Lord Jesus Christ of seeking only to *terrify* men by using terms such as "tormented day and night" and "weeping, wailing, and gnashing of teeth"? I beg every unsaved person who may read these words to repent, be born again, and prepare to meet God. Receive the Lord Jesus Christ this moment by faith, and He will save you—for God's Word says, "As many as received Him, to them gave He power to become the sons of God, even to them that believe on His name" (John 1:12).

Verse 43: *"Then shall the righteous shine forth as the sun in the Kingdom of their Father. Who hath ears to hear, let him hear."*

"Then shall the righteous shine forth as the sun in the Kingdom of their Father." All born-again

believers will enter into the joys of the Lord, and they will shine forth as the sun. While we tabernacle among men we are under the shadows of wickedness and unrighteousness; but in that glorious day the wicked will be removed, and then we will shine as the brightness of the firmament *forever and forever:* "They that be wise shall shine as the brightness of the firmament; and they that turn many to righteousness as the stars for ever and ever" (Dan. 12:3).

Man, by nature, is totally depraved, lost—without God and without hope in the world. But God, in His great mercy and love, through His great grace provided salvation for mankind. In Ephesians 2:1-3 we have a word-picture of the sinner which is sordid and ugly. Then in verses 4 through 7 we read: *"But God,* who is *rich in mercy,* for His *great love* wherewith He loved us, even when we were dead in sins, hath quickened us together with Christ, (by grace ye are saved;) *and hath RAISED US UP TOGETHER, and made us SIT TOGETHER IN HEAVENLY PLACES IN CHRIST JESUS: THAT IN THE AGES TO COME HE MIGHT SHEW THE EXCEEDING RICHES OF HIS GRACE in His kindness toward us THROUGH CHRIST JESUS."*

God will put His Church, made up of all born-again believers, in the Pearly White City suspended between heaven and earth. All of God's creation will walk in the light of that city, according to

Revelation 21:24, and all creatures will witness the exceeding riches of God's grace in His kindness toward us through Christ Jesus. What a glorious thing it will be to abide in the Pearly White City with Jesus throughout the endless ages of eternity!

"Who hath ears to hear, let him hear." We read this statement many times in the Word of God; and when we do so, we should also stop, look, and listen, spiritually speaking. We should hear God's warnings, His admonitions, and His instructions, and we should be very careful to follow His teachings in all things and never lean on the arm of the flesh.

The Fifth Mystery:
The Treasure Hidden in the Field

As stated earlier, the seven parables pertaining to the Kingdom (here in Matthew 13) are divided into two parts. The four parables previously studied show how impossible it is for men to produce anything but failure and disaster apart from Christ. He said on one occasion, *"Without me ye can do nothing"* (John 15:5). Man has attempted to bring in the Kingdom, but he has failed—and will *continue* to fail, because the Bible distinctly declares that as it was in the days of Noah and in the days of Lot, so shall it be when Jesus returns the second time (Luke 17:26-30). Paul adds that *"evil men and seducers shall wax worse and worse,* deceiving, and being deceived" (II Tim. 3:13).

The remaining three parables in our study show God's thoughts and purposes perfectly worked out. God's program and plan *cannot* fail.

Verse 44: *"Again, the Kingdom of Heaven is like unto treasure hid in a field; the which when a man hath found, he hideth, and for joy thereof goeth and selleth all that he hath, and buyeth that field."*

"The Kingdom of Heaven is like unto treasure hid in a field." The "treasure" is *Israel*, who is now "hidden" in the field (the world). (Verse 38 of this chapter clearly states that the field is the world.) The Divine Merchant buys the field because there is a treasure there—the nation Israel, beloved by God the Father (Isa. 43:1-4). In the Old Testament, Israel is referred to as the "wife of Jehovah" and the "beloved of Jehovah." This peculiar treasure, the nation Israel, will be saved, restored, and made secure.

Even though hidden now, one day God's "peculiar treasure" will be brought forth in glory, as foretold by the Prophet Isaiah: "ISRAEL SHALL BLOSSOM AND BUD, AND FILL THE FACE OF THE WORLD WITH FRUIT" (Isa. 27:6). This will *literally occur,* and in that day His people will remember and obey His Word. The Lord promised Israel, "If ye will obey my voice indeed, and keep my covenant, then ye shall be *a peculiar treasure unto me* above all people: for all the earth is mine: and ye shall be unto me a kingdom of priests, and an holy nation" (Ex. 19:5, 6). The Psalmist repeats this promise: "For the Lord hath chosen Jacob unto Himself, *and Israel for His peculiar treasure*" (Psalm 135:4).

"*. . . which when a man hath found, he hideth, and for joy thereof goeth and selleth all that he hath, and buyeth that field.*" The *"man"* who in his joy goes and sells all that he has and then buys the field is none other than *the Lord Jesus Christ.* He purchased the world at the awful cost and the tremendous price of His own blood: "Forasmuch as ye know that ye were not redeemed with corruptible things, as silver and gold, from your vain conversation received by tradition from your fathers; *but with the precious blood of Christ,* as of a lamb without blemish and without spot" (I Pet. 1:18, 19). By right of *purchase* as well as by right of *creation,* the world belongs to Him: "*The earth is the Lord's, and the fulness thereof; the world, and they that dwell therein*" (Psalm 24:1).

The *"joy"* here is the result of the fact that Israel will be restored in that glorious day when Jesus comes again. (Please study Deuteronomy 30:9; Isaiah 49:13; 52:1-3, 8, 9; 62:4-7; 65:18, 19; and Romans 11.)

There are those who interpret this parable to mean that the buyer is the sinner seeking Christ, but this is wrongly dividing the Word of God. As pointed out earlier, verse 38 clearly declares "the field is the world." The seeking sinner does not *buy* Christ—the seeking sinner *receives* Christ. The sinner has nothing to sell with which he can buy the treasure, because he is a pauper. Also, *Christ* is *not for sale;* He is the *gift of God*—and a gift is not bought, but *received.* Christ is not "hidden in the field" (or in the world)—nor having found Christ does the sinner *hide* Him, but rather makes known to all that he has found the Saviour. There is no logical way that anyone can make this parable mean that the sinner is the "buyer" buying Christ and hiding Him in the field.

The Sixth Mystery:
The Pearl of Great Price

Verses 45 and 46: *"Again, the Kingdom of Heaven is like unto a merchant man, seeking goodly pearls: who, when he had found one pearl of great price, went and sold all that he had, and bought it."*

When Jesus purchased the treasure of the nation Israel with His shed blood, the tremendous price He paid included the pearl—the New Testament Church. There is no doubt that the *"pearl of great price"* is the true Church of God, of which Jesus is the head and the foundation. The Church of the living God is valuable, as seen by "the riches of the glory of His inheritance in the saints" (Eph. 1:18).

300

Here, as in the preceding parable, the *"man"* is none other than the Lord Jesus Christ, the Son of God who died on the cross. He came into the world *"seeking goodly pearls."* He came seeking those who were lost—valuable indeed, "for what is a man profited, if he shall gain the whole world, and lose his own soul?" (Matt. 16:26).

We know that pearls are found at the bottom of the sea, and the sea in Scripture is symbolic of the Gentile world. The Word of God tells us that Jesus did come to visit the Gentiles (Matt. 12:15-21). He will take a Gentile bride, which is the New Testament Church. We have a perfect outline of God's plan in Acts 15:13-18:

"Men and brethren, hearken unto me: Simeon hath declared how God at the first did visit the Gentiles, to take out of them a people for His name. And to this agree the words of the prophets; as it is written, After this I will return, and will build again the tabernacle of David, which is fallen down; and I will build again the ruins thereof, and I will set it up: that the residue of men might seek after the Lord, and all the Gentiles, upon whom my name is called, saith the Lord, who doeth all these things. Known unto God are all His works from the beginning of the world."

Please notice that the pearl is *one,* typifying that the New Testament Church is one body. A pearl has no divisions, seams, or schisms—a perfect symbol of unity. The unity of the New

Testament Church is described in I Corinthians 12:12-14: "For as the body is one, and hath many members, and all the members of that one body, being many, are one body: *so also is Christ. For by one Spirit are we all baptized into one body, whether we be Jews or Gentiles, whether we be bond or free; and have been all made to drink into one Spirit.* For the body is not one member, but many." (Also please study I Corinthians 10:17 and Ephesians 4:4-6.) So the one pearl is definitely the symbol of the one Church, of which all true believers are members.

Let me point out also that pearls are not formed mechanically or by man's hands. Neither is the true Church. It is formed by the Holy Spirit. We are born into the body of Christ by the Holy Spirit (John 3:1-7). We are baptized into the body by the Holy Spirit (I Cor. 12:13), and we are sealed by the Spirit (Eph. 4:30). There can be no more perfect symbol of the true Church than a pearl.

A pearl is formed by *accretion*—that is, by growth in size, especially by addition or accumulation. Just so, Christ *adds to the Church* by means of His precious blood, the price that He paid for the pearl (I Pet. 1:18, 19). (Also please study Acts 2:41-47; 5:14; 11:24; Ephesians 2:21; and Colossians 2:19.) Jesus purchased the pearl with His own blood, and now He is preparing the pearl for presentation to Himself—and it will be *perfect* (Eph. 5:25-33). The visible church is not perfect;

but the body of Christ, of which each true believer is a part, will be presented to Christ without spot and without blemish. The prophetic Kingdom of Heaven is not the Church, but *a literal Kingdom* that will be set up right here upon this earth. The Church, the bride of Christ, will reign with Jesus, the Bridegroom, in the Millennium and throughout the endless ages of eternity.

The Seventh Mystery: The Dragnet

Verse 47: *"Again, the Kingdom of Heaven is like unto a net, that was cast into the sea, and gathered of every kind."*

Matthew is the only one of the Gospel writers who records this parable. The *"net"* spoken of here is one that is drawn over the bottom of the water, permitting nothing to escape. The idea set forth in this parable is the same as that in the parable of the wheat and the tares—that is, ultimate separation of the wicked from the righteous, the holy from the unholy, the wheat from the tares. The holy will be selected for the Master's use, and the unholy will be cast into the furnace of fire.

It is most interesting to me to note that *the fishermen* are not mentioned at all in this parable. We are not told how many men cast the net into the sea or who they were; they are ignored completely.

Please notice that *"every kind"* speaks of *fish,* for the net does not gather sticks, mud, weeds, and other debris.

Verse 48: *"Which, when it was full, they drew to shore, and sat down, and gathered the good into vessels, but cast the bad away."*

When the net was full it was drawn to the shore. The good fish were collected and put in the vessel, the bad fish were cast away to be destroyed.

The net is the *visible church*—not the true Church, but the visible, local assembly—Christendom. The sea is a type of the nations, throughout all of Scripture. (Please study carefully Revelation 17:15, Isaiah 8:7, and Psalm 65:7.) The gathering is from *all nations,* from all the world. When the net is filled and drawn to the bank, then the separation occurs.

Verse 49: *"So shall it be at the end of the world: the angels shall come forth, and sever the wicked from among the just."*

It is the *angels* that sever the wicked from the just. The angels here are *not* the *fishermen.* In the parable of the tares, the *servants* and the *reapers* are definitely and clearly distinguished. Here in this parable we read that the *angels* shall gather out the wicked *"from among the just"* and will cast them into everlasting punishment.

304

Verse 50: *"And shall cast them into the furnace of fire: there shall be wailing and gnashing of teeth."*

In parables we must never strain the comparisons and symbols beyond their limits. Jesus shows us clearly here that the earthly gives but a faint outline of the heavenly. If you will, compare the mild statement "cast . . . away" in verse 48 with the fearful anti-type found in verses 49 and 50, where the bad will be *cast "into the furnace of fire"* where there is screaming, *"wailing, and gnashing of teeth."*   There are no words in any language of the world to describe such torment, which will go on forever.

Verse 51:   *"Jesus saith unto them, Have ye understood all these things? They say unto Him, Yea, Lord."*

In verses 51 and 52 we have the solemn conclusion of these seven parables. When our Lord asks, *"Have ye understood all these things?"* and the disciples answer, *"Yea, Lord,"* the reply must be taken as spoken from the point of instruction and knowledge they had at that time. Jesus said to them later that there were many things He had to say to them, which they could not understand or receive at that time (John 16:12). Later the Spirit unfolded deeper truths to these men—and certainly to those of us who live in this day and study the Word of God in the light of current events.

Verse 52:   *"Then said He unto them, Therefore every scribe which is instructed unto the Kingdom of Heaven is like unto a man that is an householder, which bringeth forth out of his treasure things new and old."*

The *great* "Householder" is the Lord Jesus Himself—but each instructed disciple is like *"an householder"* who puts forth from his store of knowledge *new things* and *old things.* Those instructed by Jesus were *scribes "instructed unto the Kingdom of Heaven."* They understood then, but they would understand more fully later. Therefore, they would not only bring out spiritual truths from their present understanding, but would ever bring out new and deeper meanings. Every true scribe, every real Spirit-taught scribe of the Kingdom of Heaven, from the ever-increasing stores of his genuine experimental knowledge of the Scriptures is able to bring forth new things as well as old.

Before leaving this section of our chapter, let us observe how naturally this wonderful cycle of parables given by Jesus evolved from the objects and the associations surrounding Him at the time. When He began to teach, He was sitting in a boat in the Sea of Galilee, looking out on the beach at the masses gathered there. His eyes went beyond the people and saw the rich plain of Gennesaret. He saw the paths made by the people as they went to and from their homes to the fields. He saw plots of rich and deep soil, and He also saw the stony places and the neglected spots choked with thorn bushes.

The parables of the sower and the seed, the tares and the wheat, the mustard seed, and the leaven—these had to do with the land and man. Then Jesus left the little boat and went with His disciples into the house, and there He gave to them the explanation of the tares of the field mixed with the wheat. As Jesus continued to speak in parables, He moved from the sower sowing the seed to a man finding a treasure in a field, and then to the pearl of great price. In the pearl we have the treasure of the deep (the sea). All this is simple and natural, because the people in that area were acquainted with the sower, the seed, the leaven, and the practice of men hiding their treasures in the earth. They were also acquainted with pearls found in oysters—and when Jesus spoke of the pearl, that reminded the fishermen of the sea and their nets, and He gave the parable of the net and the fishes.

These seven parables compose in their inner depth of connection one great united whole. As mentioned earlier, we must not stretch or strain a parable too far—because, although the light of prophecy sometimes glimmers, they are given primarily to *teach* and not to *foretell*. We know that parables do point to events that have happened and will happen, but Jesus used them in His

307

The Gospel According to Matthew

teachings to make great truths simple so that the people of His day—and even our day—could better understand the deep things of God.

Jesus Returns to Nazareth;
Rejected by the People There

Verse 53: *"And it came to pass, that when Jesus had finished these parables, He departed thence."*

When Jesus finished giving the parables we have just studied, He did not remain in that area. Jesus was always on a mission; He did not make trips by accident or by chance. He always traveled with one thing in view—to seek and to save "that which was lost" and to make known God's love to poor, lost, dying sinners.   So when He finished His teaching in that particular area, He *"departed thence."*

Verse 54: *"And when He was come into His own country, He taught them in their synagogue, insomuch that they were astonished, and said, Whence hath this Man this wisdom, and these mighty works?"*

"His own country" means the district or the city of *Nazareth.*   It does not refer to Galilee in general, because He was already in Galilee when He gave the parables.

Jesus went into the synagogue in Nazareth

and taught the people in their own place of worship. As He taught them, *"they were astonished"* at His wisdom, His understanding, and the things that He taught. The people to whom He was speaking did not accept Him as very God in flesh. If they had, they would not have asked the question, *"Whence hath this Man this wisdom, and these mighty works?"* They looked upon Jesus as a great teacher but not as the Son of God and their Messiah.

Verse 55: *"Is not this the carpenter's son? Is not His mother called Mary? and His brethren, James, and Joses, and Simon, and Judas?"*

You will note that the first question they asked was *"Is not this the carpenter's son?"* No, He was *not*. He had declared Himself to be the Son of God on more than one occasion, but they did not believe Him.

There is no doubt in my mind that Jesus was very proud of His foster father and that He learned Joseph's trade. This seems to be borne out by Mark's Gospel, where it is recorded, "Is not this the *carpenter*, the son of Mary . . . ?" (Mark 6:3). Indeed He was the carpenter's son by *marriage*—but not by natural birth. No doubt Jesus was proud to be seen working with Joseph—because I am sure that Joseph was a master carpenter, not an ordinary one. It was the custom of the Jews in that day to teach their sons a trade, even though

the father might be a rich man. (You remember
the Apostle Paul learned tent making—and earned
his living this way during part of his ministry.)

The religious leaders thought that Jesus was
conceived out of wedlock and said so in public. In
John chapter 8 Jesus said, "If the Son therefore
shall make you free, ye shall be free indeed." As
He continued speaking with the Pharisees, the
scribes, and the elders, He declared that He was
the Son of God. They declared that they were
Abraham's seed. Jesus said, "If ye were Abraham's
children, ye would do the works of Abraham. But
now ye seek to kill me, a Man that hath told you
the truth, which I have heard of God: this did not
Abraham. Ye do the deeds of your father." Then
they said—and made no apology for it, "WE BE
NOT BORN OF FORNICATION; WE HAVE ONE
FATHER, EVEN GOD" (John 8:36-41). They said
openly that Jesus was an illegitimate, a son of
fornication. These people to whom Jesus was
speaking did not believe that He was virgin born.

*"Is not His mother called Mary? and His breth-
ren, James, and Joses, and Simon, and Judas?"*
Yes, Mary was His mother, and these were His
brothers—but God Almighty was His Father! In
Luke 1:26-35 we find the record that God sent
Gabriel to announce to Mary that she would be
the mother of His Son by the Holy Spirit over-
shadowing her.

It is most interesting to notice that in spite of

their unbelief, their hostility toward Jesus, and their desire to kill Him, they did not question the reality of His mighty miracles. Those people had more respect for Jesus than do the liberals and modernists of our day, who question and even *deny* His miracles. The liberals and modernists will occupy a much lower place in hell than will the scribes and the Pharisees, who said He was a child of fornication and rejected Him.

Verse 56: *"And His sisters, are they not all with us? Whence then hath this Man all these things?"*

"And His sisters, are they not all with us?" We do not have the names of His sisters, but we have the clear statement that He did have sisters. There are various and sundry interpretations concerning the brothers and sisters of Jesus. The only thing I know to do is accept the Word of God and reject all the rest. There is no doubt in my mind that Mary later gave birth to other children, who would actually have been the half-brothers and half-sisters of our Lord.

"Whence then hath this Man all these things?" They asked the question again—"How can this Man do what He is doing? Why is He so different from all the rest of the family to which He belongs?" He *was* different! He was God's Son— He was their Messiah!

Verse 57: *"And they were offended in Him.*

311

*But Jesus said unto them, A prophet is not without
honour, save in his own country, and in his own
house."*

The word *"offended"* means "caused to stum-
ble," as we find in Matthew 11:6. The people
found in Jesus obstacles to believing. They did
not go beyond the natural to look for an answer.
When Jesus said to Nicodemus, "Ye must be born
again," Nicodemus thought only in terms of the
natural. He asked, "How can a man be born
when he is old? Can he enter the second time
into his mother's womb, and be born?" (John 3:4).
He was not thinking of the *supernatural;* he was
thinking only of flesh, and not of spirit.

The same was true in the case of these people
in Nazareth. They stumbled at the humble birth
of Jesus; and in their blind unbelief they would
not listen to His wisdom nor heed His miracles,
but rejected Him without further inquiry or re-
flection.

The things of God are accepted by *faith,* not
by human reason. We cannot take the Bible, God,
Christ, or the Holy Spirit into a laboratory and
examine them under a microscope. Whatever
we receive from God must come by *faith,* and
"without faith it is impossible to *please* Him"
(Heb. 11:6). We disobey God when we do not
believe Him—for "whatsoever is *not* of faith is
sin" (Rom. 14:23).

The Jews stumbled at the humble *life* of Jesus.

They were expecting a mighty king—He was a humble carpenter.

They stumbled at His *lack of training* in the schools of the rabbis—He was trained in a carpenter's shop. In their blindness and unbelief, they refused to listen to His wisdom and accept Him as their Messiah. They did not believe His wisdom was real and genuine, because He did not attain it through their teachers.

Today it is the same. If a young minister wants to really get ahead, he must go to the "right" schools and be taught by the "right" professors, or the denomination will reject him.

"A prophet is not without honour, save in his own country, and in his own house." In ordinary matters of life, a man will be more kindly received among his own kinsmen and early friends than among strangers. But this is not true when the man appears greatly their superior. The neighbors and relatives seem to think of him only as they knew him in the early days, and they are slow to believe that he has become superior to themselves.

Mark adds in his Gospel, ". . . among His own kin" (Mark 6:4). According to John, "Neither did His brethren believe in Him" (John 7:5). They looked upon Jesus as one of their own, and they refused to believe that He was anything *except* just one of the brethren. But He was God in the flesh! He was their Messiah! How sad it is that they rubbed shoulders with Him, they ate with Him, they traveled with Him—but they did not recognize Him as the Promised One.

Verse 58: *"And He did not many mighty works there because of their unbelief."*

The people did not attempt any violence at this time, as they did on the occasion of His former visit to the area (Luke 4:28-30); but they still refused to believe on Him. They persisted in their unbelief so much that Jesus marveled and wondered at their lack of faith (Mark 6:6). Jesus *"did not many mighty works"* or miracles in that area. This was not because of the lack of ability or power on His part, but *"because of their unbelief."* Unbelief is the *ugliest sin* that mortal man can commit against Almighty God.

The Lord's power to work miracles was not *dependent* on men's faith, however. Many times He *healed* without faith on the part of the one healed (Matt. 8:13; 15:28; Luke 22:51; and others). So it was *possible* for Him to work miracles in that area—but He did not because of their unbelief. Let me emphasize that we are not to suppose that the power of Jesus was *limited* by their unbelief. But they were so prejudiced against Him and hated Him so much that they were not in a condition to judge the evidence and to be convinced through miracles that He was divine. Therefore, Jesus knew that it would avail nothing if He performed mighty works and miracles there. Jesus *never* performed a miracle simply to display His power; it was always to the glory of God and the salvation of souls. Study all of the miracles of Jesus, and you will see clearly that He did not perform them simply to make men comfortable or happy, or to remove pain.

Had Jesus performed mighty miracles in that area, the people probably would have declared that He was doing them by the power of the devil. (The *Pharisees* had accused Him of *casting out devils* by the power of the devil—Matt. 9:34; 12:24.) Jesus was omniscient, and He knew the hearts of these people; He knew it would be to no avail to work miracles in that area. The miracles that He did perform were ones of benevolence and of such a nature that they could not very easily be attributed to the devil. He did enough to prove to the people that He was the Son of God if they desired to know the truth. He left them in their unbelief, but He left them *without excuse.*

I cannot emphasize too strongly that in spiritual matters God requires faith—yea, God *demands* faith. As previously pointed out, Jesus said to His disciples, "Have faith in God" (Mark 11:22). And Paul tells us, "Without faith it is impossible to please Him" (Heb. 11:6), and "whatsoever is not of faith is sin" (Rom. 14:23). Mark tells us that after the resurrection of Jesus, He appeared to the eleven disciples and rebuked them sternly because of their lack of faith: "Afterward He appeared unto the eleven as they sat at meat, and *upbraided them with their unbelief and hardness of heart,* because they believed not them which had seen Him after He was risen" (Mark 16:14).

A Terrible Day for Nazareth

Chapter 13 closes with this brief account of the visit of Jesus to Nazareth. As we have seen in these verses, the people of Nazareth were spiritually blind, and they rejected Him. What a terrible day that was for the city of Nazareth! God was in their midst, and they knew Him not. "That Prophet that should come," of whom their prophets spoke (John 6:14; Deut. 18:15, 18), was in their midst—and they did not know Him. The Lamb of God who had come into the world to seek and to save that which was lost was there to save them; but He could not, because of their unbelief. Yes, that was a terrible day for Nazareth—a tragic day. The god of this age, the devil, had blinded their minds, and they refused to see with the eye of the inner man who Jesus was and why He was there. That was a tragic day for Nazareth because Jesus *never passed that way again*—that was His last journey through the city, and it was their *last opportunity.*

Are you born again? Are you saved by God's grace? Are you washed in the blood? If not, this could be *your* last opportunity. Is God speaking to you through this message? If so, I plead with you to receive Jesus now. Believe on the Lord Jesus Christ, accept Him by faith—and He will save you and put within your heart peace and assurance. *Today* is the day of salvation; *now* is the accepted time. God grant that as you read and as you study, if you are not born again these words will cut their way into your heart and the Word of God will find its way into your very soul. The entrance of the Word gives light, and light brings *life*. I beseech you not to do to-day as the people of Nazareth did that terrible day when Jesus passed through their city for the last time and they rejected Him and turned Him away.

Chapter XIV

1. At that time Herod the tetrarch heard of the fame of Jesus,

2. And said unto his servants, This is John the Baptist; he is risen from the dead; and therefore mighty works do shew forth themselves in him.

3. For Herod had laid hold on John, and bound him, and put him in prison for Herodias' sake, his brother Philip's wife.

4. For John said unto him, It is not lawful for thee to have her.

5. And when he would have put him to death, he feared the multitude, because they counted him as a prophet.

6. But when Herod's birthday was kept, the daughter of Herodias danced before them, and pleased Herod.

7. Whereupon he promised with an oath to give her whatsoever she would ask.

8. And she, being before instructed of her mother, said, Give me here John Baptist's head in a charger.

9. And the king was sorry: nevertheless for the oath's sake, and them which sat with him at meat, he commanded it to be given her.

10. And he sent, and beheaded John in the prison.

11. And his head was brought in a charger, and given to the damsel: and she brought it to her mother.

12. And his disciples came, and took up the body, and buried it, and went and told Jesus.

13. When Jesus heard of it, he departed thence by ship into a desert place apart: and when the people had heard thereof, they followed him on foot out of the cities.

14. And Jesus went forth, and saw a great multitude, and was moved with compassion toward them, and he healed their sick.

15. And when it was evening, his disciples came to him, saying, This is a desert place, and the time is now past; send the multitude away, that they may go into the villages, and buy themselves victuals.

16. But Jesus said unto them, They need not depart; give ye them to eat.

17. And they say unto him, We have here but five loaves, and two fishes.

18. He said, Bring them hither to me.

19. And he commanded the multitude to sit down on the grass, and took the five loaves, and the two fishes, and looking up to heaven, he blessed, and brake, and gave the loaves to his disciples, and the disciples to the multitude.

20. And they did all eat, and were filled: and they took up of the fragments that remained twelve baskets full.

21. And they that had eaten were about five thousand men, beside women and children.

22. And straightway Jesus constrained his disciples to get into a ship, and to go before him unto the other side, while he sent the multitudes away.

23. And when he had sent the multitudes away, he went up into a mountain apart to pray: and when the evening was come, he was there alone.

24. But the ship was now in the midst of the sea, tossed with waves: for the wind was contrary.

25. And in the fourth watch of the night Jesus went unto them, walking on the sea.

26. And when the disciples saw him walking on the sea, they were troubled, saying, It is a spirit; and they cried out for fear.

27. But straightway Jesus spake unto them, saying, Be of good cheer; it is I; be not afraid.

28. And Peter answered him and said, Lord, if it be thou, bid me come unto thee on the water.

29. And he said, Come. And when Peter was come down out of the ship, he walked on the water, to go to Jesus.

30. But when he saw the wind boisterous, he was afraid; and beginning to sink, he cried, saying, Lord, save me.

31. And immediately Jesus stretched forth his hand, and caught him, and said unto him, O thou of little faith, wherefore didst thou doubt?

32. And when they were come into the ship, the wind ceased.

33. Then they that were in the ship came and worshipped him, saying, Of a truth thou art the Son of God.

34. And when they were gone over, they came into the land of Gennesaret.

35. And when the men of that place had knowledge of him, they sent out into all that country round about, and brought unto him all that were diseased;

36. And besought him that they might only touch the hem of his garment: and as many as touched were made perfectly whole.

Herod's Troubled Conscience; the Murder of John the Baptist

Verse 1: *"At that time Herod the tetrarch heard of the fame of Jesus."*

"Herod the tetrarch" (also called *Antipas*) was a son of Herod the Great. Herod the Great died probably in the first year after the birth of Jesus and left his kingdom to his three sons, of whom this Herod Antipas was one. He ruled over Galilee and Peraea. The title *"tetrarch"* literally denotes "one who rules over one-fourth of any country." However, after the death of Herod the Great, the term finally came to signify the governor or ruler of any province subject to the Roman emperor.

Herod Antipas was born to a Samaritan woman named Malthace and was the brother of Archelaus. He married the daughter of the Arabian king, Aretas. However, when his half-brother, Herod Philip, came to visit him, he fell in love with Philip's wife, Herodias, and prevailed upon her to leave her husband and marry him. No doubt Herodias was vain and thought this was a great opportunity for her to become a famous woman.

In order for Herod Antipas to marry Herodias he was forced to divorce the daughter of Aretas, which caused his father-in-law to declare war on him later. In that war, Herod Antipas was totally defeated and his army destroyed by Aretas. The Jews believed this was divine vengeance, the wrath of God poured out upon Herod because of the wicked sin of divorcing his own wife to make Herodias his wife.

About A.D. 37 Herodias' brother Agrippa (the Herod mentioned in Acts 12) was through the friendship of the emporer Caligula appointed king over the area that Philip formerly reigned over, and this ambitious woman was consumed with envy. She did not give her husband any rest at all, in spite of his love of ease and his caution. Therefore he went with her to the city of Rome to see if he could not also be formally declared king, but Agrippa sent letters to the emperor of Rome accusing Antipas of treason in corresponding with the Parthians. When the emporer received these letters, he believed their message and Antipas was thrown out of office and banished to Gaul, where he died in great misery.

It may be a bit confusing to distinguish between the three Herods called by that name in the New Testament. *Herod the Great* murdered the infants when Jesus was born. The wise men came seeking the locality of the birth of Jesus, and Herod instructed them to return to him when they found the baby so that he could worship Him also. However, God warned the wise men to return home another way; and when Herod saw that he was mocked, he murdered all the babies in the city in an attempt to destroy this new King.

The second Herod, *Herod Antipas,* is the one we are studying now—the one who beheaded John the Baptist.

The third was *Herod Agrippa,* who killed James and put Peter in prison (Acts chapter 12).

These are the three main Herods, but we know

from the historian Josephus that many others of the family bore the name of the founder, Herod the Great.

Herod *"heard of the fame of Jesus."* He heard a report concerning a Man who was very famous — One who performed miracles and did marvelous things. History tells us that during the latter years of his reign, Herod usually lived at Tiberias. This was a town located on the west shore of the Sea of Galilee, also called the Sea of Tiberias (John 6:1). We have no account of our Lord visiting this town, and perhaps He stayed away to avoid exciting the hostility of Herod, who might be jealous of One beginning to be popularly regarded as King of the Jews. However, the teachings and miracles of Jesus were reported throughout the known world, even to the courts of Herod.

Herod was not a religious man by any means, and therefore he paid very little attention to religious movements among the subjects of his domain. If he had paid attention to what was being said, he would have heard of Jesus much earlier than this — for Jesus had been actively at work in Galilee — teaching, performing great miracles — and His fame had spread throughout that part of the land.

Verse 2: *"And said unto his servants, This is John the Baptist; he is risen from the dead; and therefore mighty works do shew forth themselves in him."*

"And said unto his servants . . . ." I personally believe that the servants of the king had heard the teachings of Jesus and witnessed some of His miracles. It seems to me that since he made this announcement to his servants, undoubtedly it was the servants who made known to him the fame of Jesus. We know according to Luke's Gospel that Joanna, the wife of Chuza, Herod's *steward,* was converted. She accompanied Jesus in His journey and ministered to Him and to His followers in her home: "And it came to pass afterward, that He went throughout every city and village, preaching and shewing the glad tidings of the Kingdom of God: and the twelve were with Him, and certain women, which had been healed of evil spirits and infirmities, Mary called Magdalene, out of whom went seven devils, and *Joanna the wife of Chuza Herod's steward,* and Susanna, and many others, which *ministered unto Him of their substance"* (Luke 8:1-3).

We learn in Acts 13:1 that a foster brother of Herod the tetrarch was converted, probably at a later time: "There were in the church that was at Antioch certain prophets and teachers; as Barnabas, and Simeon that was called Niger, and Lucius of Cyrene, and *Manaen, which had been brought up with Herod the tetrarch,* and Saul."

". . . This is John the Baptist; he is risen from the dead." When Herod heard of this Person performing mighty miracles, he made a definite

325

statement that it was John risen from the dead. The emphasis is on *"he,"* implying that this remarkable Person of whom they heard was no one else but John the Baptist come to life again. The notion that John had come back from the dead did not originate with Herod, but was the belief of some who had expressed their feelings about Jesus. Luke tells us, "Now Herod the tetrarch heard of all that was done by Him: and *he was perplexed, because that it was said of some, that John was risen from the dead;* and of some, that Elias had appeared; and of others, that one of the old prophets was risen again. And Herod said, John have I beheaded: but who is this, of whom I hear such things? And he desired to see Him" (Luke 9:7-9).

In Matthew 16:13-16 we read: "When Jesus came into the coasts of Caesarea Philippi, He asked His disciples, saying, Whom do men say that I the Son of man am? And they said, *Some say that thou art John the Baptist:* some, Elias; and others, Jeremias, or one of the prophets. He saith unto them, But whom say ye that I am? And Simon Peter answered and said, Thou art the Christ, the Son of the living God."

As Jesus traveled toward Jerusalem teaching, preaching, and working miracles, some of the people came to Him and warned Him to flee for fear Herod would kill Him. But Jesus said, "Go ye, and tell that fox, Behold, I cast out devils, and I do cures to day and to morrow, and the third day I shall be perfected" (Luke 13:31, 32). Jesus called Herod a *fox*—and as far as I can find in the Word of God, this is the *only place* that Jesus or God ever referred to a man as an animal. Herod was cunning and sly like a fox.

Herod's desire to see the Lord Jesus (Luke 9:9) was perhaps partly that he desired to settle the question as to His identity. At any rate, Herod was curious and desired to see Jesus work a miracle in his presence. We know that later he desired to see Jesus perform some great miracle, but Jesus did not do so; neither did He answer him one word—the only man that I can find in the Scriptures to whom Jesus flatly *refused to speak.* This is a very solemn passage to me. We have the account in Luke 23:6-12:

"When Pilate heard of Galilee, he asked whether the Man were a Galilaean. And as soon as he knew that He belonged unto Herod's jurisdiction, he sent Him to Herod, who himself also was at Jerusalem at that time. And *when Herod saw Jesus, he was exceeding glad: for he was desirous to see Him of a long season, because he had heard many things of Him; and he hoped to have seen some miracle done by Him.* Then he questioned with Him in many words; *but He answered him nothing.* And the chief priests and scribes stood and vehemently accused Him. And Herod with his men of war set Him at nought, and mocked

Him, and arrayed Him in a gorgeous robe, and sent Him again to Pilate. And the same day Pilate and Herod were made friends together: for before they were at enmity between themselves.''

"*. . . therefore mighty works do shew forth themselves in Him*"—or, since this was one who had returned from the dead, this would answer why He was able to perform the tremendous miracles that were reported of Him. According to this statement by Herod, we know that he was not an atheist. He was not a complete unbeliever in that he denied the existence of God, God's power, and the ability of men to do miracles through the power of God. He did at least believe that one from the other world had power not possessed by one in this world.

Imprisonment and Death of John the Baptist

Verse 3: *"For Herod had laid hold on John, and bound him, and put him in prison for Herodias' sake, his brother Philip's wife."*

Matthew here stops to tell about Herod's putting John the Baptist to death; and as an introduction to that, he tells of John's imprisonment, in verses 3 through 10. No doubt it was about a year earlier that John was put in prison. In Matthew 4:12 we read, "When Jesus had heard that John was cast into prison, He departed into Galilee." In Matthew 11:2-6 we read that John, who was in prison, sent his disciples to question Jesus concerning whether or not He was the Messiah.

The historian Josephus tells us that the place where John was placed in prison and finally beheaded was Machaerus, which was about seven miles from the Dead Sea on the northeast side. Machaerus was first fortified by one of the Maccabean princes about 100 B.C. It was destroyed by the Roman conquerors but later rebuilt and very strongly fortified by Herod the Great. Machaerus lies on mountains that are much higher than those around Jerusalem. Ruins of a city covering more than a square mile have been found by archaeologists in the very spot pinpointed by Josephus as the place where John was imprisoned and beheaded.

The prison was on a very high mountain peak and was well fortified by a valley that was more than a mile long, making it almost impossible for anyone to reach the place without being seen. The top of this particular hill was one hundred yards in diameter and was fortified by an impregnable citadel. In this citadel have been found two dungeons—one of them deep, with its side still intact and with scarcely a break in them. In the sides of these two dungeons small holes are still visible in the masonry. In these holes it is clearly seen that staples of wood and iron had once been fixed securely. Without a doubt one of these dungeons was the place where John the Baptist was imprisoned.

329

On this high hill, Herod the Great built an expensive and beautiful palace. The vicinity of the fortress and city was remarkable for mineral fountains—bitter and sweet, hot and cold—whose mingled waters were used for baths. These mineral baths were reported to be good for various diseases—especially nervous disorders. The most outstanding of these baths was located north of Machaerus and was called Callirhoe, which means "fair-flow." History tells us that Herod the Great was carried to this fountain not very long before he died. Machaerus was a lovely place in the summer, as well as being a very strong fortress on the boundary between Peraea and Arabia.

Herod Antipas visited Machaerus often because of the beautiful mountains and palace and the luxurious baths. Some Bible scholars believe that while visiting that area, Herod sent for John the Baptist and asked him about his marriage to Herodias. (John did much of his preaching on the eastern bank of Jordan; therefore it would have been near this spot.) These Bible scholars believe that when John visited Herod to discuss Herod's marriage to Herodias, Herod *"laid hold on John, and bound him, and put him in prison for Herodias' sake, his brother Philip's wife."* In that remote, hopeless prison, in one of those deep, dark dungeons, the great baptizer existed for probably more than a year, until he was beheaded. He was allowed visitors occasionally, who brought news to him of the outside world—and they told him about the works of Jesus (Matt. 11:1-6).

John the Baptist did not have, as we do, a New Testament containing Romans 8:28. But I am sure that he knew in his heart that all things *do* "work together for good to them that love God, to them who are the called according to His purpose." We learn from John's experience that God's thoughts are not our thoughts and God's ways are not our ways. God *could have* delivered John the Baptist from prison (and from death), but He did not. From man's viewpoint, the life of John the Baptist was a pitiful failure and his death a dreadful calamity. However, from *God's* point of view, John the Baptist lived a glowing, successful life—and his death was just as glorious as his life. God was in the midst of it all, making the wrath of men to praise Him and in due time delivering His faithful witness from the horrors of a filthy Roman dungeon to the glories of the throne room of the Eternal. As we look upon this episode, it appears to us the humiliating death of a defeated soldier; but when we see what really happened, it is the account of an honorable promotion of a victorious soldier in the greatest army ever—*the army of the Lord*.

John the Baptist did not have *these* words either—"Yea, and *ALL that will live godly in Christ Jesus SHALL SUFFER PERSECUTION*" (II Tim. 3:12). The appointed path of a true servant of God in this world that *hates* God, is the path of persecution and suffering. But if we suffer with Christ, we will *reign* with Him. If we deny Him, He will also deny us (II Tim. 2:12). This is God's plan for His servants. If we suffer because we live wrong, there is no glory in such suffering; but if we are living right and glorifying God in our lives, then we glorify God in suffering. Listen to these words in I Peter 2:19-25:

"This is thankworthy, if a man for conscience toward God endure grief, suffering wrongfully. For what glory is it, if, when ye be buffeted for your faults, ye shall take it patiently? but if, when ye do well, and suffer for it, ye take it patiently, this is acceptable with God. For even hereunto were ye called: because Christ also suffered for us, leaving us an example, that ye should follow His steps: who did no sin, neither was guile found in His mouth: who, when He was reviled, reviled not again; when He suffered, He threatened not; but committed Himself to Him that judgeth righteously: who His own self bare our sins in His own body on the tree, that we, being dead to sins, should live unto righteousness: by whose stripes ye were healed. For ye were as sheep going astray: but are now returned unto the Shepherd and Bishop of your souls.*"

Verse 4: *"For John said unto him, It is not lawful for thee to have her."*

John stood before Herod exactly as he stood before the Pharisees, when he declared that they were a "generation of vipers" (Matt. 3:7). He stood before him in the spirit and the power of Elijah—just as Elijah stood before Ahab and Jezebel. (Certainly Herod and Herodias had much in common with Ahab and Jezebel.) John the Baptist had fearlessly rebuked the Pharisees and Sadducees, as well as the masses of common people, for their evil. Now he stands before a *powerful political monarch,* and he reproves him just as *sternly* and *clearly* as he did the religionists and others to whom he preached. John did not rebuke and condemn Herod only because he married Herodias, but for *all* his acts of evil and ungodliness: "Herod the tetrarch, being reproved by him for Herodias his brother Philip's wife, *and for all the evils which Herod had done"* (Luke 3:19).

John the Baptist did not put any frills on what he said to Herod. He made it very clear— *"IT IS NOT LAWFUL FOR THEE TO HAVE HER."* The statement means "it is not permissible." The Law of Moses strictly forbade such a marriage: "Thou shalt not uncover the nakedness of thy brother's wife: it is thy brother's nakedness" (Lev. 18:16). Such an act is further condemned in Leviticus 20:21: *"If a man shall take his brother's wife, it is an unclean thing:* he hath uncovered his brother's nakedness; they shall be childless."

The law required a man to marry his *deceased*

brother's wife if there were no children; but here the brother was living, and there was a daughter. Also, Herodias was the *niece* of Herod, and the law also forbade the marriage on these grounds (Lev. 18:12-17). But John said that it was not lawful for Herod to have Herodias because she was his brother's wife. The Jewish customs of that time allowed a man to divorce his wife for almost any cause at all (Matt. 19:3-8), but for a woman to remarry while that divorced husband was alive was certainly not lawful.

Thank God for John the Baptist—and for preachers down through the ages who have not been afraid to preach against sin in high places. We have too little stern, clear preaching against sin today. I believe a minister should *name* sin and point out to those in high places where they are disobeying God. God forbid that I ever allow a man's position or a man's money to close my mouth against sin. We are commanded to *"preach the Word:* be instant in season, out of season; *reprove, rebuke, exhort* with all longsuffering and doctrine" (II Tim. 4:2). We need to name sin and then to make clear the only remedy for such sin—the blood of the Lamb of God: "Almost all things are by the law purged with blood; and *without shedding of blood is no remission"* (Heb. 9:22). It is His blood that cleanses us from all sin: "If we walk in the light, as He is in the light, we have fellowship one with another, and

*the blood of Jesus Christ His Son cleanseth us
from all sin"* (I John 1:7).

Verse 5: *"And when he would have put him
to death, he feared the multitude, because they
counted him as a prophet."*

Herod desired to put John to death but was
afraid to do so because the masses regarded John
the Baptist *"as a prophet."* They believed that
he was a man sent from God. Please notice that
it was the masses of *common* people who had this
opinion of John—not the Jewish religious rulers
and leaders (Matt. 21:25-27, 32).

Mark gives a very interesting fact concerning
the desire of Herod to put John to death: "John
had said unto Herod, It is not lawful for thee to
have thy brother's wife. Therefore Herodias had a
quarrel (grudge) against him, and would have
killed him; but she could not: *for Herod feared
John, knowing that he was a just man and an
holy, and observed him; and when he heard him,
he did many things, and heard him gladly"* (Mark
6:18-20).

There may be those who say that this contra-
dicts Matthew's statement that Herod desired to
put John to death. But remember that John was
in prison for a year or more. At the first, no
doubt, Herod was very angry when John condemned his marriage; but from time to time as he
witnessed John in prison, he came to realize that

John the Baptist was more than an ordinary prisoner. So there is no conflict between the words of Matthew here and the words in Mark's account. It is possible that while Herod generally favored John and desired to protect him from the wrath of his wife, sometimes he felt inclined to yield to Herodias' murderous desire but was restrained from doing so by his fear of the masses, who thought John was a prophet. One thing is clear: Herodias was watching for a chance to carry out her desire to get rid of John. "And when a convenient day was come" (Mark 6:21), she carried out her murderous scheme against God's prophet.

Verse 6: *"But when Herod's birthday was kept, the daughter of Herodias danced before them, and pleased Herod."*

"When Herod's birthday was kept . . . ." Some Bible scholars suggest that this does not necessarily mean Herod's birthday from the standpoint of the day he was *born*—it could mean the day that he became ruler in that area. However, we have no Scripture to prove this or even suggest it. It may be that in those days kings did refer to their ascension to the throne as a "birthday," but to me it seems that this was a celebration of the date of Herod's *birth*. It is not unreasonable to believe that he was at Machaerus for that occasion and was accompanied by some of the leading cabinet members and officials of his domain. In Mark 6:21

we see there were many dignitaries present on that occasion: "When a convenient day was come . . . Herod on his birthday made a supper to his *lords, high captains*, and *chief estates* of Galilee."

"*The daughter of Herodias . . . .*" This daughter was born to Herodias by her former marriage to Philip. According to historians, her name was *Salome*, and also apparently she was sometimes called by her mother's name, Herodias—even as so many men of the family were called Herod.

". . . *danced before them*"—that is, in the midst of them. The Greek used here denotes *publicity*, indicating that the girl danced in full view of all present. The Holy Spirit did not see fit to reveal to us through the inspired pen of any of the Gospel writers just how far her indecorous act went. It could be that she removed most of her clothing; it could be that she went through bodily contortions that so inflamed the men that they lost all of their ability to reason. In that day, it was considered improper for a female to even *dance* in public at all, so perhaps she did not go nearly so far as ungodly women go today to entice men. However, this girl had been instructed by her mother, and there is no way of knowing how far her mother would go to carry out her diabolical plans.

Men of that day did hire women to dance at their entertainments; but the business was highly disreputable, and it was commonly taken for granted

that the women were of low character. It is true
that Jewish women lived in less seclusion than in
other eastern nations, and there are instances
recorded in the Word of God where women took
part in songs and dancing in public rejoicing. But
this was considered a religious act and quite different from taking the place of dancing girls at a
feast. One such instance is recorded in I Samuel
18:6: "It came to pass as they came, when David
was returned from the slaughter of the Philistine,
that *the women came out of all cities of Israel,
singing and dancing, to meet king Saul, with
tabrets, with joy, and with instruments of musick.*"
(Also compare Exodus 15:20.)

In that day it was disgraceful both to dance
and for a *virgin* to come into a banquet hall to
men who had drunk freely. Considering this viewpoint, the only conclusion that we can reach is
that if a respectable maiden came in to dance at
a feast, it would be very surprising to the guests.
It could hardly fail to be regarded as very *un-
becoming* to a princess. It was, therefore, a very
bold and daring thing for Herodias to send her
daughter to dance before Herod and his cabinet
members. Would they be shocked by the im-
modest exposure of a princess? Or would they be
fascinated by the voluptuous movements of her
body in an oriental dance? Regardless of what
Herodias thought, her wicked scheme worked. Her
daughter *"PLEASED HEROD."*

When those who were invited to the supper saw that Herod was pleased, they were also pleased because they dare not go against Herod. In fact, Mark tells us, "When the daughter of the said Herodias came in, and danced, and pleased Herod *and them that sat with him,* the king said unto the damsel, Ask of me whatsoever thou wilt, and I will give it thee" (Mark 6:22). No doubt the babbling, half-drunk dignitaries burst out in expressions of satisfaction when they saw Salome performing her lewd, suggestive dance before their very eyes. We do not have any way of knowing just how long the dance lasted, but we know it lasted long enough to inflame the passion of Herod to the point that he lost all ability to think or to reason. When the lewd dancer finished her act, the king made one of the most foolish and unreasonable promises that any king ever made.

Verse 7: *"Whereupon he promised with an oath to give her whatsoever she would ask."*

Do you see what I see in that promise? She could have asked for *his* head. He made the promise *"with an oath"*—and if she had asked for his head, the soldiers would have been forced to carry out the request of the damsel. When a king swears that he will do something, then he must do it or lose all respect of the people of his domain. Mark tells us that the king promised "unto the half of my kingdom," but he does not tell us that the king excluded his own head or his jewels (Mark 6:23). The girl could have asked for *anything* up to half of the kingdom; she could have been co-ruler with Herod. This shows what a demented, twisted mind will do. However, instead of asking for something worthwhile that could have brought her great pleasure, she carried out the wicked desire of her ungodly mother.

Verse 8: *"And she, being before instructed of her mother, said, Give me here John Baptist's head in a charger."*

"... being before instructed of her mother." I can imagine the look of satisfaction on the face of Herodias when she realized how well her bold scheme had succeeded. As pointed out earlier, Herod was afraid to kill John because the masses looked upon him as a prophet; but Herodias was determined to see him dead, and now she is about to carry out her vengeance against the preacher she hated so much. The daughter, of course, carried out the wish of her mother. In Mark 6:25 we read that she went "with haste unto the king." The Greek word translated correctly means "with zeal" or "eagerly, happily." She ran to the king in much haste and said, *"Give me here John Baptist's head in a charger."*

The word *"charger"* actually means a dish or a platter. Bible scholars agree that this dish was taken from the table where the food at the banquet had been devoured by the half-drunk officials. They simply reached over on the table, removed a dish, and sent the executioner to chop off John's head.

To us it may seem a very strange request to bring John's head on a platter, but it was customary in that day for princes and princesses to require the heads of persons ordered for execution to be brought to them. They were gratified by the sight of the bloody head as proof that their one-time enemy would bother them no more. These men and women were so bloodthirsty that they received great joy upon beholding the bloody head of one they hated.

Verse 9: *"And the king was sorry: nevertheless for the oath's sake, and them which sat with him at meat, he commanded it to be given her."*

"The king was sorry." The young woman's request to bring John's head on a platter shocked the king; and regardless of how drunk he may have been, he came to himself and realized what a fool he had been. We know that Herod did respect John as a man sent from God, and he *feared* John because the people believed that he was a prophet of God (Mark 6:20). Herod had saved John from death earlier, because Herodias would have put him to death immediately if it had not been for the king (Mark 6:19). Herod was an ungodly man, but many times even the most ungodly of men

have a fear of God—not that they fear Him in the right manner, but they are afraid of what may happen to them if they do something against God.

This was a terrible price to pay for a few moments of lustful entertainment, and Herod's conscience was now at work. He would have preferred another request not so wicked, one that would not have involved him in such a risky thing as the damsel had asked him to do.

". . . nevertheless for the oath's sake, and them which sat with him at meat . . . ." Herod felt that he had no alternative—he was bound by the oath he made. He was not thinking of what the act would do to God's prophet nor how God would feel toward him for committing such an act, but he was thinking of his reputation in the eyes of those present. I personally believe that the strongest reason for murdering John was not because of the oath, but because of *"them which sat with him at meat."* He was afraid of what they would say if he made a promise to this damsel and then deliberately broke his word—so *"he commanded it to be given her."*

"Them which sat with him at meat" simply means those who sat with him at the table. The word "meat" in that day meant food of all kinds in general; now, however, it is restricted to the flesh of animals and does not convey the full idea of the original.

Verse 10: *"And he sent, and beheaded John in the prison."*

Herod granted the girl's request. Mark tells us that Herod murdered John immediately: "And *immediately* the king sent an executioner, and commanded his head to be brought: and he went and beheaded him in the prison" (Mark 6:27).

A feast such as this one usually began about sundown; therefore it was probably late in the night when the executioner came to John's cell, woke him up, and chopped off his head. The great prophet, the forerunner of our Lord, John the Baptist, was now delivered from a dungeon and promoted to the paradise of God. It was only a matter of seconds—the knife struck his neck, his head fell to the floor, and his body lay quivering—but his spirit took its flight to paradise. There is no time element between the last breath and the appearance in the presence of God. The Apostle Paul tells us about it in II Corinthians 5:1-8:

"For we know that if our earthly house of this tabernacle were dissolved, we have a building of God, an house not made with hands, eternal in the heavens. For in this we groan, earnestly desiring to be clothed upon with our house which is from heaven: if so be that being clothed we shall not be found naked. For we that are in this tabernacle do groan, being burdened: not for that we would be unclothed, but clothed upon, that mortality might be swallowed up of life. Now He that hath wrought us for the selfsame thing is God, who also hath given unto us the earnest of the Spirit. Therefore we are always confident, knowing that, whilst we are at home in the body, we are absent from the Lord: (for we walk by faith, not by sight:) we are confident, I say, and willing rather *to be absent from the body, and to be present with the Lord."*

John the Baptist finished his work on earth. He had announced the coming King, preaching and baptizing as God ordained him to do. Since he had completed his ministry upon this earth, for John the Baptist to die was *gain.* For any believer who is faithful and is prepared to meet God, death is not tragic at all, because his spirit is immediately in the presence of God. John had been suffering in prison over a year, and I am sure that he was ready to go Home.

Verse 11: *"And his head was brought in a charger, and given to the damsel: and she brought it to her mother."*

Some have said that this cannot be taken literally because it would have ruined the festivities that were in progress at the time. But the Bible clearly states that Herod sent an executioner *immediately* to the cell and beheaded John, brought his head on a platter, and gave it to the girl — *"and she brought it to her mother."* The historian Josephus tells us that Alexander Janneus (an an-

cestor of Herodias), while holding a feast with his
concubines, commanded that eight hundred rebels
be crucified in their view. Not only the rebels
but their wives and children were murdered before
the eyes of these women. History tells us of many
such bloody massacres just to satisfy the lust of
ungodly powerful rulers.

Whether or not Salome lifted John's head from
the platter we do not know, because the Word of
God does not tell us. But she undoubtedly danced
away to her mother with the head of John as if
bearing to her some choice dish of food from the
king's table. This shows just how criminal and
animal-like human beings can become when they
completely sell out to the devil.

Herod Antipas and his family are not mentioned
anymore in Matthew's Gospel; however, he is
mentioned in Luke 13:31-33 and in Luke 23:7-12.

Verse 12: *"And his disciples came, and took up
the body, and buried it, and went and told Jesus."*

"His disciples came . . . ." There were still
many who regarded themselves as the disciples of
John the Baptist. (Please notice Matthew 9:14.)
This was not the fault of John, because those who
declared they were his disciples knew very well
how constantly John had pointed them to Jesus,
declaring that He was the Messiah. When John
sent messengers to inquire of Jesus whether or not
He was the Messiah (Matt. 11:2, 3), the report

brought back by them must have had a deep impression upon the men who claimed John as their leader. Some, however, continued to regard John as the Messiah for many years.

"... *and took up the body, and buried it* ...." The *head* of the great prophet, John the Baptist, was with Herodias. What she did with it we do not know. But his *body* was in the hands of John's disciples. They buried their beloved prophet with tenderness and care, and then they "*went and told Jesus*" what had happened.

Probably the reason they went to Jesus was threefold: (1) Jesus and John were closely connected in their ministry, since John was our Lord's forerunner, the man who had announced His coming. (2) No doubt they also needed consolation in that hour—not only because of John's death, but also because of the possibility that *they* would be killed. (3) They probably thought that Jesus was in danger too, because He was preaching the same message that John had preached—the coming of the Kingdom.

Verse 13: "*When Jesus heard of it, He departed thence by ship into a desert place apart: and when the people had heard thereof, they followed Him on foot out of the cities.*"

"*When Jesus heard of it* ...." What Jesus heard may have been either the news of the death of John or that Herod considered Him to be John

the Baptist, risen from the dead. There is some
difficulty here in conceiving how the narration is
to proceed continuously. The death of John the
Baptist is evidently parenthetically inserted; and
yet the retirement of our Lord in this verse seems
to be the immediate consequence of His hearing
of that occurence. But this may well have been
so, for: (1) The disciples of John would be some
days in bringing the news, and the fame of Jesus
mentioned in verse 1 could have reached Herod
in the meantime. (2) The expression "at that time"
(v. 1) could extend over a considerable space of
time.

"He departed thence by ship . . . ." Mark says
that Jesus and the apostles departed "by ship
privately" — or *secretly* (Mark 6:32). He crossed
the Sea of Galilee and went *"into a desert place
apart."* According to Luke 9:10, this was "a desert
place belonging to the city called Bethsaida." A
"desert place" simply means a place that is not
cultivated, where there are few or no people living.
East of the Sea of Galilee there were many acres
of country that were rough, uncultivated, and used
primarily by the shepherds to graze their flocks.

Many believe that Jesus went to this desert
place because it would be safer — and it is true that
Jesus never threw Himself unnecessarily into the
path of danger. When Satan invited Him to leap
from the pinnacle of the temple, He said, "Thou
shalt not tempt the Lord thy God" (Matt. 4:7).

347

So there is a possibility that He went to the desert because it was safer there. Jesus knew that He would die—He came into the world to die—but He knew it was not *time* for Him to die.

According to Mark 6:31, however, Jesus went into the desert to be away from the crowd. I feel that He had a peculiar love for John the Baptist. (Even though Jesus was God, He was also *man*—and as the Son of man He could feel as we feel.) Although He was omniscient and knew all about the death of John, when John's disciples brought the news it touched Him very deeply. (Jesus *wept* at the tomb of *Lazarus,* whom He loved—John 11:5-36.) So I personally believe that though He may have gone to the desert for safety, He also went for consolation.

However, if Jesus went to the desert to get away from the crowd, He did not have the blessedness of being alone very long, because *"when the people had heard thereof, they followed Him on foot out of the cities."*

Verse 14: *"And Jesus went forth, and saw a great multitude, and was moved with compassion toward them, and He healed their sick."*

Mark tells us that when the people saw Jesus and the disciples departing, they "ran afoot thither out of all cities, and outwent them, and came together unto Him" (Mark 6:33). Then *"Jesus went forth, and saw a great multitude"*—and when

He saw them He was *"moved with compassion . . . and He healed their sick."* He, the Great Physician, had come to seek and to save the lost; but as He traveled the path to Calvary, He performed miracles for the needy people He met along the way.

In Mark 6:34 we read that Jesus was moved with compassion when He saw the multitude because they reminded Him of sheep not having a shepherd. A shepherd cares for his flock, feeds them and defends them from wolves and other wild beasts that would kill them. He cares for the young and feeble; he leads them into green pastures and beside the still waters. In the country where Jesus was at this particular time, the land was used chiefly to pasture flocks.

When Jesus saw the multitude He was moved with compassion toward them, for they were as *sheep without a shepherd*—meaning that they had no teacher to guide them, no preachers or prophets who cared for them. The religious leaders, who boasted that they were custodians of the law of God, were proud and haughty. They cared for those who were rich but were not concerned about the masses of poor people. They did not attempt to teach or lead them—they never spent any time helping the poor and the needy. The multitudes therefore flocked to Jesus when He came on the scene preaching the Gospel to the poor: "The blind receive their sight, and the lame walk, the lepers are cleansed, and the deaf hear, the dead are raised up, *and the poor have the Gospel preached to them"* (Matt. 11:5).

Christ the All-Sufficient One; the Feeding of the Five Thousand

Verse 15: *"And when it was evening His disciples came to Him, saying, This is a desert place, and the time is now past; send the multitude away, that they may go into the villages, and buy themselves victuals."*

The feeding of the five thousand is the only miracle of Jesus that is recorded by all four Gospel writers. The fact that Matthew, Mark, Luke, and John all recorded this miracle is an indication of its importance and the universality of its application. There are many practical, spiritual, typical, and dispensational lessons to be learned from the account of the feeding of the five thousand. We see Jesus in this story as the all-sufficient Saviour; no need is too great for Him. Regardless of what may arise, His resources are sufficient.

The Son is co-equal with the Father in providing our salvation and spiritual needs. He created the heavens, and the earth is the work of His hands: *"ALL THINGS were made by Him; and without Him was not any thing made that was made"* (John 1:3). He *made* all things, and all things are upheld by His power (Col. 1:16, 17;

Heb. 1:3). He opens His mighty hands and feeds every living creature upon the face of the earth. If it were not for His goodness, there would be no food, no water, no sunshine. Every good gift and every perfect gift is from God (James 1:17). Jesus—God in flesh—is not only sufficient for us and for our needs, but He is able to supply the need of all of His vast creation: "Not that we are sufficient of ourselves to think any thing as of ourselves; but *our sufficiency is of God*" (II Cor. 3:5).

All that is accomplished in our lives is done through the grace of God, as seen in II Corinthians 9:8-11: *"God is able to make all grace abound toward you;* that ye, always having all sufficiency in all things, may abound to every good work: (as it is written, He hath dispersed abroad; He hath given to the poor: His righteousness remaineth for ever. Now He that ministereth seed to the sower both minister bread for your food, and multiply your seed sown, and increase the fruits of your righteousness;) being enriched in every thing to all bountifulness, which causeth through us thanksgiving to God."

Also, in Philippians 4:19 Paul said, "My God shall supply all your need according to His riches in glory by Christ Jesus." With God there is no such thing as an impossible task. God never sets before us a ministry or a job that we cannot do. Whatever He calls us to do, He is able to supply the need, the strength, and the power to do it.

351

Not only does this miracle of the feeding of the five thousand set forth the omnipotent power of Christ, but it points to the giving of His body that we might have life—and have it abundantly. It sets forth His mighty power, by which He could lay down His life and take it again so that we might have life through His death, burial, and resurrection.

In the preceding verses, we learned that Jesus crossed over the Sea of Galilee, evidently to get away from the crowd—for Mark tells us that "there were many coming and going, and they had no leisure so much as to eat" (Mark 6:31). But the multitude learned very quickly where Jesus was, and they followed Him. This does not mean that all who followed Jesus believed that He was their Messiah nor that all of them believed He was able to save them from sin. But they saw His miracles, they saw their diseased loved ones healed; and, as a whole, the multitude followed Him out of curiosity and for excitement, hoping to see Him perform some other miracle: "And a great multitude followed Him, *because they saw His miracles which He did on them that were diseased*" (John 6:2).

According to John 6:4, the feast of the Passover was nigh, and there were thousands of Jews from all over the known world on their way to Jerusalem at that time. There were more people in that area at that particular time than at any other time of the year. Notice that Jesus did not go to Jerusalem to observe the Passover, because the persecution of the early Christians in the city was so severe. Instead, He chose to observe the Passover in Galilee.

It was not by accident that Jesus performed this specific miracle at this particular time. The Passover feast was a time when the minds of the Jewish people were centered on the flesh of the lamb they would be eating and on the blood that would be sprinkled. Jesus was always alert to every opportunity to present Himself to His people as their own sacrificial Lamb and to use every occasion to speak of the flesh and the blood which must be appropriated by those who wish to escape the damnation of hell.

In John chapter 6 we have a much fuller account of the feeding of the five thousand than Matthew gives us, and following the miracle is the message concerning the Bread of Life. The Gospel of Matthew is the *Kingdom* book and emphasizes the Kingdom more than the plan of salvation, while the Gospel of John is the *salvation* book (John 20:30, 31) and emphasizes the Bread of Life which we must eat in order to live eternally.

Jesus lifted up His eyes and saw the great multitude of people—but that does not mean that He did not know they were there until He saw them with His physical eyes. He knew they would be there before they ever came. He loved them, and His heart was moved when He realized that they were there, not only without *physical* food, but in total ignorance concerning *spiritual* food.

When evening came, *"His disciples came to Him, saying, This is a desert place, and the time is now past."* Then they suggested that He *"send the multitude away, that they may go into the villages"* and buy food.

Verse 16: *"But Jesus said unto them, They need not depart; give ye them to eat."*

In verse 15, the disciples suggested that Jesus send the multitude away to get food. But Jesus replied, *"They need not depart; give ye them to eat."*

John tells us that Jesus asked Philip, "Whence shall we buy bread, that these may eat?" (John 6:5). Philip was the logical one to be asked this question—for he was a native of Bethsaida, and if anyone knew where bread could be bought in large quantities in that area, Philip would certainly be the one to know. But Jesus had another motive in asking the question: "This He said *to prove him:* for He Himself knew what He would do" (John 6:6).

Five thousand hungry men plus the women and children comprise a tremendous crowd of people; and since bread in that day was made by hand and baked in small ovens, there would not have been enough bread in the entire area to feed so great a mass of people. But Jesus knew exactly what would happen. He knew the lad was there with his few loaves and fishes. He knew how the multitude would be fed; but He was dealing with men of slow hearts, and He therefore dealt with them as man would deal with man—that is, up to the point of the miracle of multiplying the loaves and fishes.

This was no accident—it did not just "happen." It was foreordained of God before the world was. Jesus came to do the work the Father had given Him to finish (John 5:36). The feeding of the multitude at the Passover time was one of those works foreordained of God for that particular time, to set the stage for the wonderful lesson on the Bread of Life given to us in John chapter 6.

John 6:7 reveals that Philip spoke to Jesus and said, "Two hundred pennyworth of bread is not sufficient for them, that every one of them may take a little." I do not know exactly how much two hundred pennyworth of bread would be compared to our money today, but certainly it would not be enough to feed so great a mass of people. Like Nicodemus, Philip was thinking in the realm of the natural. He had not yet realized that this One whom he followed could supply bread for *five thousand* as easily as He could supply it for *one*.

Undoubtedly, this two hundred pennies was the amount of money in the common purse of the disciple band. Since *Judas* carried the bag (John 12:6), we do not know how Philip knew how much money it contained. But when Jesus asked him where to buy bread for the people to eat, Philip answered by giving Him a report on the state of the treasury.

Verse 17: *"And they say unto Him, We have here but five loaves, and two fishes."*

While Judas, no doubt, and Philip, counted the pennies, there was another disciple very busy. Matthew does not mention him, but John does: "One of His disciples, *Andrew*, Simon Peter's brother, saith unto Him, There is a lad here, which hath five barley loaves, and two small fishes: but what are they among so many?" (John 6:8,9). Andrew was searching for bread. It is true that he did not find *very much* bread—but while others counted the money, he searched for bread. (There are a lot of folks in our churches today who are willing to count the money, but there are very few who are willing to go out and search for souls and point them to the living Bread who came down from heaven.) I can almost see Andrew now as he moves about in that mass of people until he finally finds one little boy with a lunch—*"five loaves, and two fishes."*

Have you ever attempted to persuade a man to surrender his lunch to you? Have you ever asked a boy to give you his lunch? Try it sometime, and see how far you get. There must have been something very unusual about Andrew. It was Andrew who brought Peter to Jesus (John 1:40, 41), and it was Andrew who approached Jesus concerning the Greeks (John 12:20-22). Now it is Andrew who not only finds the lad with the lunch, but *secures* the lunch and presents it to Jesus.

Andrew had been with Jesus since the beginning of the Lord's ministry and had witnessed His miracles—even the changing of the water into wine at the marriage in Cana. I believe that he knew Jesus could and would do the impossible with the lad's lunch. If he did not believe this, why did he search for even a small portion of food and then persuade the lad to surrender it into the Lord's hands? Even though he asked, "What are they among so many?" it seems evident to me that Andrew expected a miracle that would be adequate to the occasion. When we *expect* things from God, we *receive* them.

Verse 18: *"He said, Bring them hither to me."*

I like this sentence recorded by Matthew—*"Bring them hither to me."* Do you know that Jesus could have performed the miracle *without* the five loaves and two fishes being brought to Him? But He allowed Andrew to have a part in this miracle. Andrew brought what they had, he laid it in the hands of Jesus, and Jesus took over from there and supplied the need.

Verse 19: *"And He commanded the multitude to sit down on the grass, and took the five loaves, and the two fishes, and looking up to heaven, He blessed, and brake, and gave the loaves to His disciples, and the disciples to the multitude."*

"He commanded the multitude to sit down on the grass." What a majestic contrast is presented here. Concerning the five loaves and two fishes, Andrew had asked, "What are they among so many?" Jesus answered very simply, "MAKE THE MEN SIT DOWN" (John 6:10). There was no excitement, no confusion, no fretting, no irritation on His part because of the seeming lack of faith among His disciples. He simply instructed them to seat the people. Mark tells us "they sat down in ranks, by hundreds, and by fifties" (Mark 6:40). There was no disorder. Jesus is not the author of confusion, but He is the author of peace and quietness. Jesus did not get in a hurry—He never did anything hurriedly or in a haphazard way. The Word of God clearly tells us, *"Let ALL things be done decently and IN ORDER"* (I Cor. 14:40).

There was "much grass" in that area (John 6:10), and it was in the springtime just before the Passover. In the Holy Land the spring is the most beautiful time of the year. I had the wonderful privilege of visiting the area in the spring of the year, where Jesus performed this miracle. Not only was there much grass, but thousands of beautiful poppies of all colors were blooming on the hillsides. Against such a background, what a beautiful sight it must have been to see five thousand men with their families seated in groups of fifties and hundreds.

". . . *and took the five loaves, and the two fishes, and looking up to heaven, He blessed, and brake . . . .*" John speaks of Jesus having "given thanks" (John 6:11). It is interesting to point out that the Greek word used in John 6:11 for "thanks" is also used in the parallel miracle to this one (the feeding of the four thousand, in Matthew 15:36); and the same word is used by Matthew, Mark, Luke, and Paul in speaking of the Lord's Supper— where Jesus "gave thanks" and passed the bread and cup to His disciples (Matt. 26:27; Mark 14:23; Luke 22:19; I Cor. 11:23-25). The bread and the cup were symbols of His broken body and His shed blood, as the broken bread in this miracle is a symbol of His broken body for us.

". . . *and gave the loaves to His disciples, and the disciples to the multitude.*" Jesus took the five loaves and two fishes—and when He had given thanks, He broke the bread and fishes and distributed the food to the disciples. The disciples then passed it on to those who were seated on the grass.

Let me point out something here that is very significant: Jesus did not make a big show by creating a *great heap* of loaves and fishes. He could have spoken the word and there would have been a huge pile of food; but He did not do this. Jesus did not put a lot of emphasis on the spectacular. He took the lad's lunch, He gave thanks, He broke the bread and fishes, and He gave it to the disciples to feed the people. As Jesus broke the bread and gave it to His followers, a miraculous multiplication of the bread took place. There was a continual creation of bread—the bread was constantly replenished, and the same thing happened as He broke the fishes.

Jesus could have multiplied the loaves without breaking them, but in breaking the bread He was showing the necessity of His broken body. His manner of distribution of the loaves also shows us that the Bread from heaven is sufficient for all. When one poor, hungry sinner receives the Bread of Life there is no less bread than before—there is *enough for all.* God's grace abounds for all; and when one sinner is saved, there is still as much grace as before. Jesus is the Bread of Life—and His body was broken and His blood was shed for us. We are saved by receiving Him, the living Word; and His precious blood washes away all sin for the believer. Jesus was setting forth in this miracle the truth that the Bread from the Father had come down from heaven to man and that the Bread would be broken and His blood would be shed for the remission of sins.

That must have been a wonderful experience

for the disciples. Would it not have been wonderful to watch Jesus with His tender hands take a little barley loaf, break it — and where He had broken the bread immediately more appeared? He kept on breaking, and the disciples kept on carrying food to the people, until five thousand men and their families were satisfied. What a day that must have been for the disciples!

Verse 20: *"And they did all eat, and were filled: and they took up of the fragments that remained twelve baskets full."*

"They did all eat, and were filled." No one went away hungry. The same is true in the spiritual sense. If you are hungry spiritually, it is *your* fault, not God's. There is bread enough, there is milk enough, there is living water enough, to satisfy *all* saints *at all times.*

The statement *"were filled"* gives proof positive that the miracle was real and genuine, not *spiritual.* Jesus served actual bread and literal fish. It was not a sensation or something the people simply imagined. They ate real food until they were filled and completely satisfied.

". . . and they took up of the fragments that remained . . . ." Here is set forth a Christian principle that we are not to be wasteful. It is a sin to waste. How well do I remember my old-fashioned parents instructing us not to waste food. When my father served our plates, he gave us

what he felt we should eat, and we were expected to eat it. Jesus instructed the disciples to "Gather up the fragments that remain, that nothing be lost" (John 6:12). Not only is it a sin to waste *food*, it is a sin to waste money, time, health, or opportunity.

"*. . . twelve baskets full.*" They gathered twelve baskets of fragments left over from five little barley loaves and two fishes! Certainly no one could deny that a mighty miracle had been wrought. Some Bible scholars declare that this was the greatest miracle of our Lord's earthly ministry. Certainly this miracle did manifest His creative power—but since "without Him was not any thing made that was made," it was not at all difficult for Him to take the loaves and fishes and multiply them to feed more than five thousand hungry people. If we believe "In the beginning God," then we should have no trouble believing that God in flesh could take five loaves and two fishes, bless them, break them, feed multitudes, and have twelve baskets full left over!

Verse 21: "*And they that had eaten were about five thousand men, beside women and children.*"

Here Matthew tells us that "*about five thousand men, BESIDE WOMEN AND CHILDREN*" were fed. Some outstanding Bible scholars suggest that, conservatively speaking, there were probably ten thousand in the crowd. If just fifty per cent of the men present were married and had one child per family, that would be another five thousand people to feed. To feed so many was certainly a stupendous miracle, but Jesus can do that which is beyond the imagination of man.

Jesus Walks on the Water

Verse 22: *"And straightway Jesus constrained His disciples to get into a ship, and to go before Him unto the other side, while He sent the multitudes away."*

Matthew and Mark both tell us that the Lord *"CONSTRAINED His disciples to get into a ship"* and travel to *"the other side"* of the sea. *"Constrained"* is more exactly rendered "obliged, or compelled." It could be that the disciples were hesitant to leave the scene where so great a miracle had just been wrought, or that they sympathized a little with the crowd, who sought to put Jesus on the throne and proclaim Him King. But whatever the cause of their reluctance to leave, Jesus *compelled* them to get into the ship. (We know the Jews were looking for a powerful monarch to rule over them and deliver them from the tyranny of the Romans. In John 6:15 we read, "When Jesus therefore perceived that they would come and take Him by force, *to make Him a king*, He departed again into a mountain Himself alone.")

It is easy to see why the Jews thought that

One who could work such a miracle as they had just witnessed could certainly lead them out of Roman bondage. They were much more concerned about their slavery under Rome than they were about the slavery of sin that bound them. They were looking for a mighty deliverer, but not a *spiritual* deliverer. They wanted someone to deliver them from the Romans, not a Messiah to save them from sin.

Jesus had not come to be enthroned by force at the demand of a mob. He knew that He would be King indeed and sit on the throne of David, but this was not the hour for that. He would be King of kings and Lord of lords, but the *crown of thorns* must precede the kingly crown. He came the first time to pay the sin-debt; He will come the second time to sit on the throne and reign in righteousness.

The Word of God does not tell us to whom the ship mentioned in this verse belonged. Probably it belonged to Peter or one of the other fishermen there on the Sea of Galilee. They had left their nets to follow Jesus (Matt. 4:18-22), but that does not necessarily mean that they had disposed of all of their fishing equipment.

(John says the disciples "went over the sea *toward Capernaum*," while Mark says they were to "go to the other side before *unto Bethsaida*." Many Bible scholars believe that Bethsaida, the city of Philip and Andrew and Peter, was distinct

from the Bethsaida in whose neighborhood the
feeding of the five thousand took place.)

Verse 23: *"And when He had sent the multitudes away, He went up into a mountain apart to
pray: and when the evening was come, He was
there alone."*

Jesus sent the disciples to the other side of the
sea, He *"sent the multitudes away,"* and then *"He
went into a mountain...to pray."* Yes, Jesus, very
God in flesh, loved to be alone at special times to
pray. (Read Matthew 26:39; Mark 1:35; Luke 5:16
and 6:12.) Although the Word of God commands
us to fail not "the assembling of ourselves together" (Heb. 10:25), to pray together, worship together,
and to bear one another's burdens, it is also wonderful to be *alone* with God. It seems that we can
get a little closer to God when we are alone in
prayer. How well I remember that shortly after I
was converted I had a favorite spot on my father's
farm where I would go after the noonday meal and
commune with God alone. Those were some of the
sweetest hours of my Christian experience.

Verse 24: *"But the ship was now in the midst
of the sea, tossed with waves: for the wind was
contrary."*

The disciples had gotten on the ship and had
started across the Sea of Galilee. Jesus then sent
the multitudes away, and He remained alone to

pray. *"But the ship was now in the midst of the sea, tossed with waves . . . ."* Jesus could see the little ship in the middle of the Sea of Galilee as the storm arose, for Mark says, *"He saw them toiling in rowing"* (Mark 6:48). The Greek reads, "The sea was being raised, stirred." The waves were beginning to lash against the sides of the ship. Although Jesus saw them thus harassed He did not go to them for a long time.

The disciples' experience in the storm-tossed waters is a type of the storms we face as believers today in this wicked, storm-tossed world. They had just enjoyed a mountain-top experience with the Lord—they had just witnessed the miracle of the feeding of the five thousand—and this experience was followed by the darkness of the midnight hour. It was followed by a very bad storm in the midst of the Sea of Galilee. Christians today enjoy the miracle of the new birth and become possessors of the Holy Spirit and the divine nature, being made new in Christ (John 3:3-7; Rom. 8:9, 14, 16; Eph. 4:30; and II Pet. 1:4). When one is born again he is a new creation in Christ, and he enjoys the glorious experience of his "first love." Then suddenly the storm clouds lower and the tempest begins to sweep in. Temptations begin to beat upon him, trials beset him— but thank God, "we are *more than conquerors* through Him that loved us" (Rom. 8:37).

Jesus had become the object of the disciples'

faith in the matter of material provision, as they witnessed the miracle of the loaves and the fishes. Now He makes Himself the object of their faith as having to do with fear and danger as they traveled this pilgrim journey. He who had given thanks as He broke the bread and literally created food for thousands, was also Creator and Commander of the wind and the waves. The purpose of the storm was, in the plan and program of God, to lead the disciples into a deeper faith and more complete trust in Jesus.

As we grow in grace, we increase in faith. If every day, spiritually speaking, was a sunshiny, calm day; if there were no storm clouds, if the tempest did not ever come upon us, then I am afraid we would be sluggish and careless Christians. God allows the storms to come, but the God who permits them is able to deliver us out of them. When the storms beat upon us, we know they are for our good and God's glory: *"We know that ALL things work together for good to them that love God, to them who are the called according to His purpose. . . . What shall we then say to these things? If God be for us, who can be against us?"* (Rom. 8:28, 31).

Verse 25: *"And in the fourth watch of the night Jesus went unto them, walking on the sea."*

According to Roman time, *"the fourth watch of the night"* was between three o'clock and six o'clock in the morning. The darkest time of the night is just before the dawn—and it was sometime between 3:00 A.M. and 6:00 A.M. that Jesus saw that the little ship was about to sink and went to the disciples, *"walking on the sea."* There are those who try to spiritualize this event, but the words "walking on the sea" are used by all three of the Gospel writers who record this incident (Matthew, Mark, and John). These words have no other meaning here, than that the Lord Jesus walked *bodily* on the surface of the water there that night.

Job says concerning the Almighty, "Which alone spreadeth out the heavens, and *treadeth upon the waves of the sea"* (Job 9:8). Would it be difficult for God, who *created* the waters, to walk upon the surface of those waters? If you believe God, then you will have no trouble believing that Jesus actually walked on the surface of the water that night.

In John's Gospel we read that the disciples had rowed about twenty-five or thirty furlongs, which would be about three miles. According to *The International Standard Bible Encyclopaedia,* the greatest breadth of the Sea of Galilee is in the North and is about seven miles. Therefore the disciples were literally right in the middle of the sea. Matthew and Mark both tell us that the wind was "contrary," and we gather from this that the wind was *against* them—which would account for their rowing instead of using sails.

Someone may ask why the Scripture does not say *exactly* where they were and give the exact distance from shore. But let it be remembered that the disciples were in a boat which was being tossed to and fro on a stormy sea. Besides, it was a very dark night, and they could not be expected to give the exact measurement of their distance from the shore. The *Holy Spirit* knew exactly where they were and could have told John the precise number of furlongs, even to the fraction of an inch; but it so pleased Him to let John use a popular mode of expression—*about* twenty-five or thirty furlongs.

Verse 26: *"And when the disciples saw Him walking on the sea, they were troubled, saying, It is a spirit; and they cried out for fear."*

When the disciples saw a figure approaching them, walking on the water, *"they were troubled"* —and naturally so. (How do you think *you* would feel if you were in a boat on a lake in a storm at three o'clock in the morning and saw someone approaching your boat?) They said, *"It is a spirit* (a ghost)"—*"and they cried out for fear."* I believe they literally cried out in anguish because they were so terrified.

We see in this miracle the suspension of all laws of nature. Jesus was walking across the stormy sea as you and I would walk on a concrete sidewalk! It was as easy for Him to *walk* on the waters as it was for Him to *create* the waters upon which He was walking. The entire miracle was of the supernatural—and there is nothing that can unnerve and alarm human nature quite as much as being brought suddenly face to face with supernatural powers (or beings) thought to be connected with the spirit world. The disciples were human; they did not have the New Testament as we do today, and while they accepted Jesus as their Messiah they had known Him personally but a short while—and certainly they had never seen any man walk on water!

Verse 27: *"But straightway Jesus spake unto them, saying, Be of good cheer; it is I; be not afraid."*

Immediately Jesus spoke to calm and cheer the disciples. He knew they were terrified beyond words. So *"straightway"*—or immediately—He spoke to them and said, *"Be of good cheer; it is I; be not afraid."*

Peter's Little Faith

Verse 28: *"And Peter answered Him and said, Lord, if it be thou, bid me come unto thee on the water."*

This incident respecting Peter is peculiar to Matthew's Gospel alone. The account is in very strict accordance with Peter's confident and impetuous character.

It seems to me that the disciples would have recognized the Lord's voice and His Person, but apparently they did not. Peter answered Jesus, saying, *"Lord, IF IT BE THOU, bid me come unto thee . . . ."* The form of the request implies that Peter was not fully convinced it was Jesus who had spoken the words of comfort.

Verse 29: *"And He said, Come. And when Peter was come down out of the ship, he walked on the water, to go to Jesus."*

Not only did *Jesus* walk on the water, but He gave *Peter* the power to do the same thing. Peter got out of the boat, stepped down on the water, and *"he walked* (at least a few steps) *on the water."* When Peter said, "Lord, if it be thou, bid me come unto thee on the water," Jesus did not say, "Peter, IT IS I." No, Jesus did exactly what Peter asked Him to do. Peter said, "Bid me come," and Jesus simply said, *"COME."* So Peter actually walked on the WORD—he left the boat upon the invitation, *"Come."*

Verse 30: *"But when he saw the wind boisterous, he was afraid; and beginning to sink, he cried, saying, Lord, save me."*

As long as Peter kept his eyes on Jesus, all was well. But the moment he turned his gaze to the angry waves around him, *"he was afraid"* and he began *"to sink."* Then *"he cried . . . Lord, save me!"* You will notice that when Peter began to sink, he did not dress up his prayer with beautiful adjectives. If he had taken time to make a "pretty prayer," the fish would have been nibbling his toes before he had finished the words of introduction to his prayer.

There was no time for hypocrisy; Peter needed help immediately. He was sinking, he would drown, he would be lost in the storm in a few seconds of time. So he prayed from his heart—three words— *"LORD, SAVE ME!"*

Verse 31: *"And immediately Jesus stretched forth His hand, and caught him, and said unto him, O thou of little faith, wherefore didst thou doubt?"*

Just three little words, but Jesus heard them— *"and immediately"* He stretched out His hand, caught Peter and lifted him up. Then He reprimanded Peter for his *"little faith"* and asked him, *"Wherefore didst thou doubt?"*

Verse 32: *"And when they were come into the ship, the wind ceased."*

When Jesus and Peter entered into the ship, the great storm was over at that instant. John tells us that *"immediately* the ship was at the land whither they went"* (John 6:21).

The Apostle Peter

Since I first started to study the Word of God,

Peter has been my favorite disciple. John the Beloved was a great disciple and extraordinary in many ways, but somehow Peter was so human and so like most of us in many ways. He did many praiseworthy things during his lifetime, but this episode of walking on the water certainly ranks as one of the greatest things Peter ever did.

Peter was just an ordinary fisherman. He knew the Sea of Galilee and how extremely stormy it could become even in a moment. (When we were in that area several years ago, we crossed this sea in a small boat. We left the shore in bright sunshine; but while we were out on the sea a cloud appeared, and the missionary who was with us became quite concerned before we reached the shore.) Storms sweep down upon the Sea of Galilee very quickly. Peter knew this, and he knew how treacherous the water was; but in spite of all that, he stepped out of the ship onto the waves when Jesus said, "Come."

Peter has been criticized by some for *sinking* after he stepped out of the boat, stood on the water, and realized that he was walking on it. Some say there was absolutely no excuse for him beginning to sink. However, we must never underestimate the greatness of this achievement of this fisherman. Surrounded by the waves, knowing the danger of the sea, faced with absolute impossibilities, Peter found strength in the word of Jesus— a word that was actually a command. When Jesus said, "Come," Peter forgot everything else. He forgot the waves, the storm, the water. He stepped into the midst of the rolling tempest, and he did not sink. He stood for a time.

We have a tremendous lesson here for all born-again believers. When we become a child of God, we are safe and secure in God's grace. We might refer to this as the little "salvation ship." But eventually the command of Jesus calls us to step out into the unknown. We can always rest assured, however, that Jesus will be there. We may not be able to *see,* we may not be able to *understand;* but we know that He has promised never to leave us nor forsake us. We might argue with ourselves and with our God-given conscience and say, "I cannot do that," or "I cannot go there." But we hear the words of the Holy Spirit penned down by Paul: *"I can do ALL things through Christ which strengtheneth me"* (Phil. 4:13). God gives grace sufficient in the hour that we need it the most.

The true born-again Christian knows that God will never allow a believer to be engulfed by temptation while he is steadfastly looking into the face of Jesus. As long as Peter kept his eyes on Jesus, things went well—and if we keep *our* eyes on Jesus, His all-sufficient grace and power make it possible for us to trample under foot the very waves that would overwhelm and destroy us. Yet even the *greatest* saint is endangered when he takes his eyes off Jesus. When Peter "SAW THE WIND BOISTEROUS, HE WAS AFRAID." At first, Peter was trusting—but frantic despair gripped his heart when he looked at the waves around his feet. When he ceased listening to and looking into the face of his Master, he began to sink and was forced to cry out for Jesus to rescue him.

I pointed out earlier that Peter prayed a short, sincere, and powerful prayer—one of the greatest on record. He said just three little words—"LORD, SAVE ME." There are three things that I would like to point out about these three words that Peter used:

First, *Peter realized the terrible predicament he was in.* He was sinking and would drown in only a matter of seconds. His predicament was grave, dangerous, and deadly—which is a true picture of any sinner. *Peter* was not a sinner; but we have here the *picture* of a sinner, whose predicament is grave, dangerous, and deadly.

Second, *Peter knew that Christ was near and was able to perform another miracle to save him.* All of this happened in the mind of Peter in a fraction of a second. He was drowning, but he knew Jesus was near and would save him from a watery grave.

Third, *I would like to emphasize again the sincerity and simplicity of Peter's prayer.* There was no time to put together an elaborate prayer—no time to tell Jesus that he had left his nets and followed Him or how much good he had done and *would* do if Jesus would spare him. Only one thing mattered—instant salvation from a watery grave.

There is a time for long prayers, and there are times when one will pray all night; but this is not pertaining to a sinner. There are ministers who instruct the sinner to pray until he is saved—but the only prayer that a poor sinner needs to pray is, "Lord, save me." If the sinner has heard the Word of God, is under conviction, and realizes that Jesus is the only Saviour, all he need do is cry out for the Lord to save him. A simple, short prayer *from the heart* will bring salvation to the vilest; and when a *believer* is in dire need, all he need do is make known to God the need, and God will deliver.

God does not answer all prayers of a Christian as quickly as He answered Peter's prayer, however. We read that *"IMMEDIATELY* Jesus stretched forth His hand, and caught him, and said unto him, O thou of little faith, wherefore didst thou doubt?" Jesus could have spoken the word and they would have been standing in the boat, but He did not do so. Peter realized that the waves were still surging around his feet, and they were still some distance from the boat; but all fear had disappeared. Peter was no longer afraid, because the hand of the One who had power over the wind and the waves was resting on his shoulder. He was now walking on the water that would have taken his life had it not been for Jesus. The all-sufficient Saviour had saved him from a watery grave—and finally he and Jesus were in the boat.

Verse 33: *"Then they that were in the ship came and worshipped Him, saying, Of a truth thou art the Son of God."*

When those who were in the boat realized what had taken place, they confessed that Jesus was *"the Son of God"* and they *"worshipped Him."* Mark says, "They were sore amazed in themselves beyond measure, and wondered" (Mark 6:51). What had just occurred was additional proof of the power of Jesus—He had authority over the winds and the waves. (See also Matthew 8:23-27.)

Verse 34: *"And when they were gone over, they came into the land of Gennesaret."*

When the boat reached the other side with Jesus and the disciples, they went into the land of Gennesaret. This was a district extending along the western shore of the Sea of Galilee. Josephus gives a glowing description of the beauty of the land, its fertility, its plains, the beautiful flowers, and the crops that grew in abundance. At the northern end of the Sea of Galilee was Capernaum, near which our Lord landed—as would appear from John 6:24, 25.

Verse 35: *"And when the men of that place*

had knowledge of Him, they sent out into all that country round about, and brought unto Him all that were diseased."

The fame of Jesus had spread like wildfire all over the countryside. And when the men in that area learned that Jesus was there, *"they sent out into all that country round about, and brought unto Him all that were diseased."* Mark says that the people "ran through that whole region round about, and began to carry about in beds those that were sick, where they heard He was. And whithersoever He entered, into villages, or cities, or country, they laid the sick in the streets . . ." (Mark 6:55, 56).

Verse 36: *"And besought Him that they might only touch the hem of His garment: and as many as touched were made perfectly whole."*

The people besought that Jesus would just allow them to *"touch the hem of His garment"*—for they knew that in so doing, they would be made whole. To a Jew, the hem of the garment had a certain sanctity (Num. 15:38, 39). At each corner of their robes was a tassel which had a conspicuous blue thread, symbolic of the heavenly origin of the commandments.

"AS MANY AS TOUCHED WERE MADE PERFECTLY WHOLE." Faith reached out and touched the hem of His garment, and faith made the sick "perfectly whole." This reminds us of the dear

378

woman we studied in Matthew 9, who made her way through the crowd to Jesus, touched the hem of His garment, and was instantly healed (Matt. 9:20-22).

Jesus was the Great Physician. He did not come specifically to heal the sick; He came "to seek and to save that which was lost" (Luke 19:10). But He opened the eyes of the blind, He straightened crooked limbs, and He even raised the dead. All of these things He did as He traveled toward the one purpose for which He came into the world — to die on the Cross.

As I have stated many times, I believe in divine healing today; but I do not believe in the methods used by some modern "healers." *All* healing is *divine*—for no man can heal another man. Thank God for doctors who can operate and prescribe healing drugs; but if there is any healing, *God does it.* Thank God for His healing power. I am alive today and preparing this commentary because I have been divinely healed more than once. I have been at death's door three times. I know what it is to be rolled into a hospital and into an operating room in a dying condition, but I also know that God is able to raise us up and make us strong.

It is not always God's will to heal a sick person, however, even though that person may be a saint. But just because a person is sick does not mean that he does not have enough faith to be healed, nor is it necessarily a result of his sins. God permits things to happen to His children for a purpose, and we should always be willing for His purpose to be carried out in our lives. If God can get more glory out of our lives as we sit in a wheel chair or as we are on a hospital bed, then we should say in the words of our Saviour, "Not as I will, but as thou wilt" (Matt. 26:39).

Chapter XV

1. Then came to Jesus scribes and Pharisees, which were of Jerusalem, saying,

2. Why do thy disciples transgress the tradition of the elders? for they wash not their hands when they eat bread.

3. But he answered and said unto them, Why do ye also transgress the commandment of God by your tradition?

4. For God commanded, saying, Honour thy father and mother: and, He that curseth father or mother, let him die the death.

5. But ye say, Whosoever shall say to his father or his mother, It is a gift, by whatsoever thou mightest be profited by me;

6. And honour not his father or his mother, he shall be free. Thus have ye made the commandment of God of none effect by your tradition.

7. Ye hypocrites, well did Esaias prophesy of you, saying,

8. This people draweth nigh unto me with their mouth, and honoureth me with their lips; but their heart is far from me.

9. But in vain they do worship me, teaching for doctrines the commandments of men.

10. And he called the multitude, and said unto them, Hear, and understand:

11. Not that which goeth into the mouth defileth a man; but that which cometh out of the mouth, this defileth a man.

12. Then came his disciples, and said unto him, Knowest thou that the Pharisees were offended, after they heard this saying?

13. But he answered and said, Every plant, which my heavenly Father hath not planted, shall be rooted up.

14. Let them alone: they be blind leaders of the blind. And if the blind lead the blind, both shall fall into the ditch.

15. Then answered Peter and said unto him, Declare unto us this parable.

16. And Jesus said, Are ye also yet without understanding?

17. Do not ye yet understand, that whatsoever entereth in at the mouth goeth into the belly, and is cast out into the draught?

18. But those things which proceed out of the mouth come forth from the heart; and they defile the man.

19. For out of the heart proceed evil thoughts, murders, adulteries, fornications, thefts, false witness, blasphemies:

20. These are the things which defile a man: but to eat with unwashen hands defileth not a man.

21. Then Jesus went thence, and departed into the coasts of Tyre and Sidon.

22. And, behold, a woman of Canaan came out of the same coasts, and cried unto him, saying, Have mercy on me, O Lord, thou son of David; my daughter is grievously vexed with a devil.

23. But he answered her not a word. And his disciples came and besought him, saying, Send her away; for she crieth after us.

24. But he answered and said, I am not sent but unto the lost sheep of the house of Israel.

25. Then came she and worshipped him, saying, Lord, help me.

26. But he answered and said, It is not meet to take the children's bread, and cast it to dogs.

27. And she said, Truth, Lord: yet the dogs eat of the crumbs which fall from their masters' table.

28. Then Jesus answered and said unto her, O woman, great is thy faith: be it unto thee even as thou wilt. And her daughter was made whole from that very hour.

29. And Jesus departed from thence, and came nigh unto the sea of Galilee; and went up into a mountain, and sat down there.

30. And great multitudes came unto him, having with them those that were lame, blind, dumb, maimed, and many others, and cast them down at Jesus' feet; and he healed them:

31. Insomuch that the multitude wondered, when they saw the dumb to speak, the maimed to be whole, the lame to walk, and the blind to see: and they glorified the God of Israel.

32. Then Jesus called his disciples unto him, and said, I have compassion on the multitude, because they continue with me now three days, and have nothing to eat: and I will not send them away fasting, lest they faint in the way.

33. And his disciples say unto him, Whence should we have so much bread in the wilderness, as to fill so great a multitude?

34. And Jesus saith unto them, How many loaves have ye? And they said, Seven, and a few little fishes.

35. And he commanded the multitude to sit down on the ground.

36. And he took the seven loaves and the fishes, and gave thanks, and brake them, and gave to his disciples, and the disciples to the multitude.

37. And they did all eat, and were filled: and they took up of the broken meat that was left seven baskets full.

38. And they that did eat were four thousand men, beside women and children.

39. And he sent away the multitude, and took ship, and came into the coasts of Magdala.

Jesus Rebukes the Scribes and Pharisees

Verses 1 and 2: *"Then came to Jesus scribes and Pharisees, which were of Jerusalem, saying, Why do thy disciples transgress the tradition of the elders? for they wash not their hands when they eat bread."*

When the great miracle of the feeding of the five thousand was wrought, the Jewish Passover was near at hand (John 6:4). According to the view of most Bible scholars, this was the third Passover during our Lord's public ministry and about one year before His death. To this last year of the ministry of Christ belong half the chapters and considerably more than half the pages of Matthew's Gospel, and a still larger proportion of the Gospels of Mark, Luke, and John.

Jesus did not go to the Passover feast that year because the people in Judaea were seeking to kill Him (John 7:1), but continued His labors in Galilee as described in general terms in Matthew 14:35, 36. The particular incident here seems to have occurred a little time after the Passover, as it would

384

not have been natural for the Pharisees to leave
Jerusalem before the Passover feast.

The scene of this occurrence was somewhere in
Galilee in the plain of Gennesaret (Matt. 14:34-36),
probably in the city of Capernaum, where Jesus
usually abode (Matt. 4:13). The faultfinding inquiry by the Pharisees and scribes is turned back
upon them by the Lord (vv. 3-9) and then answered
by a most important general principle to which
the special attention of all present is called (vv.
10, 11) and of which the disciples afterwards sought
an explanation in private.

"Then" does not necessarily mean at the time
just before mentioned in Matthew 14:34-36 but
is naturally so taken unless there be proof to the
contrary, which is not the case here. The scribes
and Pharisees, the religious leaders of that day,
made a trip from Jerusalem to bring the accusation
against the Lord Jesus concerning the habits of
His disciples.

The city of Jerusalem was the seat of the great
religious schools as well as the temple worship.
The most eminent men were congregated there
especially at the Passover season, and these persons were regarded with special reverence and
dignity in Galilee. Their object in coming may
have been partly to satisfy their own curiosity
about the Lord Jesus, excited by accounts told at
the Passover of the great miracles Jesus was performing, and partly to prevent Him from gaining

too much influence in Galilee. It is not unlikely that they were sent as a deputation to observe Jesus and later report on what they witnessed. We have other accounts in Scripture where the religious headquarters in Jerusalem did send out men to observe Jesus and also John the Baptist (Matt. 12:24; 22:15,16; Mark 3:2; Luke 11:53,54; and John 1:19-24).

"Why do thy disciples transgress the tradition of the elders?" The word rendered *"tradition"* signifies that which is passed along or given from one to another—handed down from father to son to grandson. It is sometimes applied by Paul to Christian doctrine in general, handed over by him to the churches for their observance: "Therefore, brethren, stand fast, and *hold the traditions which ye have been taught, whether by word, or our epistle"* (II Thess. 2:15). Paul uses the expression again in the next chapter of this epistle: "Now we command you, brethren, in the name of our Lord Jesus Christ, that ye withdraw yourselves from every brother that walketh disorderly, and not after *the tradition which he received of us"* (II Thess. 3:6). The same word is translated "ordinances" in I Corinthians 11:2: "Now I praise you, brethren, that ye remember me in all things, and *keep the ordinances, as I delivered them to you."* However, here in Matthew, as well as in Galatians 1:14 and I Peter 1:18, the word denotes things handed down from generation to generation.

It is also very important to point out here that *"elders"* does not speak of men of authority in the church but of men of former times, the old men who had passed on—the forefathers of Israel. The same word is used in Hebrews 11:2: "For by it *the elders* obtained a good report." We have a similar thought in the Sermon on the Mount: "Ye have heard that it was said *by them of old time,* Thou shalt not kill; and whosoever shall kill shall be in danger of the judgment" (Matt. 5:21).

The supreme authority of the Word of God is the question brought to our attention in the opening verses of this chapter. The Jewish religious leaders had placed numerous rules and regulations of their religion alongside the Word of God and declared that their ideas had equal authority with the Scriptures. In fact, wherever there was a conflict between the two, the traditions of the Jews were counted as having higher authority than the Scripture text itself.

The tremendous mass of traditions which the later Jews so reverenced were held by them to consist partly of *oral* laws given by Moses (in addition to the written law) which they supposed to be referred to in Deuteronomy 4:14: "The Lord commanded me at that time to teach you statutes and judgments, that ye might do them in the land whither ye go over to possess it." They also believed that these traditions were partly decisions made on occasion by some of the judges (Deut.

17:9-12). You can see that these oral traditions would accumulate after a time and finally would be written down. If the scribes had some favorite tradition, they would slip it in as they copied the Scriptures. I am not suggesting that the Word of God has been changed, because I believe that God has preserved and protected His infallible Word. However, some of the books of religion that the Jews in that day held in high esteem were made up more of the traditions of the fathers than of the Word of God.

The only group who did not hold the traditions of the fathers in high esteem were the Sadducees. The Talmud of Jerusalem says this: "The words of the scribes are more lovely than the words of the law, for the words of the law are weighty and light, but the words of the scribes are all weighty." Also, in the Talmud is written, "My son, attend to the words of the scribes, more than the words of the law."

There are many religions today that emphasize tradition more than "thus saith the Lord God Almighty." In some of our Protestant churches which claim to be extremely fundamental, many times a greater emphasis is put upon the observance of custom and tradition than on Scripture, and more emphasis is placed upon "the rule of the denomination" than on the law of Almighty God. We need to listen to the Word of God—study and rightly divide the Word—then we can say with the Apostle Paul, "I know whom I have believed, and am persuaded that He is able to keep that which I have committed unto Him against that day" (II Tim. 1:12).

"They wash not their hands . . . ." Time and space will not permit us to discuss fully the different Greek words which are all translated "wash" in our Bible. However, I will mention five: One word *(nipto)* is used chiefly of washing a part of the body, such as the face, the hands, or the feet. *Brecho,* another word, means to wet, moisten, or sprinkle; and another *(pluno)* speaks of washing inanimate objects, nets, or clothes. A fourth word *(louo)* means to bathe or to wash the entire body, as in John 13:10: "He that is washed *(louo)* needeth not save to wash *(nipto)* his feet . . . ." Then there is a fifth word *(baptizo)*, which means to immerse or put completely under water.

". . . when they eat bread." Mark, in writing his account of the scribes and Pharisees condemning the disciples for not washing their hands before eating, pauses to give details about the elaborate purifications of the Jewish people in their religion (Mark 7:3-8). The law required frequent and sometimes very thorough washings, purifications, bathing completely—and in some cases, washing beds, saddles, and vessels (Lev. 15). In Leviticus 11:32 we note that in the washing of these vessels, they must be "put into water." In Hebrews 9:10 Paul speaks of "divers washings." The strict Jews

adopted the most thorough purification and washing rites even when not required by law. Mark 7:4 tells us that when they would "come from the market, except they wash (the word means to be put under the water, to completely immerse or submerge), they eat not"—which may mean they immersed their *hands* for thorough washing, but more probably means *themselves.*

This ceremonial hand washing before eating was supported by the rabbis, using Leviticus 15:11. It was natural that this should arise—along with the washing after the meal—from the fact that the ancient Jews ate with their fingers. They always washed *after* eating, and so someone decreed that they should also wash *before* eating—which would be more sanitary and healthy. According to Bible history, someone later added another washing—in the middle of the meal—making a total of three washings.

The Jewish rabbis taught in the days of our Lord that for one to neglect washing his hands before eating was just as grievous a sin as a gross crime. One rabbi said, "It is better to go four miles to water than to incur guilt by neglecting hand washing." Historians tell us that the famous Rabbi Akiba, when imprisoned and limited to water scarcely sufficient to sustain life, preferred dying of thirst to eating with unwashen hands.

How sad it is that today religions of works are growing by leaps and bounds—and new works, customs, and traditions are being added all the time. But in this Dispensation of Grace, it is *all* grace or *no* grace. Salvation is not by washings, baptisms, ceremonies, holy days, or works. It is *by grace through faith, PLUS NOTHING:* "For by grace are ye saved through faith; and that not of yourselves: *it is the gift of God: not of works,* lest any man should boast" (Eph. 2:8, 9).

Verse 3: *"But He answered and said unto them, Why do ye also transgress the commandment of God by your tradition?"*

Remember that Jesus knew the hearts of these men as He knows the hearts of all men. Before He proceeded to the great principle given in verse 11, involved in His justification of the disciples' neglect of hand washing, Jesus asked the Pharisees and the scribes a question which charged them with transgression: *"Why do ye also transgress the commandment of God by your tradition?"* They had accused the disciples of transgressing the traditions of the elders, but Jesus said the Pharisees and scribes were transgressing the commandments of Almighty God by their strict obedience to tradition.

The scribes and Pharisees had said "the tradition of the elders" in verse 2; but here Jesus says simply, *"your* tradition." However, no matter what was its origin, they were now making it an occasion of transgressing the law of God. This

391

charge He proves by an example not connected with hand washing or any other purification.

Verse 4: *"For God commanded, saying, Honour thy father and mother: and, He that curseth father or mother, let him die the death."*

Jesus was the greatest Preacher and the greatest Teacher that ever walked upon the face of this earth, and He always made His sermons clear and understandable. Therefore He proceeds to prove this charge against the Jewish leaders. On other occasions He taught in parables, but now He is giving an example taken from a most sacred duty, as acknowledged by mankind, and a solemn command of God's law: "Honour thy father and mother; which is the first commandment with promise" (Eph. 6:2).

"For God commanded . . . ." God's commandment on this matter is found in Exodus 20:12: "Honour thy father and thy mother: that thy days may be long upon the land which the Lord thy God giveth thee." The importance of this commandment is seen in Exodus 21:17: "He that curseth his father, or his mother, shall surely be put to death."

". . . Honour thy father and mother." The first part of this verse in Matthew 15 is a quote from Exodus 20:12 and the second part from Exodus 21:17, which we have just quoted.

". . . He that curseth . . . ." "Speaketh evil of"

or "reviles, belittles, or makes light of" is the exact rendering; so this commandment is extremely broad. The connection here reveals to us clearly that we must honor our father and mother, not just in our feelings but also by our actions. The Apostle Paul said, "If any widow have children or nephews, *let them learn first to shew piety at home, and to requite their parents:* for that is good and acceptable before God" (I Tim. 5:4).

". . . *let him die the death*"—or better, "LET HIM SURELY DIE."   This term is used much in the Old Testament Scriptures and more often denotes the *certainty* rather than the *severity* of the punishment. The great importance of this commandment is shown by the sure penalty of death for breaking it. Notice the strong language on this subject in Deuteronomy 27:16: *"CURSED be he that setteth light by his father or his mother. And all the people shall say, Amen."* The breaking of this commandment is also strongly condemned in Proverbs 20:20: "Whoso curseth his father or his mother, his lamp shall be put out in obscure darkness." A similar condemnation is found in Proverbs 30:17:   "The eye that mocketh at his father, and despiseth to obey his mother, the ravens of the valley shall pick it out, and the young eagles shall eat it."

Verses 5 and 6:   *"But ye say, Whosoever shall say to his father or his mother, It is a gift, by whatsoever thou mightest be profited by me; and*

*honour not his father or his mother, he shall be
free. Thus have ye made the commandment of
God of none effect by your tradition."*

"But ye say . . . ." The word *"ye"* is especially
expressed in the original, and therefore is very
strong and emphatic. It is no *little matter* for
men to say that which is directly opposed to what
God has already said. Yet these men had done so,
and at the same time they condemned the disciples
of Jesus because they did not wash their hands
before eating.

". . . Whosoever shall say . . . ." Mark mentions
the word "Corban" in his record of this incident:
"But ye say, If a man shall say to his father or
mother, It is *Corban,* that is to say, a gift, by
whatsoever thou mightest be profited by me; he
shall be free" (Mark 7:11). If a man's father or
mother wanted any article from him—it might be
food, or clothing, or money—he could just say,
"It is Corban, it is a *gift,* a thing consecrated to
God"—and he was then, according to the tradi-
tional rules, free from any obligation to his parents
and at liberty to withhold the article from them.

The Jews used religion as a scapegoat to ease
their conscience. They said that these words, "It
is a gift," even when pronounced in spite and
anger against parents, would excuse the son from
his duty toward his parents. One outstanding
Bible scholar says on this verse that the expression
cited by Jesus here did not always bind the one

who made the statement to actually dedicate his property to religious use, but the utterance of the statement was sufficient to absolve him from the duty of caring for his parents.

The Jewish traditions said that when a son had once made this vow, he was not bound by the law, but must observe the *vow* in *preference* to the law of God: "And ye suffer him no more to do ought for his father or his mother" (Mark 7:12). Therefore, such a man was certainly not honoring his father nor his mother as the law required him to do. Through their traditions, Jesus said they *"made the commandment of God of none effect."* They had not only transgressed the law of God, but they had declared it *void*. It is *most dangerous* to declare void the Word of God.

Verses 7 and 8: *"Ye hypocrites, well did Esaias prophesy of you, saying, This people draweth nigh unto me with their mouth, and honoureth me with their lips; but their heart is far from me."*

"Ye hypocrites . . . ." The people called hypocrites here made great pretense of devotion to God—they had a great outward show but no inward possession. They were ready to set aside God's express commands for their traditions. The persons to whom Jesus particularly referred were the ones from Jerusalem (verse 1)—the men sent down by the religious leaders to spy on Jesus. This seems to be the first instance of our Lord

openly rebuking these counterfeit religionists; however, we will often hear Him denounce them from here on until the end of His ministry.

"... *well did Esaias prophesy of you ....*" It is true that Isaiah spoke directly to the men of his own day and hour, but his words are prophetic, nonetheless, and designed by the Holy Spirit to refer to the contemporaries of Christ.

The words quoted by Jesus are found in Isaiah 29:13: "Wherefore the Lord said, Forasmuch as this people draw near me with their mouth, and with their lips do honour me, but have removed their heart far from me, and their fear toward me is taught by the precept of men." The same message is given in Ezekiel 33:31: "They come unto thee as the people cometh, and they sit before thee as my people, and they hear thy words, but they will not do them: for with their mouth they shew much love, but their heart goeth after their covetousness."

It is very possible for a man to honor God with his lips but down in his heart have no real love for nor fear of God. He is simply putting on a religious show to make an impression on people—as Jesus said of the Pharisees: "All their works they do for to be seen of men" (Matt. 23:5a). Vain glory is the desire of that person's heart. However, "Man looketh on the outward appearance, but *the Lord* looketh on the *heart*" (I Sam. 16:7). Titus 1:16 says: "They profess that they know God;

but in works they deny Him, being abominable, and disobedient, and unto every good work reprobate."

Verse 9: *"But in vain they do worship me, teaching for doctrines the commandments of men."*

"In vain they do worship me . . . ." This means that the worship of these hypocrites was neither acceptable to God nor profitable to themselves or anyone else. Their worship was dead, formal, and empty. The *Spirit* must lead, guide, and direct for there to be true worship. Jesus told His disciples in John 16:12, 13 that He had many things to say to them but they could not bear them at that time; but when the Holy Spirit came, He would guide them into all truth. So it is today: Unless the minister is speaking in the Spirit, the words he speaks are words of emptiness and the worship is vain.

". . . teaching for doctrines the commandments of men." These men were teaching the precepts and commandments of men rather than the precepts and commandments of God. They held their traditions to be superior to the written Word of God, and taught them as *doctrines* binding the consciences. Today there are thousands of ministers who teach doctrines and commandments that please men, but they are not acceptable to God or profitable to anyone because they are of human origin. True believers are under no obliga-

tion to conform to these rules of men, but instead they should rebuke them openly wherever and whenever there is the opportunity. When a minister teaches anything that is in direct violation of the Word of God, or when he neglects to preach the Word of God, he should be rebuked by those who are true born-again believers. Just be sure that the rebuke is given *in the Spirit* and not in the flesh.

It is natural for us to desire things of beauty, and many times a church service is planned and organized to be beautiful to the eyes of men and pleasant to their ears. We must remember that our human nature is prone to be intent upon the *forms* of religion rather than upon the *spirit.* Let us do all things to *glorify God*—never to glorify the flesh or to please men.

In this day of liberalism and modernism, I feel it would be to our advantage to read an admonition given to us under inspiration by the Apostle Paul:

"I marvel that ye are so soon removed from Him that called you into the grace of Christ unto another gospel: which is not another; but *there be some that trouble you, and would pervert the Gospel of Christ.* But though we, or an angel from heaven, preach any other gospel unto you than that which we have preached unto you, let him be accursed. As we said before, so say I now again, If any man preach any other gospel unto you than that ye have received, let him be accursed.

"For do I now persuade men, or God? or do I seek to please men? for *if I yet pleased men, I should not be the servant of Christ.* But I certify you, brethren, that *the Gospel which was preached of me is not after man. For I neither received it of man, neither was I taught it, but BY THE REVELATION OF JESUS CHRIST.*

"For ye have heard of my conversation in time past in the Jews' religion, how that beyond measure I persecuted the Church of God, and wasted it: and profited in the Jews' religion above many my equals in mine own nation, being more exceedingly zealous of the traditions of my fathers. But when it pleased God, who separated me from my mother's womb, and called me by His grace, to reveal His Son in me, that I might preach Him among the heathen; immediately I conferred not with flesh and blood: neither went I up to Jerusalem to them which were apostles before me; but I went into Arabia, and returned again unto Damascus. Then after three years I went up to Jerusalem to see Peter, and abode with him fifteen days. But other of the apostles saw I none, save James the Lord's brother.

"Now the things which I write unto you, behold, before God, I lie not. Afterwards I came into the regions of Syria and Cilicia; and was unknown by face unto the churches of Judaea which were in Christ: but they had heard only, That he which persecuted us in times past now preacheth *the faith which once he destroyed.* And they glorified God in me" (Gal. 1:6-24).

Verse 10: *"And He called the multitude, and said unto them, Hear, and understand."*

"He called the multitude . . . ." At this point Jesus begins speaking to the multitude. The foregoing dialogue, even though it was in the people's hearing, was between Jesus and the Pharisees and scribes, whom He called hypocrites. The object of these hypocrites was to discourage the masses of the people from listening to the words of Jesus. But Jesus, having put down the hypocrites, turns to the multitude, who were more likely to receive what He was about to say.

". . . and said unto them, HEAR, AND UNDER-STAND." Jesus calls for their complete and undivided attention. What He was about to say was something extremely important, and it demanded attentive consideration on the part of His listeners. The disciples referred to it as a parable in verse 15 of this chapter; however, He was not using the obscure expressions of a parable (Matt. 13:13). With deep love and desire as only Jesus could have for poor lost souls, He wanted all to understand. In Mark 7:14 we read, "When He had called all the people to Him, He said unto them, *Hearken unto me every one of you, and understand."* They

must not just hear with the ear, but they must understand with the heart. Jesus was not about to speak words of tradition as the scribes did, but He would speak by His *own* authority (Matt. 7:29), directly to the understanding and conscience of the people.

Verse 11: *"Not that which goeth into the mouth defileth a man; but that which cometh out of the mouth, this defileth a man."*

"Not that which goeth into the mouth defileth a man." The Greek word translated *"defileth"* means "makes common, profane, unclean; defiles; pollutes." There were certain foods especially set apart to be used by God's chosen people, and in a certain sense these foods were sacred and all other food was common. Devout Jews refused to eat of this unclean or common food. *Peter* said, "Not so, Lord; for *I have never eaten any thing that is common or unclean"* (Acts 10:14). For a Jew to partake of the forbidden foods would make him common and unclean.

This statement of Jesus amazed and astonished the Jews. They realized at once that it applied not just to bathing the hands before eating, but to the whole matter of clean and unclean food—and this seemed to them one of the most important and vital parts of the law. Even the disciples of the Lord Jesus failed to understand it, as we will see later in this chapter.

401

". . . but that which cometh out of the mouth, this defileth a man." Ceremonially, various things did defile the man by entering the mouth; but this was designed only to represent the idea of moral pollution, while the great mass of the Jews, however scrupulous about this outward purity, were careless about *inward* purity. They would wash their hands, go through all the ceremonies, abstain from certain meats and certain foods—but they cared very little about the cleanliness of heart and spirit. Therefore Jesus directed their attention to the heart and that which really counts—inward holiness and purity. If one is impure in his heart, the washing of hands and abstaining from food will not clean the inner man.

Jesus declared in the Sermon on the Mount that He had not come to destroy the law but to fulfill it (Matt. 5:17). And here, as in so many points in the Sermon on the Mount, He is leading the people to deeper and more spiritual views of the morality which the law was designed to teach. Thus He was not correcting or doing away with the law but *completing* the law. His teachings prepared the way for the laying aside of ceremonies, holy days, partaking of certain foods and wearing certain garments, but this only by developing these things into something higher, greater, and nobler. Accordingly, Jesus did not repeal the Mosaic directions concerning clean and unclean food, but He laid down a general principle that deals with the point at hand. We will study more about this in verse 20 of our present chapter. Many of the things that Jesus taught in principle were fully developed by His followers after His crucifixion, when men were more prepared to understand and receive them. (Please study John 16: 12-15.)

The law concerning clean and unclean food in the Mosaic system was not given just to teach moral purity among the Israelites, but was also given to separate them from other nations. However, Peter was taught to set this aside when the time came to preach salvation to the Gentiles. In a dream, Peter saw something like a "great sheet" let down from heaven containing all kinds of animals. He was hungry, and he was commanded to "kill and eat"—but he said that he had never eaten anything common or unclean. God then showed him that *all men* were included in God's grace, whereas during the Mosaic economy only the Israelites were God's chosen people (Acts 10).

Verse 12: *"Then came His disciples, and said unto Him, Knowest thou that the Pharisees were offended, after they heard this saying?"*

Only Matthew records the statement given here concerning the Pharisees being offended. It seems that this conversation took place after Jesus and His disciples had retired from the crowd and returned into a house (Mark 7:17). There had been a little interval since the saying in verse 11, and the disciples had heard the Pharisees talking about what Jesus had said concerning that which enters the mouth. The Pharisees were offended and angry about this teaching of Jesus, which was in direct opposition to the law about clean and unclean food.

The disciples undoubtedly thought the opinion of these distinguished religious leaders from Jerusalem was very important. They said, *"Knowest thou that the Pharisees were offended . . . ?"* They probably thought that Jesus did not know He had offended them or He would be busy trying to explain what He meant and trying to appease them. Evidently the disciples looked upon the statement of Jesus as extremely obscure and very strange (v. 15), and no doubt they sympathized with the offended Pharisees. But Jesus did not regard man; He came to do the will of the Father. He declared on many occasions that the words He uttered were not *His* but the words that God the Father gave Him to speak. He came to speak God's words, to do God's will, and to finish the work that God gave Him to do. But the Pharisees were willingly ignorant and refused to accept Him as God's Son.

Verse 13: *"But He answered and said, Every plant, which my heavenly Father hath not planted, shall be rooted up."*

404

When Jesus spoke these words concerning plants, He was using the plant to represent the man-made *doctrine* of the Pharisees and the scribes. What He is teaching here is simply that every doctrine that is not from God will not stand. Doctrine of human origin (verse 9) will lose its influence and will be rejected by those who sincerely seek the truth. Jesus said on one occasion, "Ye shall know the truth, and the truth shall make you free" (John 8:32). And in verse 36 of that same chapter, He said, "If the Son therefore shall make you free, ye shall be free indeed." Today we have much man-made doctrine in our religions. But thank God there is *true doctrine* and we can *know* what is the truth—for the Holy Spirit will guide us into all truth if we are a true believer (John 16:13; I Pet. 2:6).

Verse 14: *"Let them alone: they be blind leaders of the blind. And if the blind lead the blind, both shall fall into the ditch."*

"Let them alone." In other words, Jesus told the disciples, "Do not trouble yourselves about these men, as to what they teach or whether they approve of my teachings." Jesus was the greatest of all teachers, but He did not expect—nor *try*—to please all of His hearers. No minister of the Gospel ever has or ever will please all who hear his message. Many people are blinded by the god of this age, many are blinded by prejudice, many are

hardened in unbelief and are willful in their opposition to pure doctrine—*"let them alone."* In the Old Testament God said, "Ephraim is joined to idols: *let him alone"* (Hosea 4:17).

"They be blind leaders of the blind." Of course, when a blind man leads another blind man, the result is evident—they both will fall. There is no person on earth that has a warmer spot in my heart than an unsighted person; but there is something many times sadder—and that is for one to be *spiritually* blind. The devil, the god of this age, blinds the minds of unbelievers (II Cor. 4:3, 4)—and for one to be blind in his *mind* is much worse than to be blind in his *eyes.* There are some people whom God cannot help, for they have their minds made up. They are willingly ignorant, willingly hardened, and willingly blind. They are following men, and they refuse to hear the voice of God.

". . . both shall fall into the ditch." The Greek word translated *"ditch"* literally means "a pit or cistern." It is the same Greek word as that in Matthew 12:11, denoting a pit dug in the field to catch rain water—which was a very common practice. The use of our English word "ditch" gives the image of two blind men walking down the road and falling into a ditch beside the road. However, most Bible scholars choose the translation "pit," which gives the image of a blind man leading another blind man in an open field.

Eventually they both will fall into a pit filled with rain water—which, of course, is a more serious tragedy than falling into a ditch beside the road.

Liberal ministers who deny the Virgin Birth, the Blood Atonement, and the verbal inspiration of the Bible—and all who follow them—will fall into a pit; but it will not be filled with water—it will be the *"bottomless pit,"* burning with *fire and brimstone.* God pity anyone who reads these words and continues to support a liberal minister, church, or denomination. Any minister, church, or denomination that denies any of the fundamentals of the faith does not deserve your support, but rather you should come out from among them. You should not give comfort or aid to the enemies of the pure Gospel of God's saving grace.

Verse 15: *"Then answered Peter and said unto Him, Declare unto us this parable."*

Peter is the spokesman here for the group. Notice he said, *"Declare unto US,"* which shows he is speaking for all the disciples. This is not the only time that Peter was the spokesman for the twelve disciples (Matt. 16:15, 16). Peter is not asking for an explanation of what Jesus said in verse 14; he is referring to what was said in verse 11, where Jesus spoke of defilement coming from within a man.

Verse 16: *"And Jesus said, Are ye also yet without understanding?"*

The Gospel According to Matthew

There is a mild rebuke in these words. Although Jesus had not given any instructions that we know of on this particular subject, the disciples had heard the Sermon on the Mount and His many parables and other teachings in chapters 5 through 13. Surely all of these instructions and His own personal influence ought to have prepared them to take a spiritual view of things.

Verse 17: *"Do not ye yet understand, that whatsoever entereth in at the mouth goeth into the belly, and is cast out into the draught?"*

It is common knowledge that that which enters a man's mouth goes *"into the belly and is cast out into the draught."* It has nothing to do with what he may possess in his heart. The Jews had come to the place that they did not distinguish between ceremonial and moral defilement. To correct the confusion, Jesus pointed out that *food* cannot pollute a soul or affect the spiritual nature of an individual, because it passes through the body; it does not enter into the heart.

In the Gospel of Mark, Jesus explains that it is not that which is from without that defiles a man: "And He said unto them, Are ye so without understanding also? Do ye not perceive, that *whatsoever thing from without entereth into the man, it CANNOT DEFILE HIM; BECAUSE it entereth not into his HEART*, but into the belly, and goeth out into the draught, purging all meats?" (Mark 7:18,19).

It seems here that Jesus declared all articles of food clean or acceptable. Also see Acts 10:15.

Verse 18:   *"But those things which proceed out of the mouth come forth from the heart; and they defile the man."*

Jesus is teaching here that the seat of corruption is *within.*   It is the heart itself—and if men would be made pure, the heart must be cleansed. If the heart is corrupt, the whole man is corrupt. Through the mouth enter food and drink, this corruptible body's corruptible nourishment; but *from* the mouth come forth *words* that declare what the real man is and to whom he belongs. Words express thoughts, and thoughts are born in the heart. Jesus said, "By thy *words* thou shalt be justified, and by thy words thou shalt be condemned" (Matt. 12:37). When James reminds us that sweet and bitter water cannot flow from the same fountain (James 3:11), he is speaking of *words* uttered by the tongue.

Verse 19:   *"For out of the heart proceed evil thoughts, murders, adulteries, fornications, thefts, false witness, blasphemies."*

Our Lord does not confine Himself only to evil things that are *spoken,* but passes to the more general idea that whatever comes forth from the heart has its origin within us. *"Evil thoughts"* proceed from the *heart,* not the brain—because it is from the heart that the issues of life come

409

forth (Prov. 4:23). If a person's heart is clean, evil thoughts will not proceed from his heart. The heart is responsible for that which is harbored in the mind and that which proceeds out of the mouth.

"Murders" also originate in the heart. There are thousands of murderers upon the earth today who have never literally killed someone in the eyes of the law. Murder comes from the heart— and God's Word says that if we *hate* our brother, we are guilty of murder (I John 3:15; Matt. 5:21, 22). And, of course, there are ways of murdering without actually shedding blood. People murder their loved ones by living lives that cause worry, sorrow, and fretting. Many mothers wet their pillows with tears at night, weeping over a prodigal son or daughter. Whether such sons and daughters realize it or not, they are slowly murdering their mother. But whichever type of murder we may be talking about, it is a result of a wicked and sinful heart.

". . . adulteries." We think of adultery as being committed by a person who is unfaithful to his or her marriage partner. But Jesus tells us in the Sermon on the Mount that if a man looks upon a woman to lust after her, he has committed adultery with her already *in his heart* (Matt. 5:27, 28). If a man looks upon a woman to lust after her, an evil heart is responsible for the looking and the lusting. There are thousands of men and women walking upon the face of this earth who are guilty of

410

adultery in the eyes of God, who have never literally taken up with another man or woman. Adultery comes from the heart—and if a person has a
clean, pure heart controlled by the Holy Spirit,
no adultery can abide there.

In this day when many women wear so little
(and such suggestive) clothing, many times they
actually contribute to adulterous thoughts. Therefore, men and women should be very careful how
they dress and how they conduct themselves, because they may influence someone to have evil
thoughts that would lead to rape, assault, or even
murder, upon an innocent victim. Paul tells us
that "none of us liveth to himself, and no man
dieth to himself" (Rom. 14:7). Whether we like it
or not, the way we dress, the way we act, the way
we talk, and the places we go, certainly influence
the lives of people around about us.

"Fornications" also come from the heart. The
dictionary defines fornication as illicit sex between
the unmarried; however, in our Bible the word is
used interchangeably with adultery. Fornication
does not come from an ungodly mind, nor does it
come through association with ungodly friends.
If one's *heart* is right, his friends will be right, and
his mind will be right. Fornication cannot live or
abide in a heart that is filled with righteousness
and the Spirit of God.

". . . thefts." We usually think of one who steals
as one who is in need—or of one who *habitually*

411

steals as being a kleptomaniac. But the sin of taking that which does not belong to us originates in the heart. People steal because they have a wicked and sinful heart. One who is born again and right with God will not be forced to steal in order to eat. God has promised to provide our physical needs as well as the spiritual: "Seek ye first the Kingdom of God, and His righteousness; and *all these things shall be added unto you*" (Matt. 6:33). In Philippians 4:19 we have another great promise of God's provision: *"My God shall supply ALL YOUR NEED* according to His riches in glory by Christ Jesus."

"*. . . false witness.*" One who bears false witness does so because of a wicked heart. If we have Jesus in our heart, truth abides there and fills the heart, and we will utter words of soberness and truth. We need to be very careful what we say, because we will give an account to God for every word that we speak: "But I say unto you, That *every idle word that men shall speak, they shall give account thereof in the day of judgment*" (Matt. 12:36).

"*. . . blasphemies.*" One of the most uncalled-for things that any man will ever do is to curse, to blaspheme, to use God's name in vain. There are so many good and righteous words that we can speak. Instead of cursing and swearing, we should *praise* God for the sunshine, the air, the beautiful world, and all of the marvelous things that we see

412

and come in contact with every day. Everything that is beautiful and good comes from God: "Every good gift and every perfect gift is from above, and cometh down from the Father of lights, with whom is no variableness, neither shadow of turning" (James 1:17).

Blasphemy does not come from a heart filled with righteousness and possessed by the Holy Spirit. Jesus is speaking here primarily of blasphemy against God, but it can also extend to one's fellow man and even to the things around him. One of the commandments definitely states, "Thou shalt not take the name of the Lord thy God in vain" (Ex. 20:7). If you are guilty of this sin of blasphemy, it does not originate in your mouth; it originates in your *heart*. You do not need a new tongue—you need a new heart; you need to be born again.

When Christ comes into our hearts, we are changed completely: *"If any man be in Christ, he is A NEW CREATURE:* old things are passed away; behold, all things are become new" (II Cor. 5:17). When we are born again, God puts within us a new heart: *"A new heart also will I give you, and a new spirit will I put within you:* and I will take away the stony heart out of your flesh, and I will give you an heart of flesh" (Ezek. 36:26).

Let me point out that Mark names several sins that come from the heart, which Matthew does not mention: "For from within, out of the heart of

413

The Gospel According to Matthew

men, proceed evil thoughts, adulteries, fornications, murders, thefts, COVETOUSNESS, WICKEDNESS, DECEIT, LASCIVIOUSNESS, AN EVIL EYE, blasphemy, PRIDE, FOOLISHNESS: all these evil things come from within, and defile the man" (Mark 7:21-23). Matthew does not mention covetousness, wickedness, deceit, lasciviousness, an evil eye, pride, or foolishness; but these and *all other* wickedness and ungodliness originate in a wicked heart, and these are the things that defile a man. How important it is for us to be sure our hearts are right with God at all times: *"Keep thy heart with all diligence; for out of it are the issues of life"* (Prov. 4:23).

Verse 20: *"These are the things which defile a man: but to eat with unwashen hands defileth not a man."*

I am sure you will agree that it is right and profitable for one to wash his hands before eating. But Jesus assured His disciples that real defilement does not come through dirt or germs that may be on the hands, but defilement that destroys comes from *within*—not from dirty *hands* but from a *dirty heart*. We need to recognize daily that we will give an account to God for what we do and what we are.

And so verse 20 ends our Lord's defense of His disciples and His answer to the Pharisees' criticism of the disciples' eating with unwashen hands.

The *Apostle Paul* had much trouble with legalism and tradition. In almost all of the early churches, there were divisions among the people concerning eating meat and various other matters of law. Paul taught the believers in Rome that they should be careful how they lived and how they conducted themselves, but they were not to judge their brothers, as these Pharisees and scribes (here in Matthew) were judging the disciples of Jesus.

God forbid that we judge our fellow man by what he eats or by what he wears—for one day Jesus will judge in righteous judgment, and each one of us will get his just reward. Listen to the words of Paul in Romans 14:11-20:

"It is written, As I live, saith the Lord, every knee shall bow to me, and every tongue shall confess to God. So then *every one of us shall give account of himself to God. LET US NOT THEREFORE JUDGE ONE ANOTHER any more:* but judge this rather, that no man put a stumbling-block or an occasion to fall in his brother's way. . . . Destroy not him with thy meat, for whom Christ died.

"Let not then your good be evil spoken of: for the Kingdom of God is not meat and drink; but righteousness, and peace, and joy in the Holy Ghost. . . . For meat destroy not the work of God. All things indeed are pure; but it is evil for that man who eateth with offence."

The Syrophenician Woman's Daughter Healed

Verse 21: *"Then Jesus went thence, and departed into the coasts of Tyre and Sidon."*

We have here an account of Jesus ministering to a Gentile. She was a woman who had a broken heart and a deep desire to see her daugher delivered from demons. The account of the Syrophenician woman is also found in Mark 7:24-30 in the same setting as here in Matthew.

"Jesus went thence . . . ." The jealousy and hatred of Herod (Matt. 14:1-14), the hostility and threatenings of the Pharisees (Matt. 12:14; 15:1-12), and the fanaticism of the masses (John 6:15), required Jesus to withdraw from Galilee. He left probably from Capernaum and set out to travel in a different direction than heretofore. He journeyed toward the northwest into Phoenicia, and in so doing, He would be beyond the jurisdiction of Herod. The distance from Capernaum to Phoenicia was about thirty miles.

". . . and departed into the coasts of Tyre and Sidon." The meaning here is that Jesus departed into the area around these two cities—that part of the country, or region, belonging to these two cities. Mark 7:24 uses the word "borders," rather than *"coasts."* Some Bible scholars, because of the indefinite terms *coasts* and *borders,* insist that He stopped at the *boundary* and did not go into Phoenicia. But, since "borders" often denotes the

territory inclosed thereby (according to the Greek dictionary), we believe He crossed the border and went into this heathen land. (See verse 22, where the woman *"came out of the same coasts"* — meaning that territory.)

This does not conflict with the true fact that the mission of Jesus was to the Jews. In verse 24 of this chapter, He clearly declared that He had come to "the lost sheep of the house of Israel" — but this did not prohibit Him from traveling into the heathen land where the Syrophenician woman lived, for He did not go there to minister to those people. As soon as He was induced to perform this miracle, which He knew would attract attention and gather a crowd, He went away again. Mark tells us that He entered into a house because He wished to stay out of the sight of the masses (Mark 7:24). He wanted to be in seclusion.

God commanded *Elijah* to go to the house of the widow at Zarephath, in the same country of Phoenicia: *"The word of the Lord came unto him, saying, Arise, get thee to Zarephath, which belongeth to Zidon, and dwell there: behold, I have commanded a widow woman there to sustain thee.* So he arose and went to Zarephath. And when he came to the gate of the city, behold, the widow woman was there gathering of sticks: and he called to her, and said, Fetch me, I pray thee, a little water in a vessel, that I may drink. . . . And she went and did according to the saying of Elijah:

417

and she, and he, and her house, did eat many days" (I Kings 17:8-10, 15). (This incident is referred to in Luke 4:26: "But unto none of them was Elias sent, save unto Sarepta, a city of Sidon, unto a woman that was a widow.")

Jesus probably also desired rest for His disciples and Himself, as on their first withdrawal not long before (Mark 6:31), for they had been very busy. It is true that He was God; but He was also *man*, and therefore at times He needed physical rest for His body.

The cities of Tyre and Sidon were the two great seaports of the country of Phoenicia. Jesus probably at the first visited the southern part where Tyre was located, and afterwards traveled north through Sidon. We also learn from Mark 3:8 and from Luke 6:17 that great masses from the region of Tyre and Sidon went out to hear the Lord and attended His early ministry. Jesus declared in Matthew 11:21 that if the mighty works that were done in Chorazin and Bethsaida had been done in Tyre and Sidon, they would have repented. He also said that it would be more *tolerable* for Tyre and Sidon in the day of judgment than for the cities where many mighty miracles were performed by the Lord.

Verse 22: *"And, behold, a woman of Canaan came out of the same coasts, and cried unto Him, saying, Have mercy on me, O Lord, thou son of David; my daughter is grievously vexed with a devil."*

"And, behold . . . ." Something remarkable was about to occur; therefore we are urged to listen carefully and pay very close attention.

". . . a woman of Canaan . . . ." In the early times, the people of Phoenicia were spoken of as Canaanites (Judges 1:3-5). They belonged to the great tribe that occupied all the lowlands and afterwards gave its name (Canaan) to the whole land. It is probable that the Jews continued to call all of the inhabitants of Phoenicia Canaanites, even though many of the later inhabitants may have been of different origin. All Jews would recognize this woman as a Gentile. Mark calls her a Greek (a Gentile) and tells us also that she was a Syrophenician by race (Mark 7:26).

This Syrophenician woman *"came out of the same coasts"*—meaning the same region or territory. She did not come from Galilee, but from the country of Tyre and Sidon.

". . . and cried unto Him, saying, Have mercy on me, O Lord, thou son of David." The woman begged for mercy and pity on behalf of her child, and she called Jesus *"Lord."* It is not clear whether this was an expression of high respect or possibly one of sincere worship. Apparently she believed that He was the Messiah, because she addressed Him as the *"son of David."* Even though this woman lived in a heathen country, it was near the land of Israel and she must have been familiar with the religion of the Jews.

419

It is quite possible that this Syrophenician woman may have previously gone with the people from Tyre and Sidon (Mark 3:8) to attend the meetings Jesus conducted in Galilee. She could have heard Jesus teach and work miracles on several other occasions.

"... *my daughter is grievously vexed with a devil.*" (Mark says "young daughter," which implies she was a child.) The Greek reads "badly demonized." There were many people in that day who were completely controlled by demons. (See comments on Matthew 8:28.) There are also many today who are demon possessed, their lives dominated by demons. Some of the hideous crimes committed today against society could not be committed by rational human beings; they are people who are demon possessed.

Verse 23: *"But He answered her not a word. And His disciples came and besought Him, saying, Send her away; for she crieth after us."*

"He answered her not a word." Notice the strong, unique contrast here. The woman was crying out with a loud, strong voice, but Jesus was completely silent. He did not utter one word to the woman.

"... *His disciples came and besought Him, saying, Send her away; for she crieth after us.*" The disciples did not fully understand at this time that Jesus had come to seek and to save the lost

and that God so loved *the world* that He gave
His Son to die for the sins of the whole world.
They were, no doubt, half touched and half an-
noyed by this woman's loud and persistent crying.
They probably were also afraid that her crying
would draw attention to them, when they desired
to remain in the background at this time.

The disciples came up near to Jesus, and the
Greek reads, "they begged Him" to send her away.
Some scholars think that the disciples simply wanted Jesus to order her to leave them alone and to
dismiss her from their presence.   But they had
never witnessed Jesus dismiss a suppliant in any
other way than by doing what was asked; so I
doubt that the disciples even entertained the idea
that Jesus would literally run her away from their
company.   That they wanted Him to grant her
request and send her home to get rid of her seems
clear from the answer Jesus gave, stating a reason
why He should not grant it.

Verse 24: *"But He answered and said, I am not
sent but unto the lost sheep of the house of Israel."*

The answer Jesus gave for not granting the
woman's request was not given directly to her
but to the disciples.   The Father sent Jesus to
earth on a mission—He commissioned Him to go
to the lost sheep of the house of Israel.   Please
notice that Jesus said, *"I AM NOT SENT but
unto the lost sheep of the house of Israel,"* signi-

fying that God the Father *sent Him* on a specific mission. And now that He was in a Gentile country He must avoid entering upon a general ministry to Gentiles, for it was not yet time for Him to turn from the chosen nation to strangers.

Christ's ministry to the elect of Israel prepared the way for God's blessings to be poured out upon the Gentiles. In Romans 15:8-10 we read, "Now I say that Jesus Christ was a minister of the circumcision for the truth of God, to confirm the promises made unto the fathers: and that the Gentiles might glorify God for His mercy; as it is written, For this cause I will confess to thee among the Gentiles, and sing unto thy name. And again He saith, Rejoice, ye Gentiles, with His people."

When Christ's work on earth was finished, the apostles would be His witnesses. His commission to them just before His ascension was not to the Jews only, for He said: "Ye shall receive power, after that the Holy Ghost is come upon you: and ye shall be witnesses unto me *both in Jerusalem, and in all Judaea, and in Samaria, and UNTO THE UTTERMOST PART OF THE EARTH*" (Acts 1:8).

At the time the Syrophenician woman came to Jesus it would have conflicted with the nature and design of our Lord's mission had He revealed this future ministry to the disciples, although He alluded to the commission He would give them as a part of His own work, in John 10:16: "Other sheep I have, which are *not of this fold:* them also I must bring, and they shall hear my voice; and there shall be *one fold, and one Shepherd."*

The book of Acts shows plainly that the Jews were slow to receive and needed slow preparation to accept the fact that Gentiles were to share freely in the blessings the Messiah would bring. If Jesus at this time had begun a great work among the Gentiles and had announced that Gentiles were equal with Jews in every respect, that they would be included in the body of Christ and reign with Him for one thousand glorious years, no doubt the Jews would have torn Him to pieces. Here Jesus made an exception because of the great faith of the Syrophenician woman. But, in fact, this was hardly an exception—for her great faith brought her in a sense within the limits of the mission of Jesus upon the earth at that time: "Know ye therefore that *they which are of faith, the same are the children of Abraham"* (Gal. 3:7).

The message in this verse (24) is found only in the Gospel account given by Matthew. Since Matthew's Gospel is the Kingdom book, written especially to the Jews, his desire was to show them that Jesus was their Messiah.

Verse 25: *"Then came she and worshipped Him, saying, Lord, help me."*

The woman must have been a short distance

from Jesus when she cried out to Him, but here she came near. Then she *"worshipped Him,"* bowing before Him, probably prostrating herself upon the ground. She cried out to Jesus as she worshipped Him, *"Lord, help me."* In helping her Jesus would be helping her daughter, because the deep burden and the first desire of her heart was to see her daughter delivered from demons.

Verse 26: *"But He answered and said, It is not meet to take the children's bread, and cast it to dogs."*

Here Jesus said to the woman practically the same thing He had said to His disciples—that He was not sent "but unto the lost sheep of the house of Israel." He told her, *"It is not meet* (it was not good or proper) *to take the children's bread, and cast it to dogs."* Even though these words seem harsh to us, we must remember that Jesus knew the woman's heart. He knew exactly what to say to humble her and to develop her faith to claim that which she desired with all of her heart. (Jesus used just the opposite approach when dealing with the centurion in Matthew 8:7. We must always keep in mind that Jesus knew the thoughts and heart of each person who came to Him for any reason.)

The Jews looked upon themselves as God's *"children"* and spoke contemptuously of the Gentiles as *"dogs,"* unclean and vile. Gentiles in that day were accustomed to this, and therefore the expression here was not altogether so offensive and painful as it would seem to us.

Verse 27: *"And she said, Truth, Lord: yet the dogs eat of the crumbs which fall from their masters' table."*

The reply given by the Syrophenician woman not only shows a very high degree of faith and humility, but also does credit to her ability and intelligence. Instead of becoming offended and walking away in disgust, she took the next step that caused the Lord Jesus to grant the desire of her heart.

You can rest assured that the woman was not being sarcastic, for she was broken in spirit and heart and she desired a miracle for her daughter. She said, "Lord, I know it is not proper for you to take the children's bread and throw it to dogs, but you know that dogs pick up the little crumbs that fall from their masters' table." In other words, she was willing to take a dog's place under the table and to receive *"crumbs,"* or that which was left over. True, the Jews are God's chosen people and elect nation, and they have a very special place and mission in this world. However, this woman was not asking Jesus to deprive the Jews of any of their special privileges—but if He had come to bring bread to the children of the Kingdom, surely a despised Gentile could have a few crumbs that were left over. Mark states, "Let the children *first* be filled" (Mark 7:27)—which certainly implies that afterward the "dogs" would be fed. Paul said, "I am not ashamed of the Gospel of Christ: for it is the power of God unto salvation to every one that believeth; *to the Jew FIRST, and ALSO to the Greek (Gentile)*" (Rom. 1:16).

Greek scholars tell us that the word *"dogs"* here (and in Mark 7:27) is a diminutive and suggests smaller dogs or puppies allowed to run freely around the house and under the table. The woman must have used this word intentionally, for she laid hold on this point and made it her own—"If we are dogs, may we fare as such—be fed from the crumbs of thy mercy?" She was, as it were, under the edge of the table, close on the confines of Israel's feast. The common word for "dog" occurs five times in the New Testament, but the Greek word used here (and in Mark 7:27, 28) is not found anywhere else in the Bible. Dogs are spoken of as objects of dislike throughout the whole Bible.

Certainly this Syrophenician woman is a heroine of faith, and we will profit if we follow her example. Many believers grow despondent and discouraged if God does not answer their prayers immediately. God grant that we profit also from this woman's humble *perseverance*, which may be compared to that of Jacob when he wrestled all night with the same Person to whom this woman came and talked. The account is recorded in Genesis 32:24-26:

"Jacob was left alone; and there wrestled a man with him until the breaking of the day. And when he saw that he prevailed not against him, he touched the hollow of his thigh; and the hollow of Jacob's thigh was out of joint, as he wrestled with him. And he said, Let me go, for the day breaketh. *And he said, I will not let thee go, except thou bless me.*"

I am not suggesting that God forces us to beg for His grace and His blessings, but many times God does not see fit to answer us quickly. At such times we should not get discouraged. Instead, we should exercise faith and persevere in prayer and in making our requests known unto the Lord.

Verse 28: *"Then Jesus answered and said unto her, O woman, great is thy faith: be it unto thee even as thou wilt. And her daughter was made whole from that very hour."*

The phrase *"O woman"* is much more expressive than simply "woman." Then Jesus said, *"Great is thy faith."* God honors faith, and it is impossible to *please* Him *without* faith (Heb. 11:6). "The just shall *live* by faith" (Rom. 1:17), and "whatsoever is *not* of faith is *sin*" (Rom. 14:23).

". . . be it unto thee even as thou wilt." Jesus told the woman that her wish was granted. At first it seemed that He would not grant unto her

anything at all; He did not even answer her. But now He opens the treasure house of His grace to her and invites her to help herself and carry away what she will.

Jesus had shown to her for awhile—like Joseph to his brothers (Gen. chaps. 42-45)—the aspect of severity; but, like Joseph (who is a type of Jesus), He did not maintain the severity long. At least, He did not maintain it an instant longer than was needful. When the woman humbled herself before Him, Jesus declared that He had not found such faith in all of Israel. *Great faith brings great blessings from Almighty God.*

The woman showed her humility when she said that she was willing to eat the crumbs as a puppy would; but notice that Jesus did not speak of this humility, though so remarkable, for that was a *result* of her great *faith.* Unbelief produces pride, but faith gives birth to humility. The Psalmist said, "Lord, thou hast *heard the desire of the humble:* thou wilt prepare their heart, thou wilt cause thine ear to hear" (Psalm 10:17).

"And HER DAUGHTER WAS MADE WHOLE FROM THAT VERY HOUR." This reminds us of the nobleman who came to Jesus and declared that if Jesus did not come down to his house, his sick child would die. Jesus answered him, "Go thy way; thy son liveth"—and, of course, when the nobleman reached home his son was alive. He asked the servants what hour the lad began to

amend, and when they told him, he confessed that it was the same hour that Jesus said, "Thy son liveth." This is a beautiful picture of salvation. (Please study carefully John 4:46-54.)

The Omnipotence, the Patience, and the Power of Christ

There is a beautiful picture of the Saviour and salvation for the sinner in this story we have just studied. How strange it is that Jesus went into some areas and places only one time, and it seems that always such a visit led to something extraordinary and supernatural. (Jesus arrived in *Nain* at the very moment a young man was being carried to his grave. He could have arrived a little earlier or a little later, but He arrived at the very moment that He was needed to bind up the broken heart of a precious mother. Read the account in Luke 7:11-15.)

Somewhere in the locality of Tyre and Sidon a Gentile mother lived with her daughter who was possessed with demons. Periodically this mother's heart was moved with compassion as she watched the crowds moving south toward the towns where Jesus, the great Healer, was ministering and preaching (Mark 3:8; Luke 6:17). She longed to go with them—and there is a possibility that she did attend on occasion; but if she did not go, she had heard glowing reports from friends and neighbors of what Jesus was doing. She knew that Jesus was a Jew

429

and that the Jews despised and hated her people. But when Jesus visited the area where she lived, in spite of the fact that He was a Jew, in desperation she decided to go and ask Him to help her daughter.

It is interesting to note that she, a Gentile, approached Jesus as the *Son of David*—a title strictly Jewish—and He refused to answer her. This mother did not know that in God's great heart all racial barriers disappear. Therefore when she addressed Jesus merely as *"Lord,"* she received an immediate answer.

Jesus then demonstrated His power to deal with the needs of *all people.* He said to the woman, "It is not meet to take the children's bread, and cast it to dogs." But surely the warmth of His eyes and the look on His precious face must have made known to the woman that He did not look upon her as a common dog. She replied, in effect, "That is the truth, Lord; but dogs pick up the crumbs which fall from the master's table." When in our heart we prove to God that we are willing to accept *crumbs,* He always gives a *loaf.* Jesus said, "O woman, great is thy faith: be it unto thee even as thou wilt." The woman did not ask any more questions, but departed—and when she reached home, her little girl was well and waiting.

The same Jesus who healed the Syrophenician woman's demented daughter is ready and willing to heal your spirit and soul now. He is omniscient;

He knows all about you. You do not need to tell
Him what you have done or what you have not
done—just make known to Him that you desire
salvation. He has been patient with you. You
could have been cut off many times, but God has
allowed you to live until this good hour. God's
patience has been extended to you—so why not
believe on the Lord Jesus Christ and be saved?
The Apostle Paul said, "I am not ashamed of the
Gospel of Christ: for it is *the power of God unto
salvation to every one that believeth;* to the Jew
first, and also to the Greek" (Rom. 1:16).

I *believe* all of the Bible—from the first word in
Genesis through the last word in Revelation. I *love*
all of the Bible, but I especially love this portion
of God's Word.

Multitudes Healed

Verse 29: *"And Jesus departed from thence, and
came nigh unto the sea of Galilee; and went up
into a mountain, and sat down there."*

This account is also found in Mark 7:31-37. The
statement *"And Jesus departed from thence"* signifies that He departed from the country of Tyre and
Sidon. We do not know how long He stayed in
that area—certainly not very long. And we do not
have any information concerning the rest of His
journey in Phoenicia.

When Jesus left that area, He must have passed

eastward across the Jordan River and then traveled
southward until He went through the district of
the ten cities of Decapolis: "Departing from the
coasts of Tyre and Sidon, He came unto the Sea
of Galilee, through the midst of the coasts of
Decapolis" (Mark 7:31). According to Bible historians, the Decapolis was a region southeast of
the Sea of Galilee, made up of ten Greek cities.
Nine of these were east of the Jordan and one west.

This journey without a doubt climaxed somewhere in the region of the southeastern border of
the Sea of Galilee. This area was out of the
jurisdiction of Herod, like the areas to which Jesus
had previously withdrawn (Matt. 14:13; 15:21). His
desire to stay out of Herod's territory at that time
may have caused Him to make the journey just
described instead of going direct from the area of
Tyre and Sidon through Galilee and crossing the
sea. He appears not to have stopped in the area
of Caesarea Philippi, probably through desire to
revisit the cities around the sea that He had visited
earlier.

Jesus was now in the vicinity of Gadara (one of
the ten cities), the same region in which He had
healed the two demoniacs and had allowed the
legion of demons to destroy the herd of swine
(Matt. 8:28-34; Mark 5:1-13; Luke 8:26-39). According to Matthew 4:25, there were many people in
Decapolis who had heard Jesus teach months before the healing of the demon possessed men.

But when Jesus visited the area this time, His ministry produced a much greater impression— probably through the testimony of the restored demoniac mentioned in Luke's Gospel. After his healing, Jesus instructed him, *"Return to thine own house, and shew how great things God hath done unto thee.* And he went his way, *and published throughout the whole city* how great things Jesus had done unto him" (Luke 8:39).

Now we read that Jesus *"went up into a mountain, and sat down there."* Statements like this cause me to appreciate the Lord Jesus more and more. He was God in flesh, He was supernatural and divine; but He was also human, and He loved to get alone, to sit down in the mountains or by the seashore to relax and rest. The mountain referred to was the range of mountains that runs along the east of the Sea of Galilee.

Verse 30: *"And great multitudes came unto Him, having with them those that were lame, blind, dumb, maimed, and many others, and cast them down at Jesus' feet; and He healed them."*

Somehow I feel that the place Jesus picked to sit down was where He could look upon the Sea of Galilee. There He wrought many miracles of healing, and He also fed another multitude. In this case, a great number of those present must have been Gentiles, for the ten cities in that area were more Gentile than Jewish. Jesus must have spent several days in that area since it required a little time for His presence to be known, and verse 32 tells us that the multitude had been with Him for three days.

"Great multitudes" — literally, "many crowds" — is used in many other passages in the Gospels. In this verse we have a general account of several miracles. The people brought to Jesus *"those that were lame, blind, dumb, maimed . . . ."* (Compare Matthew 4:23; 8:16; 9:35; 12:15.) One of the miracles that Jesus performed here was the healing of the deaf and dumb man, described by Mark alone (Mark 7:32-37).

Let me point out that the word *"maimed"* in the Greek signifies "crooked, bent, contracted." It sometimes applies to cases of mutilation, the loss of some part of the body (Matt. 18:8). Probably the best English word we could use today for "maimed" is *crippled.*

It is very interesting to notice in the Gospel records that Jesus raised the dead and healed all manner of diseases and all kinds of infirmities — but the restoring of Malchus' ear is the only recorded instance of Jesus restoring a missing part of the body. This occurred in the Garden of Gethsemane when Peter drew his sword and cut off Malchus' ear and Jesus miraculously restored it (Luke 22: 50, 51; John 18:10, 11).

After Matthew names the lame, blind, dumb, and maimed, he adds *"and many others"* — which would include any disease or ailment that one might have. Jesus, very God in flesh, was capable of healing any type of disease and any and all crippled bodies. That must have been a sight—so many sick people with diseases and ailments too numerous to name. It is important to see that the Holy Spirit moved Matthew to name those ailments associated with the prophecies concerning the coming of the Messiah. (Please read Isaiah 35:4, 5 and Matthew 11:5.)

The friends and loved ones who brought the diseased *"cast them down at Jesus' feet."* This does not suggest that they literally threw them on the ground or that they were careless with them, but it implies hurry and bustle amid the crowd of applicants. They were placed at Jesus' feet—*"and He healed them"!*

Verse 31: *"Insomuch that the multitude wondered, when they saw the dumb to speak, the maimed to be whole, the lame to walk, and the blind to see: and they glorified the God of Israel."*

". . . the multitude wondered . . . ." They heard the dumb speak and they saw all kinds of sick people made well immediately. They confessed in their own hearts that they had never seen anything like this before.

". . . and they glorified the God of Israel." In Matthew 9:8 we read simply, "they marvelled, and *glorified God."* As pointed out earlier, these people

in Decapolis were primarily Gentiles and were looked upon as heathen, so it would be natural for Matthew to mention that they "glorified the God of *Israel.*" Most of the people knew that the Messiah would come to Israel first. Indeed He *did* come to the Jew first, but they rejected Him— and now the message is to the Gentile world and to *"whosoever will."*

Jesus Feeds the Four Thousand

Verse 32: *"Then Jesus called His disciples unto Him, and said, I have compassion on the multitude, because they continue with me now three days, and have nothing to eat: and I will not send them away fasting, lest they faint in the way."*

Here Jesus expresses pity for the people who had been with Him three days. If they brought any food with them, they had eaten it all and were now without food. Three days they had been listening to Jesus; and as He looked out over that mass of people, His heart was moved with compassion because He knew they were hungry, and He simply refused to send them away without food.

I am so happy that our Saviour is concerned not only about our spiritual welfare, but also about our daily needs. If we put Him first, He promises to supply every need. He clothes the lily, He feeds the sparrow—and He will take care of His children. He is able, willing, and ready to supply the need of any and all who will put their faith and trust in Him.

Verse 33: *"And His disciples say unto Him, Whence should we have so much bread in the wilderness, as to fill so great a multitude?"*

At first glance it seems that His disciples were slow to believe and slow to accept the fact that He was the all-sufficient One, able to supply any need. Instead of saying to Jesus, "Lord, you feed them," they asked, "Where can we find so much bread out here in the wilderness to feed such a multitude as we have present?" This wilderness was, no doubt, far from the nearest city—and even if they could have reached a city with enough money to buy bread for four thousand people, they would not have found enough bread there to feed them.

Had the disciples so soon forgotten the feeding of the five thousand with five loaves and two little fishes? I think not. Though the question here is the same as when Jesus fed the five thousand, evidently the disciples now meant no more than that they had nothing with which to feed the multitude. This is further borne out by the fact that Jesus does not now try them, as before, by saying, "They need not depart; give ye them to eat." He simply asks, "How many loaves have ye?" and then gives His directions.

Verse 34: *"And Jesus saith unto them, How many loaves have ye? And they said, Seven, and a few little fishes."*

Jesus knew how many loaves they had, but He asked them the question anyway. Jesus did not speak useless words; He never uttered one word without a reason. The reason here was to increase their faith. He was leading them, little by little, into the true knowledge of His identity. The Holy Spirit did not see fit to reveal to us where the seven loaves came from, who had them, or how the disciples knew that there were seven loaves. In answer to the Lord's question, they told Him that they had *seven loaves "and a few little fishes."* In the case of the feeding of the five thousand, we know exactly how many *fishes* they had, but here we know only that there were "a *few* little fishes."

Notice that as soon as Jesus asked about how much bread they had, the disciples immediately made known to Him what was on hand, expressing no surprise or doubt whatsoever. After He asked about the bread, it seemed that they took for granted what would follow.

Verse 35: *"And He commanded the multitude to sit down on the ground."*

As in the case of the feeding of the five thousand, Jesus commanded the multitude to sit down on the ground. We are not told here that they sat down in numbers, but it stands to reason that they did. Jesus always did things decently and in order. You can rest assured that there was no confusion in what Jesus planned or did.

I believe that organization is of the Lord. But I am afraid there is *too much* organization today, and we have just about "organized" the Holy Spirit out of our religious programs. Thank God, there are some ministers and churches who still allow the Holy Spirit to direct in all things. I do not believe that we should gather into the house of God and just sit there and wait for someone to speak or move. I believe that God is pleased and glorified when the church service has dignity— but *spirit above dignity*, always. You can rest assured if we allow the Holy Spirit to have His way, there will be dignity and true worship.

Verse 36: *"And He took the seven loaves and the fishes, and gave thanks, and brake them, and gave to His disciples, and the disciples to the multitude."*

Jesus *"took the seven loaves and the fishes, and gave thanks . . . ."* He always did give thanks. I have many pleasant memories about my father, but one of the most pleasant is that he never sat down to eat food without saying grace. Our table was a very crude one, not shiny and polished; and the children sat on a bench, with my mother and father sitting in cane-bottom chairs. That

439

table was a place where we found food and fellowship. On the wall over the table were the words, "Give us this day our daily bread." I can truthfully say that even through the depression days when things were extremely critical, we always had bread. We did not always have meat and fine foods, but we had bread and milk. My father and mother had nine children, but not one of us had to go hungry during all the days of the depression.

". . . and gave to His disciples, and the disciples to the multitude." After Jesus gave thanks, as in the case of the feeding of the five thousand, He broke the bread and the fishes and gave to the disciples to serve to the multitude.

Verse 37: *"And they did all eat, and were filled: and they took up of the broken meat that was left seven baskets full."*

The Greek word *spuris* translated *"baskets"* in this verse means "woven work." The baskets were woven out of a type of reed, and they were large baskets—sometimes large enough to contain a man's body. The Apostle Paul was let down in one of these baskets over the wall of Damascus: "But their laying await was known of Saul. And they watched the gates day and night to kill him. Then the disciples took him by night, and *let him down by the wall in a basket"* (Acts 9:24, 25).

Some Bible scholars suggest that these baskets

were used by the people to sleep in at night on the desert. The thing I want to emphasize here is that they were not *little* baskets, but *very large* ones — and there were *seven* of them *filled with fragments* left over after the four thousand were filled and satisfied with the food Jesus provided from seven loaves and a few little fishes.

Our God is able to do *exceedingly abundantly over anything we think or ask.* When Jesus fed the five thousand, there were twelve baskets of fragments left. After feeding the four thousand, there were seven baskets left. Jesus can do whatever He desires to do — and if He had wanted twelve baskets of fragments left over on this occasion, there could have been that many. This is twice that Jesus fed a great multitude with very little, and this should have been proof to the disciples — and to the whole world — that He is *all sufficient,* well able to take care of our temporal needs, regardless of how little or how great they may be. This is pointed out to the disciples later in Mark's Gospel:

"And they reasoned among themselves, saying, It is because we have no bread. And when Jesus knew it, He saith unto them, Why reason ye, because ye have no bread? Perceive ye not yet, neither understand? Have ye your heart yet hardened? Having eyes, see ye not? and having ears, hear ye not? and *do ye not remember?* When I brake the five loaves among five thousand, how

441

many baskets full of fragments took ye up? They say unto Him, Twelve. And when the seven among four thousand, how many baskets full of fragments took ye up? And they said, Seven. And He said unto them, How is it that ye do not understand?" (Mark 8:16-21).

Verse 38: *"And they that did eat were four thousand men, beside women and children."*

We see here that the four thousand were *men*, not counting the women and children. We do not know how many of the men were married or how many children there were, but certainly there must have been a great number of women and children along with the four thousand men.

We have here a very similar miracle to the feeding of the five thousand. Some have suggested that these miracles are one and the same; but this cannot be true. The following words recorded by Matthew are proof that these are two different miracles: *"Do ye not yet understand, neither remember the five loaves of the five thousand, and how many baskets ye took up? neither the seven loaves of the four thousand, and how many baskets ye took up?"* (Matt. 16:9, 10). These are the words of Jesus—and if they are not true, they are forged by Matthew and we cannot believe any of the Gospel written by him. I accept the Word of God as verbally inspired and God breathed, and I accept this as an entirely different miracle because the Holy Spirit led Matthew to record it as such. On the first occasion Jesus fed *five* thousand; in this instance, He fed *four* thousand.

Another thing that definitely points out that these are two separate miracles is the remarkable difference as to the words translated "baskets." The Greek word for "baskets" in which the fragments were collected on the occasion of the feeding of the five thousand is *kophinos*, and is used by all four evangelists. The feeding of the four thousand is recorded only by Matthew and Mark, and they use the Greek word *spuris*, also rendered "baskets." When Jesus reminds the disciples of these miracles in Matthew 16:9, 10, He also differentiates between the baskets by using the word *kophinos* with reference to the first miracle, and *spuris* with reference to the second. This means that different kinds of baskets were used on the two occasions. There were many kinds and sizes of baskets because the people used them extensively, both at home and in industry.

Some critics have suggested that if these are not two accounts of the same miracle, why did the disciples not refer to the feeding of the five thousand when Jesus said that He would not send the crowd away hungry? They maintain that if the miracles are not one, certainly the disciples would have said to Jesus, "Do the thing you did a little while ago when you fed the five thousand."

But we must remember that Jesus sternly rebuked

the crowd who shared in the first miracle and followed Him the next day, hoping to be fed again: "Jesus answered them and said, Verily, verily, I say unto you, *Ye seek me, not because ye saw the miracles, but because ye did eat of the loaves, and were filled*" (John 6:26). Jesus was very displeased at the popular determination produced by the miracle to force Him to become King at that time. He had rushed the disciples themselves unwillingly away from that area, partly because they sympathized with the masses who wanted to make Him King. We studied this in Matthew 14:22: "Straightway Jesus *constrained* His disciples to get into a ship, and to go before Him unto the other side, while He sent the multitudes away." In this state of things the disciples might naturally doubt whether Jesus would repeat a miracle which had been formerly attended by such unfavorable results. With this in mind, they might have been afraid to ask Him to repeat the miracle. (In Mark 9:32 we read, "But they understood not that saying, and *WERE AFRAID TO ASK HIM.*")

Although the two miracles are definitely not identical, they do have many things in common: They both were in the wilderness. The food was the same—loaves and fishes. The blessing and the breaking was the same, as well as the distributing to the people by the disciples. But there is nothing unusual about these features being the same, considering the area and the food the people ate in that day.

Verse 39: *"And He sent away the multitude, and took ship, and came into the coasts of Magdala."*

The multitudes were fed and satisfied, so Jesus sent them back to their homes. Then Jesus *"took ship,"* which means He entered into a boat. The boat which He and the disciples were accustomed to use was no doubt brought from Capernaum while they were there on the southeast side of the Sea of Galilee. It could have been another boat, but I like to believe that Jesus used the same boat in His crossing the sea on several occasions.

After He had sent the multitude away and had entered a ship, He *"came into the coasts of Magdala."* The exact location of this place is unknown, as is that of Dalmanutha, mentioned in the parallel passage in Mark 8:10. The locality was somewhere on the western side of the Sea of Galilee, because from this area the party crossed to the northeastern side of the sea. (Notice Matthew 16:5 and Mark 8:13.)

This place was formerly called Magadan but was changed to Magdala, which means "tower." The modern name is Mejdel. There are a few huts there; and some Bible scholars believe this was the home of Mary Magdalene, out of whom Jesus cast seven demons.

445